States of suspense

Manchester University Press

States of suspense

The nuclear age, postmodernism
and United States fiction and prose

Daniel Cordle

Manchester University Press

Manchester and New York

distributed exclusively in the USA by Palgrave

Published by Manchester University Press
Oxford Road, Manchester M13 9NR, UK
and Room 400, 175 Fifth Avenue, New York, NY 10010, USA
www.manchesteruniversitypress.co.uk

Distributed exclusively in the USA by
Palgrave, 175 Fifth Avenue, New York,
NY 10010, USA

Distributed exclusively in Canada by
UBC Press, University of British Columbia, 2029 West Mall,
Vancouver, BC, Canada V6T 1Z2

British Library Cataloguing-in-Publication Data
A catalogue record for this book is available from the British Library

Library of Congress Cataloging-in-Publication Data applied for

ISBN 978 0 7190 7712 8   *hardback*

First published 2008

17   16   15   14   13   12   11   10   09   08   10   9   8   7   6   5   4   3   2   1

Typeset
by SNP Best-set Typesetter Ltd., Hong Kong
Printed in Great Britain
by Bell & Bain Ltd, Glasgow

For Sam

Contents

Acknowledgements

I owe an enormous debt of thanks to many current and former colleagues at Nottingham Trent University. In particular, Professors Nahem Yousaf, Greg Woods, R. J. Ellis and David Worrall, and Drs Lynne Hapgood and Phil Leonard have, variously, read sections of manuscript, talked through ideas, provided encouragement and given concrete advice.

My thanks also to all those colleagues, many anonymous, who have through their conversations at conferences, or their comments as referees or editors of journal papers, edited collections, book proposals or funding applications, provided constructive feedback and suggestions that have shaped this project and the associated research and articles out of which it has come. Colleagues' generosity with time and ideas, in a highly pressured profession, is greatly appreciated.

My gratitude goes also to staff at Manchester University Press for their help and hard work in producing this book. Notwithstanding all the valuable contributions noted above, needless to say all mistakes or shortcomings herein remain mine.

Finally, thanks as ever to all friends and family whose support and good company contributed far more to this book than they probably realise. To Sandra Gell, who may have felt with justification that nuclear obsessions could border on the unhealthy and to whom this book is dedicated: thanks for everything.

A note on terminology

While, as is common practice, the terms 'atomic' and 'nuclear' are used relatively interchangeably throughout this book, I have been as consistent as is possible in a work moving across sixty years of culture, in using the former predominantly in relation to the period when it was the favoured term of reference (broadly, though not exclusively, that preceding the construction of the hydrogen bomb).

Introduction: states of suspense

This is a book about things that did not happen and the cultural consequences of their not happening. From Winston Churchill's declaration in 1946 that Europe was riven by an 'iron curtain [that] has descended across the Continent',[1] to the tearing down of the Berlin Wall forty-three years later, the Cold War fizzled and spluttered into regional conflicts around the globe but failed to explode into nuclear heat. Nor, at the time of writing, has there been any military use of nuclear weapons since. Yet the possibility that this technology might be deployed has had a profound shaping influence, politically and culturally, since the first bomb was dropped on Hiroshima on 6 August 1945. At times the nuclear threat has been palpably close, as during the Cuban Missile Crisis; in other periods, it has faded into a dull familiarity, a background hum rendered almost inaudible by the cacophony of everyday life.

This book is about the ways in which various nuclear states of suspense that pertained between 1945 and 2005 inflected United States fiction and prose. It argues that the residual crisis of Cold War life – withheld but constantly threatened destruction – shaped people's relations to the State, each other and themselves. Suspense was a signature mindset of the period. Furthermore, nuclear threats have an ongoing cultural legacy beyond the end of the Cold War. Retrospectively, the Cold War is frequently represented nostalgically as an emergency that bound us together but did not come to pass, but, even though nuclear threats are now unlikely to produce the species death that haunted the earlier period, they also persist, morphed into new fears like those of proliferation and terrorism.

Crucially, nuclear issues are a mainstream rather than a peripheral concern, and for this reason this book looks not only at conventional nuclear disaster texts, but also at 'mainstream', particularly postmodern, literature that carries within it the signatures of the nuclear presence in everyday life. By making extinction possible, nuclear weapons fundamentally changed the conditions of lived experience even though they remained undetonated in war after the attack on Nagasaki. Nuclear power, too, changed contemporary reality, at first promising unlimited cheap energy; then threatening, if only once delivering, devastating environmental contamination in accidents at Windscale (1957), Three Mile Island (1979) and

Chernobyl (1986); and most recently touted as a high-tech answer to soaring global carbon emissions. Both military and civilian nuclear technologies (although the distinction between the two is not always absolute) have inspired active campaigning by some people at some times. It is not, however, in these explicit arenas of public debate that their effects have been most broad-reaching. It is instead in more nebulous shifts in worldview, certainly during the Cold War when a world-ending conflict was possible, that their impact has been most profound. After 1945, nuclear technology became part of the fabric out of which everyday experience was woven. Its possible effects had to be assimilated, even if for most people, most of the time, this involved acceptance or denial of, not active resistance to, this new condition of reality.

Because it is suspense – anticipation of disaster rather than disaster itself – that defines the period, it is important to find ways of engaging with the psychological and cultural consequences of living with nuclear weapons that go beyond the simple delineation of depictions of disaster. One way of doing this is to read obviously nuclear texts with a subtly shifted emphasis, looking less at their representation of life during or after nuclear war and more for their depiction, direct or metaphorical, of the Cold War experience of extended anticipation, frozen just before the nuclear cusp. A second is to seek in 'mainstream' texts (in this book, largely postmodern ones), passing but revealing inflections of the nuclear context; nuclear anxieties resonate elsewhere than, as well as in, the ghettoes of standard science-fiction depictions of post-apocalyptic worlds. Such readings can uncover the everyday experience of nuclear realities, which are characteristically nagging on the edges of normal life or erupting in short bursts of anxiety, rather than at the centre of attention. Yet another strategy is to consider the traffic between nuclear and other issues: nuclear tropes as metaphors for broader social concerns and, conversely, non-specific motifs of anxiety (like a truncated sense of the future; particular forms of paranoia; a preoccupation with contamination) as revealing of a nuclear source even when it is not named as such.

The first section of the book, 'The nuclear age', addresses broad issues of psychology, literature and culture since 1945. Chapter one defines a nuclear anxiety literature, different from disaster literature and which, encompassing texts we might not normally consider to be nuclear, nevertheless carries the signature of a nuclear presence in everyday life. It does not go quite as far as Martin Amis, who argued, in a period of acute nuclear tension, that 'all writing – all art, in all times – has a bearing on nuclear weapons, in two important respects. Art celebrates life and not the other thing, not the opposite of life. And art raises the stakes, increasing the store of what might be lost.'[2] However, although it does not claim that every text is unwittingly nuclear, it does find nuclear issues erupting across the culture, not just on its margins, and demands that the nuclear context be recognised as so fundamental that an understanding of post-1945 literature is incomplete if it is not taken into account. In particular, it finds postmodern texts to have concerns overlapping with a culture of nuclear anxiety.

A new 'nuclear criticism' of the post-Cold War era, pushing beyond that produced in some English departments for about a decade from the mid-1980s, can re-evaluate Cold War literature, shifting attention from the representation of nuclear explosion and its aftermath, to the more common Cold War experience of bombs not detonating. To this extent I follow Jacqueline Foertsch in defining the Cold War as 'the tension-filled and exhausting constant deferral of [nuclear attack]'.[3] It is in this deferral of nuclear explosion, anticipated, threatened but never delivered, that some characteristic features of the Cold War lie. A contemporary nuclear criticism should also be interested in the continuation and transformation of nuclear themes in literature since 1989, a topic that is the subject of the final chapter.

Chapter two theorises the nuclear anxiety that produces the states of suspense of Cold War literature. A crucial context is the strategic balance of terror of the Cold War, with the threat of absolute destruction hanging over both sides. In the 1950s there was concern about the general impact of this threat on the citizenry. Much of the justification for civil defence was that it would transform 'terror' (directionless panic) into more socially useful 'fear', simultaneously ingraining acceptance of United States geopolitical strategy; creating the illusion, essential for deterrence, that the country could survive nuclear attack; and, in the event of war, maintaining social order. A more critical perspective was opened up by psychological research into the impact of nuclear fear which, although relatively sparse until the 1980s, then enjoyed a decade of comparative abundance. Particularly influential was Robert Lifton's hypothesis that 'psychic numbing' characterised Cold War life as people repressed and denied their nuclear fears.

A final context for understanding nuclear anxiety, indebted to provocative cultural analyses by Alan Nadel and Elaine Tyler May, is a conception of 'containment' not simply as a Cold War geopolitical strategy but as a domestic cultural ideology.[4] With its roots in the 1950s, it produced a Cold War vision of normality centred on the middle-class family home and constructed departure from this norm (through, for instance, homosexuality or rejection of consumer capitalism) as politically deviant and subversive. Following Nadel, the chapter establishes the root conditions of a broad-reaching postmodernism in the contradictions and evasions of this containment culture.

The second section of the book, 'Nuclear environments', explores the pervasive influence of nuclear anxiety, permeating Cold War spaces at every level from the personal to the global. Chapter three discusses the city, a strategic target and symbolically vulnerable in the nuclear age. Carpet- and firebombing of urban areas had, during the Second World War, been established as distinctive features of twentieth-century total warfare, but with the obliteration of Hiroshima by a single atomic device a terrible new ratio of destruction became lodged in the popular imagination. In the nuclear era, with defence against attack seemingly impossible (after all, only one bomb had to get through) and the ongoing emergency of the Cold War (with peace liable to flip swiftly into open conflict), city life was marked by fragility. As Tom Vanderbilt has argued, this was the point at which the city finally shifted from 'protective enclave', in which one might seek shelter, to a 'strategic target' from which one should flee.[5]

Two visions of the post-nuclear city haunt the metropolises of the second half of the twentieth century. The first is the flattened city, established by iconic images of Hiroshima and reinforced by John Hersey's magnificent piece of reportage, *Hiroshima* (1946). The second is the empty city, intact but, with cleared streets, a symbol of the end of civilisation. This latter image features prominently in Nevil Shute's *On the Beach* (1957), influential in the United States even though its author was not American. It also dominates contemporary press reports of bomb drills in American cities, and the chapter uses an astonishing sequence of exercises in New York between 1951 and 1961 to discuss its significance.

The city is also one of the primary loci for postmodern literature, its shifting faces and reflections, its over-abundance of signs and codes, and the ebbs and flows of its populations linked to the fractured, ephemeral and continually reconstituted subjectivities of postmodern humanity. While there are numerous root causes much more important than the nuclear context in the rise of postmodern cities and subjects (consumer capitalism; the growth of international travel; the explosion in mass media popular culture), the fragile status of the subject in both the postmodern and the nuclear-threatened city furnishes texts working the cultural territory between apocalypse and postmodernism, like Thomas Pynchon's *Gravity's Rainbow* (1973) and Paul Auster's *In the Country of Last Things* (1988), with a rich source of material.

Chapter four turns to the home, particularly the middle-class family home, which was the primary location for depictions of nuclear threat in civil defence leaflets and films and in many literary texts. Ideas of family and domesticity thus became central to discourse on nuclear issues. While families were seen as crucial in practical preparations for attack (building shelters together and taking collective responsibility for post-attack survival), they also assumed an important ideological role. Discussed as though they were natural entities, they were actually constructed by the philosophies of containment as a bulwark against what were seen as politically subversive threats from both outside and inside the nation. Judith Merril's *Shadow on the Hearth* (1950) is particularly astute on this topic, revealing contradictions in domestic ideology obscured by containment. It is precisely these contradictions which form the starting point for later postmodern novels, like Don DeLillo's *White Noise* (1984), which are shadowed by domestic and environmental disaster.

The planet, fragile in the face of nuclear holocaust, is the subject of chapter five. Very rapidly after 1945, and even in the short period before it was technologically possible, atomic technology was depicted as world-ending. This catastrophist interpretation drew on a long tradition of apocalyptic visions of end times and connected up with the broader environmental consciousness that emerged from the 1960s onwards. It also, though, generated a counter movement, drawing on concepts and images (like the earth from space) that allowed those resisting 'nuclearism' to reach out across the boundaries of national, cultural and ideological difference to posit a common, threatened humanity.[6] Texts like Kurt Vonnegut's *Cat's Cradle* (1963) frequently work this dialectic between planetary death and salvation, positing a unifying humanist perspective against the forces imperilling the earth.

The final section, 'Nuclear reactions', addresses more directly the political dimensions of representations of nuclear issues during and after the Cold War. Chapter six looks at the politics of Cold War nuclear literature. Interestingly, nuclear disaster texts are often not as politically engaged as one might expect. The post-holocaust environment can be treated frivolously, ripe, for instance, with possibilities for sexual adventure uncensored by the taboos of civilisation. Even serious depiction of disaster does not of itself imply a political perspective beyond the rather unenlightening insight that nuclear war would be pretty unpleasant and is best avoided. As Jacqueline Smetak rather pithily puts it, '[w]hile nuclear holocaust stories can describe the problem, they don't tell us anything we don't already know. All of us, left, right and center, are well aware that if you drop something that blows up, it will make an awful mess.'[7] Indeed, the simple depiction of nuclear devastation was appropriated by those both pro- and anti-disarmament to prove the urgency of their cases. Extensive psychological research into the effects of ABC's *The Day After* (1983), the most watched made-for-television film in history when it was screened, shows that it entrenched the views of those on all sides of the debate.[8] Essentially the problem is one of scale: nuclear holocaust is so overwhelming as to take on, in its representation, the status of natural disaster, liable to obscure the political circumstances that produce it, except in clunky, propagandist polemics like Philip Wylie's advocacy of civil defence in *Tomorrow!* (1954). Even a text as brilliant as Hersey's *Hiroshima* has been criticised for this.[9]

Where even the most unsubtle and sensationalist disaster texts are politically interesting is in their largely unconscious preservation of contemporary social perspectives. For instance, while Pat Frank's *Alas, Babylon* (1959) is a polemic in favour of civil defence, more politically interesting and revealing is the pleasure it takes in the accommodations its small community of survivors make to their post-nuclear environment. Nuclear war, ostensibly horrific in the text, actually emerges as a stage on which a survivalist fantasy can be played out, a corrupt political establishment eradicated as core frontier values of self-reliance and community reassert themselves. Even in its most liberal aspect, its depiction of African-Americans, subject to racial discrimination in the pre-nuclear order, as valuable members of the new society, it reveals conservative assumptions about racial difference. When the survivors arm themselves to resist outside attack, it is unsurprising that it is the black character who appears, 'teeth and eyes gleaming', with a 'six-foot spear' instead of a gun.[10]

However, the literature of nuclear anxiety (as opposed to that of disaster) is often more politically complex. Although it has no consistent political agenda, by representing anxiety about future nuclear war, rather than people's experience during or after such a war, it is forced to address the ambiguous position of the individual in relation to the complex architectures of political power in the period. This includes what Eisenhower christened the 'military-industrial complex',[11] the sprawling technologies and bureaucracies of surveillance and control, and the contradictory pressures to conform to and resist social norms. The individual can seem lost and powerless within such large and impenetrable systems and this concern signals a significant degree of overlap between fictions of nuclear anxiety and the paranoid postmodernist fictions that proliferated toward the end of the Cold War. Such texts tend both to expose the operations of power and suggest that resistance to it is fraught with compromises. Tim O'Brien's *The Nuclear Age* (1985) is particularly astute on the continuities between personal and global political realities, and the chapter uses it to explore the tensions between 'going underground' (pursuing subversive resistance) and 'digging in' (being so paralysed by terror as simply to disengage, seeking shelter from the perils of the time).

The final chapter, functioning as both conclusion and epilogue, examines the literary and cultural representation of nuclear issues after the Cold War. One reaction is to consider the Cold War as a distinct period that, now closed off, can be revisited nostalgically or even with regret that its seeming certainties have passed. An astonishing feature of contemporary discourse about the Cold War is that it should be represented as a 'safe' period, in contrast to a present portrayed as uniquely threatened by, for instance, terrorism. Such historical revisionism forgets the uncertainties and terrors of nearly half a century in which global nuclear holocaust was a possibility. While writers have tended to adopt more sophisticated positions than this, as Don DeLillo and Philip Roth have in their brilliant investigations of the American half-century in, respectively, *Underworld* (1997) and *American Pastoral* (1997), their works nevertheless frequently deploy the nostalgic mode.

In another reaction, fears of nuclear holocaust morph into new forms following the Cold War. Sometimes these terrors remain nuclear, although they are more likely to be about nuclear proliferation or terrorism than all-out war. Sometimes they undergo a more subtle transformation into anxieties about issues like non-nuclear terrorism (as in Jonathan Safran Foer's 2005 novel, *Extremely Loud and Incredibly Close*, where the anxieties induced by the 9/11 attacks are shown to be shaped by the cultural legacy of the nuclear age), health scares or environmental catastrophe. Sometimes, too, they shift into less expected forms. During the 1990s, for instance, there was a brief burst of public interest in the possibility of a species-destroying meteorite or comet strike on earth. Films like *Deep Impact* (1998) and *Armageddon* (1998) exploited this interest in ways that were Cold War in character. In *Deep Impact* a subplot about the random selection of citizens to go into extensive government shelters echoes Cold War survivalist fantasies. In *Armageddon*, the earth is saved by a nuclear detonation that blows up the approaching asteroid, in a move that simultaneously reinscribes nuclear weapons at the heart of national defence, and recalls and validates the 'Star Wars' nuclear defence programme of the Reagan Administration.

The final reaction is to contest the absolute binary divide between Cold War and post-Cold War. Arundhati Roy's essay, 'The End of Imagination' (1998), about the Indian and Pakistani nuclear programmes, demonstrates the continuity between these and the earlier Cold War standoff. Bobbie Ann Mason's novel, *An Atomic Romance* (2005), finds contemporary legacies of the Cold War in a scandal at a uranium enrichment plant, contesting the suggestion that the earlier historical phase has entirely passed. Such readings can begin to interrogate the notion of the present as uniquely threatened and show it to be the outcome of long-standing historical developments.

States of Suspense therefore seeks to cover a long period and a broad range of nuclear issues. It is not, though, a survey, and does not claim to account for every nuclear text published between 1945 and 2005. Instead, it seeks to raise two issues that deserve more sustained critical attention than they have in the past received: the 'states of suspense', the mindsets produced by the long-threatened but continually deferred possibility of nuclear war; and the continuing relevance of nuclear issues, both for our attempts retrospectively to make sense of Cold War culture, and for an understanding of the legacy of this culture in contemporary experience.

2005 is an arbitrary endpoint for the study to the extent that it was the moment at which the project crystallised, not the end of a nuclear era. Nuclear issues are of ongoing importance, their representation rooted in earlier nuclear cultures as well as in contemporary constructions like the much hyped 'War on Terror', and it is important not to assume that seemingly definitive historical moments, like 11 September 2001, mark the closing off of particular phases in nuclear culture.

The choice of texts is designed to open up the pathways between more obviously nuclear and mainstream, particularly postmodern, literatures. After section one, which establishes the theoretical groundwork for the book, each chapter generally consists of three aspects: a discussion laying out general or specific nuclear contexts; a reading of a conventionally studied nuclear text or texts; and a suggestion of the ways in which such readings might be developed in relation to a mainstream text or texts, where nuclear issues are ostensibly a minor concern, or even seemingly absent.

Postmodernism is taken as 'mainstream' because, despite its frequent association with experimentalism or other cultural margins, it is increasingly at the centre of culture during the second half of the twentieth century and beyond. Postmodern concerns are even taken to be largely latent in conventional nuclear disaster fiction and prose, even though the form of this literature is frequently deeply conservative. Nadel argues that containment narratives, from the early Cold War period, contain the germ of dynamics later intrinsic to postmodernism. Even *Hiroshima*, which appears to be realist (a detached third-person narrator reconstructs the story of the attack from interviews with survivors), 'raises formal and epistemological questions about the relationship between writing and experience foregrounded in postmodern aesthetics, as it attempts to construct a narrative of atomic warfare legible within the codes of containment culture'.[12] The nuclear subject, in other words, reveals fundamental limitations to the realist mode in which it is rendered.

Indeed, the issues of representation raised by nuclear contexts can be seen as, if not identical, certainly continuous with those associated with postmodernism. For instance, the possibility of capricious and sudden destruction of everything renders everyday life absurd and fragile, a point of view influential both on existentialist and, later, postmodernist thought. Furthermore, representational challenges posed to language and literature by the sheer scale of destruction threatened by nuclear technology are contiguous with the postmodern preoccupation with problematic relations between signifier and signified.

Given this, it is astonishing how infrequently surveys of United States literature after 1945 make reference to nuclear or even, sometimes, broader Cold War contexts. Excellent overviews of the period, or decades within the period, like Kathryn Hume's *American Dream, American Nightmare* and Kenneth Millard's *Contemporary American Fiction*, tend to contextualise literature in terms of crucial issues like race, ethnicity, gender or sexuality; specifically North American contexts like the idea of the frontier or Civil Rights struggles; or formal and cultural developments like postmodernism.[13] They tend not, however, to situate these within the larger geopolitical context.

All critical works are, of course, circumscribed: critical narratives remain coherent as much by what they exclude from consideration as by what they include. The focus on nuclear contexts is not intended to downplay the importance of, say, issues of race, but to suggest another facet that enhances our understanding of the multiple forces bearing on post-1945 United States culture, not only in overtly nuclear texts but also diffused throughout a much broader selection of literature. Before embarking on this project, two complicating factors need to be addressed: the distinction between United States and other literatures is, particularly when considering nuclear issues, a convenient artifice; and notions of suspense and anxiety are not fixed throughout the period but shift according to contingent historical, technological and cultural circumstances.

United States literature in a global context

One of the impacts of the Cold War was further to open the United States to vectors of global political and cultural exchange. While North American culture had been defined, since early European encroachments onto the continent, by the conversations between various immigrant traditions, it is fair to say that, for the United States, despite a political history of isolationism, the Cold War signalled a more self-conscious engagement with the rest of the world. In particular, United States voices and concerns began to impress themselves more strongly upon the global community. Politically, and quite self-consciously, they sought to provide an ideological and technological lead. It is not surprising that, culturally, they should also seek to seize the initiative, even if United States artists and writers spoke with myriad, and often dissenting, voices.

Yet this cultural engagement could not be one-way. The ideological, political, technological and cultural struggle with the Soviet Union forced the acknowledgement that the United States' national interests would be shaped abroad as well as at home. Arguably, after all, it was on Europe that the unresolved nuclear tension was centred. It was Berlin, carved into zones of occupation by the victors in the Second World War and sitting a vulnerable 125 miles inside the Soviet Bloc, that Nikita Khrushchev described in 1958 as the 'testicles of the West',[14] liable to be squeezed by the Soviet premier whenever he wished to exert pressure on his opponents, and it was here where some of the most dangerous of the early crises of the Cold War took place. Europe, more broadly, would have been the battleground had the Cold War ever resulted in direct confrontation between NATO and Warsaw Pact troops, with the industrial powerhouse of West Germany the target, in the minds of some Western politicians, for Soviet expansionism. Europe, too, of course, would have borne the brunt of any nuclear exchange in such a conflict, its densely packed populations vulnerable in ways that were not true of the more widely spread and distant people of the United States.

But if Europe and the threat of nuclear holocaust formed an eye to the Cold War storm that was relatively static, albeit marked by extreme tension and, as in the cases of Hungary in 1956 and Czechoslovakia in 1968, violence and direct military repression, a maelstrom of consequences swirled around the globe from this centre. Struggles for power in Europe may not have resulted in direct confrontation there, but they were deflected into devastating conflicts elsewhere. To talk of the Cold War not being fought is to dismiss the casualties in Korea, Vietnam, Afghanistan and other places.[15] While these wars had their own histories behind them, they were given shape, not to mention military hardware and hundreds of thousands of personnel, by the principal antagonists of the Cold War.

Politically, then, from 1945 the United States was implicated in the international political system to an unprecedented degree. Despite earlier, decisive contributions to two world wars, it was in the second half of the twentieth century that American political, economic and military forces were most thoroughly engaged on a global scale and most directly shaped the geopolitical system, though often by rather crudely superimposing Manichean Cold War perspectives of West against East onto struggles around the world.

Culturally too, therefore, American forces were played out on, and responsive to, a larger stage. The nuclear context itself suggested concerns that transcended national boundaries. More than any war previously, the projected nuclear conflict of the Third World War would implicate people around the planet in a common fate. Even the testing of nuclear weapons drew people together in systems and concerns that were simultaneously ecological, political and military. The displaced peoples of the Pacific, who had their lands requisitioned as test zones, the 'downwinders' from the nuclear tests in the American deserts, and the myriad recipients of fallout around the globe, especially following the Chernobyl disaster, were all casualties of the 'unfought' Cold War. In this light, novels like Masuji Ibuse's *Black Rain* (1965), about the social and cultural legacy of Hiroshima, must be seen as addressing issues of global, not just Japanese, significance.

In discussing United States fiction and prose, therefore, it is better to conceive less of an isolated national tradition, than of a network responsive to connections around the globe. For this reason, it makes sense not to be coy about leaving American shores and, for instance, crossing the Atlantic to consider *On the Beach*, written by a British author in the process of emigrating to Australia, where such texts are part of the dialogue through which United States culture is produced. Indeed, British culture, sharing a common language with America and a political class broadly aligned with the United States' stance toward the Soviet Union, provides a particularly fecund site of exchange with the United States literature with which this book is predominantly concerned. Similarly, another American voice, though not a United States one, that of the Canadian Douglas Coupland, provides a profound meditation, in a number of texts, on nuclear issues that is more broadly expressive of North American cultural responses to the bomb.

It is important, then, to embrace a spatial dynamism in addressing a United States culture constituted in part by dialogue with voices exterior to the country. For this reason, *States of Suspense* discusses foreign texts alongside United States ones where they are in some way constitutive or reflective of a United States nuclear culture. Alongside these spatial dimensions are dynamic temporal ones: nuclear anxiety has not remained static since 1945. Even during the Cold War, largely comprehensible through an organising motif of suspense, there was considerable change, as brief reference to three studies will indicate. In an article on shifting attitudes toward nuclear weapons, Kramer, Kalick and Milburn produce a bar chart showing how many opinion polls were conducted on nuclear issues each year between 1945 and 1982. Unsurprisingly, peaks accompany significant moments in nuclear history: the bombings in Japan, Russian entry into the nuclear arms race and the Cuban crisis. Interestingly, the year which overshadows all others, although it includes only four months of data, is the final one for 1982. A slightly later study by Spencer Weart – a graph showing the number of periodical articles on nuclear issues between 1900 and 1986 – coincides with Kramer, Kalick and Milburn's findings, the peaks and troughs for the years after 1945 almost exactly mirroring those of the earlier study, although it suggests a closer equivalence of interest between the early 1960s and the early 1980s. A similar study by Polyson, Hillmar and Kriek, using the same source as Weart (*The Reader's Guide to Periodical Literature*) but limited to military uses of atomic technology, produces broadly equivalent findings, but with an even more pronounced peak in the early 1980s.[16]

While such quantitative studies are inevitably limited in what they can show, they do demonstrate widely shifting levels of concern with nuclear issues. Literary responses did not simply follow these fluctuations and nor did they shift wholesale with each technological and political development of the last sixty years. Nevertheless, in order to contextualise the specific readings that will follow in this book, it is worth identifying in broad strokes some of the key phases of nuclear suspense.

Developments in nuclear anxiety: 1945–2005

What this book finds most interesting in the influence of nuclear technology, particularly the bomb, is the state of suspense it induced between 1945 and 1989. In this respect it is things not happening, it is life lived perpetually on the cusp *before* events occur, that is the main focus. This was a feature of the 'freezing' of the Cold War: an induced historical suspended animation. It seemed intransigent; it had a feeling of permanence. As John Lewes Gaddis writes, the Cold War 'went on for so long that toward its end few experts on it had experienced any other international system: comparisons across time and space faded as a result.'[17] Even until very near the end, the slow shifts that in retrospect seem inevitably to have led to its passing, appeared incapable of stopping the heavy machinery of its continuation. How could a world without the hammer and sickle, May Day parades in Moscow and the art and architecture of socialist realism, without CND marches, Conelrad and the championing of East European 'dissident' writers, and without the Berlin Wall and the threat of nuclear holocaust, be imagined? All this seemed inevitable and ongoing.

Yet, of course, beneath the surface there was much that was in flux. All of those features that had a sense of permanence to them were specific to particular phases of the Cold War. Similarly, although the state of suspense provided a thread of continuity between 1945 and 1989 (and, arguably, if to a lesser degree, since then), its character shifted with surrounding circumstances. Briefly identifying significant phases of nuclear anxiety may therefore provide a helpful, if necessarily rather schematic, contextualisation.

The first phase, *1945–49, the early atomic age*, runs from the bomb's first use to the Soviet Union's development of an atomic capability. This period has been brilliantly dissected by Paul Boyer in *By the Bomb's Early Light*, to which the reader is referred for a comprehensive survey of complex early reactions to the new era. We might nevertheless pick out a few themes from these early years. Immediate reactions to Hiroshima included horror and fear of a world-destroying atomic war. Despite initial denials by occupation forces, it also soon became apparent that survivors of Hiroshima were suffering from radiation sickness, a more nebulous and perhaps more frightening facet of the new era than the sheer explosive power of the new weapons.

Yet fear occasioned by atomic bombs also inspired hope for a system of global security, transcending nation states, to prevent atomic war. Only fourteen days after Hiroshima, the columnist Max Lerner summarised the alternatives starkly: 'world state or world doom'.[18] Such hopes were, of course, both utopian and abstract and need to be set against other, more concrete, reactions and developments.

Much as the attacks on Hiroshima and Nagasaki brought new kinds of fear, they also signalled an end to the horror of the Second World War, dramatically curtailing the long and bloody attempt to defeat Japan. From an American perspective, too, the bomb signalled the United States' pre-eminence in the emerging post-war world, even though, and perhaps even because, the team of scientists who worked on the Manhattan Project included many émigrés from Nazi persecution in Europe. The country did, after all, hold the weapon in monopoly, despite international pressure for collective control of atomic technology.

Tremendous hope was also invested in the potential for atomic energy to transform society. Numerous miracles, revolutionising transport, home life and medicine, and including the production of cheap, clean energy, were predicted for atomic technology.[19] This Janus-like nature of responses to the atom – as a bringer of deliverance as well as destruction – invested it with divine qualities with which it thereafter remained associated, although these contradictory impulses were perhaps most strongly apparent in the first decade and a half following Hiroshima. Spencer Weart argues that transmutation, the ability of atomic energy rapidly, seemingly magically, to produce change, lies at the heart of its cultural incarnation. It became a 'full symbolic representation for the entire bundle of themes involving personal, social, and cosmic destruction and rebirth'.[20] It promised – although this promise was continually deferred – the future transformation of the world, destroyed in war or delivered into a new age, freed from the constraints and conflicts produced by finite resources.

Politically, despite the Second World War alliance with the Soviet Union, the architecture of Cold War hostility between East and West emerged swiftly after 1945, creating the mould in which nuclear relations would be cast. In June 1948, the first major crisis of the new era arose when Western transport links to Berlin were cut off, precipitating a massive British and American airlift to supply West Berlin and setting the template for later deadly exercises in brinkmanship. Within a year, the creation of NATO had formalised Western alliances; little more than half a decade later, in 1955, the Warsaw Pact brought into being its Eastern Bloc corollary.

The second phase of nuclear suspense, *1949–62, the high Cold War*, is characterised by rapid technological and geopolitical developments, producing global insecurity, even if it was against a domestic background in the United States of middle-class affluence and, seemingly, security and consensus. In September 1949 tests confirmed a successful Soviet bomb test, although only two months earlier the CIA had predicted a breathing space of four years before this would happen.[21] This added urgency to calls to develop the more powerful hydrogen bomb and in 1952 the United States tested such a device, producing an explosion a thousand times greater than that over Hiroshima. The Soviet Union soon caught up and by 1955 had built one that could be dropped from an airplane. Images of bomb tests punctuated the 1950s, appearing, for instance, on the covers of magazines like *Life*,[22] as the nuclear states flexed their technological muscles.

The growing stockpiles of atomic weapons, their increased power and the diversification of the means by which they could be delivered to targets around the world, made the relative isolation of the continental United States seem increasingly irrelevant in the face of attack. In 1955 a bomber was revealed at the Moscow Air Show that had the range to reach the United States, and in 1957 the Soviet Union tested the first intercontinental ballistic missile and launched Sputnik, the first satellite.[23] Although there was a disparity between what seemed, and what was, possible, the perception of a potent Russian capability challenged the security promised by post-war affluence. Although Sputnik only broadcast simple radio signals, it had a profound symbolic impact, speaking to the United States' fears of technological inferiority; when Yuri Gagarin became the first man in space in 1961, these fears seemed to be confirmed. Sputnik also symbolised a susceptibility to attack from above: orbiting the world, it combined with the nuclear threat to make North American skies feel more vulnerable than ever before. Although Soviet capabilities proved to be less developed than was feared

– when Kennedy became president, for instance, he discovered that the 'missile gap', on which he had in part campaigned, was illusory – the general perception that the United States was in danger of losing the arms race was important.

It is in their impact on the imagination that technological developments were most strikingly influential. Aside from the strategic potential of nuclear weapons (which was actually increasingly limited: as stockpiles grew they became a weapon of last and suicidal resort), they had a psychological role to play that was lost on neither superpower. A feature of political discourse of the period was the bellicose statement of intent to use nuclear weapons. Indeed, if actually useless in a war (despite the protestations of the hawks who maintained the nuclear option was a viable strategy), their real use – the way in which they were in fact used – was in the imaginary wars threatened and projected by the superpowers to constrain each other's behaviour. Nuclear fear had, therefore, to be kept alive to some degree. While the intended audience for such fears might ideally have been limited to the political classes of the opposing superpowers, they also inevitably reached a wider public.

Civil defence was another prominent feature of this period, with bomb drills taking place in schools, plans for large public defence projects and, at the height of the Berlin crisis in 1961, much publicity about shelters available on the market to homeowners. Yet, while the illusion of effective civil defence was integral both to the effectiveness of the United States' nuclear strategy, and to gaining domestic consensus for this strategy, plans for an enormous civil defence infrastructure never got off the ground, partly for reasons of cost and partly because developments in the offensive capability of missiles swiftly outstripped the already dubious claim that surviving attack was possible. With authorities unwilling to commit capital to ineffective preparations, but with a need to maintain the myth of civil defence, the emphasis increasingly fell on the personal responsibility of private citizens to prepare their homes for attack. There was, therefore, a contradiction at the heart of public discourse about deterrence: it necessitated both that the overwhelmingly destructive power of nuclear weaponry be emphasised, and that it be seen as relatively safe, survivable with a few basic domestic preparations.

Another flaw in the notion that nuclear weapons guaranteed security emerged with the revelation that even in bomb tests the destructive power of the atom could not be contained. The *Lucky Dragon* incident in 1954, in which the crew of a Japanese fishing boat suffered radiation sickness from an unexpectedly powerful H-bomb test over eighty miles away, was a crucial moment, but there were also outcries closer to home over increased levels of strontium-90, a by-product of weapons testing, in human bones and teeth. The very bomb tests which demonstrated the United States' power and authority within the world were simultaneously contributing to environmental pollution and, potentially, killing its own citizens.

The destabilising impact of rapid technological change was matched by international political volatilities as the Cold War found its shape. Dramatic tensions and events around the world seemed to confirm the United States' suspicion that the world was dividing into opposing capitalist and communist camps. The division of Europe into East and West continued apace. The brutal suppression of the Hungarian uprising in 1956 demonstrated the Soviets' refusal to cede ground, and the division of East and West Germany, particularly in Berlin, remained a potential flashpoint for World War Three. The building of the Berlin Wall in 1961 both brought this to crisis and, in the longer term, symbolised the acceptance by both sides of the division of Europe. The wall became a symbol not only of this division but also of permanence and the fraught stasis in which this book is interested.

The Korean War produced the first major military engagements for Western forces, setting a precedent both for the sponsoring of friendly indigenous forces and for direct military intervention. It also raised the question of whether atomic weapons would be used in 'local' conflicts.[24] Mao Zedong's success in China increased Western paranoia that the momentum was with communism around the world, and the messy French withdrawal from Indochina created the conditions for the Vietnam War.

The dangers of the new technological and political eras coalesced in the Cuban crisis of 1962, the discovery of Soviet medium-range missiles so close to the Florida coast provoking the most dangerous Cold War moment. Secret recordings of White House discussions demonstrate how close war was. Richard Russell, Chairman of the Armed Services Committee and one of Kennedy's advisors during the crisis, saw, for instance, an opportunity to precipitate, on the United States' terms, a war some saw as inevitable: 'Oh, my God, I know that [it's a difficult decision]. A war, our destiny, will hinge on it. But it's coming someday, Mr. President. Will it ever be under more auspicious circumstances?'[25] Subsequently, Robert McNamara, the Secretary of Defense, considered the avoidance of war to be pure chance: 'I want to say, and this is very important, at the end we lucked out. It was luck that prevented nuclear war. . . . Rational individuals came that close to the total destruction of their societies.'[26] Yet the fact that war did not occur perhaps helped to quell specifically nuclear fears in the following decades. More formal means of communication, like the establishment of a 'hotline' between Washington and Moscow, followed the crisis and offered some reassurance. The Test Ban Treaty of 1963, preventing further atmospheric tests by the superpowers, if not by everyone (France was not a signatory), had the effect of making weapons testing less public and taking nuclear issues out of public view.

The following phase of nuclear suspense, *1963–79, détente*, saw a period of much less explicit nuclear fear. The surveys of opinion polls and periodical articles noted above all show a dramatic decline in the prominence of nuclear issues during this period,[27] although it is probably less a case of nuclear anxieties disappearing, than of their being driven beneath the surface of the culture.

One reason for this is that other Cold War events, notably the United States' involvement in the Vietnam War, distracted attention from nuclear issues. For instance, the Committee for a Sane Nuclear Policy (SANE) reoriented its protests away from the bomb toward Vietnam, dropping the word 'nuclear' from its name in 1969.[28] More broadly, turmoil within the country over issues like Civil Rights, and the relations between mainstream and increasingly vocal countercultures, also filled the spaces in which nuclear issues had previously been discussed.

There were, nevertheless, important technological and political developments. From the early 1960s, nuclear missiles housed in submarines increased the potential for surprise or retaliatory attacks. Later, Multiple Independently Targetable Re-Entry Vehicles (MIRVs), allowing individual missiles to split into individual warheads aimed at different targets, made defence against attack even less likely. One effect was to place even greater emphasis on the threat of an all-out retaliatory counterstrike as the primary defensive option, and it was in this period that Mutual Assured Destruction (MAD) was finally fully established as the central strategy.

Nevertheless, the Strategic Arms Limitation Treaty (SALT) talks in the 1970s provided temporary hope for control of the arms race. Long-term failure to make progress in these talks did, however, increase the sense that the Cold War would not thaw and that the world had entered a sustained period of struggle between East and West.[29]

At the same time, seemingly separate developments had implications for how people saw nuclear issues. Primary among these was the emergence of a modern environmentalist movement, traceable to Rachel Carson's *Silent Spring* (1962), which provided powerful ways of conceptualising what military and civilian nuclear technology might be doing to the planet. 'Green' perspectives, while not necessarily anti-nuclear, often were analogous to those of protesters against the arms race and nuclear power, and they produced vocal, if not always influential, political lobby groups. More broadly, as chapter five explains, they redefined our conception of the Earth, and of humans' place upon it, in ways that facilitated global, rather than strictly national, responses to nuclear issues.

Environmental issues were also prominent in the *war fear revival and decline, 1980–89*,[30] which constituted the final phase of the Cold War period of the nuclear era. Jonathan Schell's *The Fate of the Earth* (1982) presented nuclear war as a catastrophic eco-collapse, and the idea of 'nuclear winter', as a consequence of World War Three, also gained popular currency at this time.[31]

Most notable about this period, though, was the sudden upsurge in publicly expressed fear of nuclear war. This may have been due to the overtly bellicose postures adopted by Soviet and United States administrations as the 1980s dawned. At the end of 1979 the Soviet Union invaded Afghanistan to prop up its failing communist regime. In the United States, Ronald Reagan's government increased defence spending (up 50% during Reagan's first term in office) and insisted the country could 'prevail' in a war with the Soviet Union, implying that nuclear conflict was seen as a viable strategic option.[32] The Strategic Defense Initiative (SDI), popularly known as Star Wars, further destabilised the entrenched nuclear standoff by threatening to remove a fundamental characteristic of MAD, the guarantee of both sides' destruction.

Political debate about nuclear weapons involved unprecedented dissent from official policy. In Europe, proposals to site American Pershing II and cruise missiles on the continent focused protest and brought many onto the streets. In

Britain the Campaign for Nuclear Disarmament (CND), though over twenty years old, enjoyed by far its most significant boom in membership. The women's peace camp at Greenham Common also served to keep nuclear protest in the news.

Feeding off, and into, the cultural momentum around nuclear issues at this time were a series of significant popular texts from both sides of the Atlantic. Raymond Briggs's cartoon depiction of nuclear war, *When the Wind Blows* (1982), was translated into radio and film versions, and effectively satirised the British government's 'Protect and Survive' civil defence advice (which also gave anti-nuclear campaigners one of their most memorable slogans: 'Protest and Survive'). Two pieces of 'event' television, ABC's *The Day After* (1983) and the BBC's *Threads* (1984), brought visions of nuclear war to television screens.[33] Later, the BBC's *Edge of Darkness* (1985) made explicit links between civilian nuclear power, military nuclear technology and the threat to the environment. Hersey's *Hiroshima* was reissued in an expanded edition in 1984.

Academic engagement with nuclear issues was also reinvigorated in this period. For instance, significant work on the psychology of nuclear fear, and the literary representation of nuclear issues, emerged in the 1980s.

Yet, even as the Cold War seemed dangerous again, it was winding down toward its end. By the second half of the decade, the Soviet Union had a new kind of leader in Mikhail Gorbachev, and the Russian terms 'perestroika' (restructuring) and 'glasnost' (openness) had entered Western consciousness. Summits with Reagan seemed to produce progress toward arms control and reduction. In three short years, everything changed: in 1989, old-guard communist leaders were ousted in Poland, Hungary, Czechoslovakia, East Germany and Romania, and the Berlin Wall was torn down; in 1990, a number of Soviet republics declared their independence from Moscow; and by the end of 1991, Gorbachev himself had relinquished power and a new phase of American fears, though it may only read thus in retrospect, was signalled by the first Gulf War.[34]

The post-Cold War phases of nuclear anxiety, *1990–2001, after the Cold War*, and *2001 onwards, the 'War on Terror'*, undoubtedly have involved a lessening of the dread of global holocaust, and the United States and Russia certainly hold fewer nuclear weapons than they did. Although there were not the 'swords into ploughshares' dividends optimistically forecast immediately following the Cold War, it is now conceivable to think of the future as unshadowed by the worst terrors of the preceding half century.

Of course, nuclear issues have not disappeared. The issue of disposal of nuclear waste makes periodic appearances in the news, and the problem of reducing carbon emissions has reignited passionate debates about nuclear power. In a military context, tensions between India and Pakistan, and the prospect of North Korean and Iranian nuclear arsenals, have shifted the focus from an essentially bipolar global standoff (albeit that this ignored, for example, possible Israeli nuclear capabilities) to complex multiple nuclear relationships between relatively numerous nuclear states. Discourse about nuclear terrorism and 'dirty bombs' has become particularly insistent following the 2001 attacks on the World Trade

Center, and the subsequent construction of a global 'War on Terror'. Perhaps as importantly, the legacy of nuclear fear has given shape to contemporary non-nuclear fears of, for instance, global warming and 'conventional' terrorism. So, to take a minor example, the idea of the nuclear-imperilled city finds, after 9/11, contemporary incarnation in the terrorist-threatened city. Whereas earlier terrorist outrages tended to be conceived in more localised terms (the Hyde Park and Regent's Park bombings of 1982, for example), contemporary attacks are almost always seen as attacks on great cities (the Madrid and London bombings). This is partly to do with the scale of the attacks (multiple explosions across cities) but is perhaps also because they are presented as outrages against civilisation, just as during the Cold War projected nuclear attacks on cities functioned symbolically to denote the threat to civilisation.

While this book does not contest the idea that the nuclear fears of the Cold War were qualitatively different, it challenges the notion that there was an absolute break between the two periods. Rather than seeing the fall of the Berlin Wall as the end of the nuclear era, we could profitably conceive of the present as a second nuclear age, perhaps less dangerous than the first but nonetheless marked by significant continuities with it.

The six phases of nuclear anxiety, identified above, are intended only to capture, in the broadest strokes, some of the main developments in a long and complex period. They cannot account for differences of perception and representation between different countries, regions, individuals or texts. It is not proposed, then, that tracing literary changes, in direct accordance with these six phases, is an especially useful or revealing enterprise and *States of Suspense* does not attempt to do this. Complicating factors are: the differences of penetration of nuclear issues amongst different people, according to, for instance, upbringing, social context, geographical location and political persuasion; the tendency of motifs from one phase to bleed into those of another; the time lag between the impact of various ideas and their appearance in published writing; and the way in which the production of textual nuclear anxieties is a function of reading as well as of writing (so the fears of an earlier era, and earlier texts, may be reproduced, transfigured or nullified by those of later ones).

However, not all generalisations are futile. It is helpful to read individual texts, in all their subtlety and idiosyncrasy, against the broad sweep of more general historical and cultural developments. To reiterate: *States of Suspense* is not a survey and does not claim to be comprehensive. It intends the explication of motifs of nuclear anxiety in specific texts, but these readings and texts sit within the broad framework of the nuclear era, sketched out in the developments outlined above without being absolutely determined by them.

While a lengthy multi-volume work would be necessary to trace in full every avenue down which nuclear influences travelled, *States of Suspense* seeks, more suggestively, to flag up some of the cultural effects of nuclear technology that are easy to overlook when exploring United States literary history of the last sixty years. In particular, suspense should be recognised as an intrinsic feature of the cultural response to the world-changing events that both did – and pointedly did not – happen following the atomic explosion over Hiroshima on 6 August, 1945.

Notes

1 Jeremy Isaacs and Taylor Downing, *Cold War* (London: Bantam, 1998), p. 30.
2 Martin Amis, 'Introduction: thinkability', in Amis, *Einstein's Monsters* (1987; London: Vintage, 2003), p. 24.
3 Jacqueline Foertsch, 'Not bombshells but basketcases: gendered illness in nuclear texts', *Studies in the Novel* 31:4 (1999), 471.
4 Elaine Tyler May, *Homeward Bound: American Families in the Cold War Era*, 2nd ed. (New York: Basic Books, 1999). Alan Nadel, *Containment Culture: American Narratives, Postmodernism, and the Atomic Age* (Durham: Duke University Press, 1995).
5 Tom Vanderbilt, *Survival City: Adventures Among the Ruins of Atomic America* (New York: Princeton Architectural Press, 2002), p. 39.
6 For a definition of 'nuclearism' see the discussion of Lifton in chapter two.
7 Jacqueline R. Smetak, 'So long, Mom: the politics of nuclear holocaust fiction', *Papers on Language and Literature: A Journal for Scholars and Critics of Language and Literature* 26:1 (1990), 55.
8 Perrin L. French and Judith Van Hoorn, 'Half a nation saw nuclear war and nobody blinked?: *The Day After* in terms of a theoretical chain of causality', *International Journal of Mental Health* 15:1–3 (1986), 276–97. As the authors acknowledge, this effect was exacerbated by the film's presentation of nuclear war as something that 'simply occurred, as an earthquake, forest fire, flood, or other natural disaster might occur' (p. 286). Unfortunately a similar study is not available on the BBC's more polemical film, *Threads* (1984), scripted by Barry Hines and directed by Mick Jackson.
9 Mary McCarthy felt Hersey 'actually diminished the atomic bomb by treating it as one would a natural catastrophe – a fire, flood, or earthquake – solely for its "human interest" value.' Paul Boyer, *By the Bomb's Early Light: American Thought and Culture at the Dawn of the Atomic Age* (1985; Chapel Hill: University of North Carolina Press, new ed., 1994), p. 206. As Boyer observes, McCarthy's reading does not do justice to the task facing Hersey.
10 Pat Frank, *Alas, Babylon* (New York: HarperPerennial, 1999), p. 228.
11 Isaacs and Downing, *Cold War*, p. 248.
12 Nadel, *Containment Culture*, p. 5. While broadly following Nadel, I dispute the details of his reading of *Hiroshima*. He treats it more as a novel than a work of reportage. The limits it reveals are, surely, those of journalism not fiction. The direct product, in later culture, of the contradictions *Hiroshima* struggles to contain is not so much postmodern fiction as its journalistic equivalent, the 'new' or 'gonzo' journalism of the 1960s and 1970s.
13 Kathryn Hume, *American Dream, American Nightmare: Fiction Since 1960* (Urbana: University of Illinois Press, 2000). Kenneth Millard, *Contemporary American Fiction: An Introduction to American Fiction Since 1970* (Oxford: Oxford University Press, 2000).
14 John Lewes Gaddis, *We Now Know: Rethinking Cold War History* (Oxford: Oxford University Press, 1997), p. 140.
15 Isaacs and Downing speculate briefly on the scale of this human toll. *Cold War*, p. 420.
16 Weart's graphs are particularly helpful, distinguishing between military and civilian nuclear technology, measuring positive and negative responses to civilian technology, and showing not simply the raw number of articles dealing with nuclear issues, but the fraction of the total number of indexed articles they represent. Bernard M. Kramer, S. Michael Kalick

and Michael A. Milburn, 'Attitudes toward nuclear weapons and nuclear war: 1945–1982', *Journal of Social Issues* 39:1 (1983), 10. Spencer R. Weart, *Nuclear Fear: A History of Images* (Cambridge: Harvard University Press, 1988), p. 387. James Polyson, Jodi Hillmar and Douglas Kriek, 'Levels of public interest in nuclear war', *Journal of Social Behavior and Personality* 1:3 (1986), 399.

17 John Lewes Gaddis, *We Now Know: Rethinking Cold War History* (Oxford: Oxford University Press, 1997), p. 282.

18 Quoted in Boyer, *By the Bomb's Early Light*, p. 34.

19 For detailed information on these utopian predictions, see, in particular, part 4, 'Anodyne to terror: fantasies of a techno-atomic utopia' (pp. 107–30) and part 5, 'The social implications of atomic energy: prophecies and prescriptions' (pp. 131–78) of Boyer, *By the Bomb's Early Light*.

20 Weart, *Nuclear Fear*, p. 406.

21 Isaacs and Downing, *Cold War*, p. 146.

22 Atomic explosions were *Life*'s cover story on 27 February 1950, 19 April 1954 and 20 July 1962.

23 See 'Sputnik and the bomb: 1949–1961' in Isaacs and Downing, *Cold War*, pp. 144–63.

24 Truman had refused to rule out the use of nuclear weapons. Eisenhower, his successor as president, threatened their use in May 1953. He also considered using them to defend Taiwan against China in 1958.

25 Ernest R. May and Philip D. Zelikow (eds), *The Kennedy Tapes: Inside the White House During the Cuban Missile Crisis* (Cambridge: Harvard University Press, 1997), p. 265.

26 McNamara says these words in the documentary film, *The Fog of War* (US, Errol Morris 2003).

27 See note 16.

28 Paul Boyer, *Fallout: A Historian Reflects on America's Half-Century Encounter with Nuclear Weapons* (Columbus: Ohio State University Press, 1998), pp. 121–2.

29 After four years of talks, SALT I was signed in 1972. However, SALT II remained unratified and the terms of the first treaty, which forbade the development of new missile systems, were contravened when the US embarked on the Strategic Defense Initiative in 1983.

30 I take the phrase, 'war fear revival', from one of Weart's chapter headings. Weart, *Nuclear Fear*, pp. 375–87.

31 The idea was first proposed in R. P. Turco et al., 'Nuclear winter: global consequences of multiple nuclear explosions', *Science* 222 (23 December 1983), 1283–92.

32 Isaacs and Downing, *Cold War*, p. 334. An extended investigation of the Reagan administration's attitude to nuclear war is F. H. Knelman's *Reagan, God and the Bomb* (Toronto: McClelland and Stewart, 1985). Knelman's alarming claims about Reagan's hawkishness should be balanced against the progress made toward détente in various summits between Reagan and Gorbachev in the second half of the 1980s.

33 The BBC's 1965 drama about nuclear war, *The War Game* (dir. Peter Watkins), had been kept off television screens, although it was released in cinemas in 1966.

34 For a good general introduction to the final years of the Cold War, see the chapters on 'Gorbachev, 1984–88' (pp. 354–73), 'People power, 1989' (pp. 374–97) and 'Endings, 1990–1991' (pp. 398–421) in Isaacs and Downing, *Cold War*.

I
The nuclear age

1

The literatures of the nuclear age: fictions of disaster and anxiety

It's time to move on. (Paul Brians, 'Farewell to the first atomic age', 1992)[1]

It is not surprising that our view of what is significant in literature should shift with the social and historical context from which we view it. With a technology definitive in so many ways of the struggle between East and West between 1945 and 1989, nuclear literature provides a particularly stark instance of these revaluations. Over a decade and a half into a post-Cold War environment, contemporary nuclear criticism is freed from the siren song of hypothetical global holocausts. In particular, it can move from fictions of nuclear disaster to those of nuclear anxiety. This can mean looking at entirely new texts; it can also mean valuing established nuclear texts in different ways.

If this new environment opens up possibilities for nuclear criticism, it did not always seem thus. Indeed, at first the end of the Cold War induced a sense of crisis in the field: the threat it sought to resist seemed to have passed. Bidding farewell in 1992 to his editorship of the scholarly newsletter, *Nuclear Texts and Contexts*, the critic Paul Brians noted this juncture: 'we have gone through a major historical transition, from an era during which nuclear holocaust seemed imminent to many people to an era during which it is a remote prospect indeed'.[2] This impacted both on literature (Brians identifies a 'steep decline' in the number of nuclear holocaust fictions published in the 1990s) and criticism (he points out that his own work, *Nuclear Holocausts*, had been remaindered, and an updated edition was now unlikely to appear).[3]

'Moving on', therefore, meant leaving behind a number of things: it was not only the end of Brians' editorship, but also of the Cold War, of the threat of global nuclear holocaust and of this topic as a live subject for fiction. Nuclear criticism, not yet a decade old (its birth is best dated to a special edition of *Diacritics* on nuclear issues in 1984),[4] no longer seemed necessary. A year after Brians' farewell, in a brilliant analysis of the field, Ken Ruthven predicted that his own book, and one by Patrick Mannix on the same subject, would be seen as 'belated examples by a couple of yesterday's men of a defunct critical mode'.[5]

But moving on need not only mean leaving something behind. It can also mean taking things forward. I have dealt elsewhere with the complex movement from a first phase (Cold War) to a second phase (post-Cold War) of nuclear criticism,[6] but it is worth picking out here one feature of the former – the peculiar ethico-political context in which it operated – in order to demonstrate the scope opened up for the latter.

A primary motivation for the development of first-phase nuclear criticism was a widespread resurfacing in the 1980s of fear of nuclear war. Although this critical endeavour comprised a complex set of sometimes contradictory perspectives (Ruthven distinguishes between two main branches, each expressive of broader contemporary practices in literary studies: 'Nuclear Criticism as a state-of-the-art critical theory . . . [and] nuclear criticism as a comparatively untheorised critical practice')[7] it was united by its sense of the urgency of the nuclear debate. The value of addressing nuclear issues 'now' was that nuclear war was a pressing possibility demanding immediate attention before it was too late. Discussion of nuclear issues was seen, in part, as a consciousness-raising exercise loosely contributory to the prevention of nuclear war. For example, Patrick Mannix suggested that antinuclear fiction 'strengthens our resolve' to resist armageddon, Paul Brians wrote that it could have 'an admonitory effect which may be valuable in a world perpetually perched on the brink of an atomic holocaust', I. F. Clarke claimed that '[l]earn or perish . . . is the common text for . . . tales of nuclear catastrophe', and David Dowling wrote that we 'call on the power of the word to de-fuse the power of the fused atom' and that we 'try to speak it [the world's end] so that we might not know it'.[8] Although some of these first-phase critical texts appeared just after the end of the Cold War, either their production was rooted in the earlier fearful atmosphere or, like Ruthven, they found themselves apologising for their own redundancy.

Being opposed to nuclear war, as this first-phase criticism was, was not in itself, of course, a radical position. Even most hawks were not 'for' nuclear war *per se*, arguing that armament and a strong line with the Soviet Union were the best ways to preserve the peace. What distinguished nuclear critics from such conservative perspectives was that they frequently sought to undermine the presumptions underpinning the nuclear state and nuclear strategy; they broadly opposed what Robert Jay Lifton called 'nuclearism'.[9]

A general goal of this first-phase criticism was to raise consciousness about the possibility of nuclear war. Such a goal produces a particular critical subject: the representation of nuclear war itself. Fictions of nuclear disaster were the primary focus for first-phase nuclear criticism because they drew attention to the worst consequences of the Cold War arms race, looming in the future.

Freed of this Cold War imperative, second-phase nuclear criticism does not have to keep returning to the possible imminence of nuclear war. It is liberated to look at other dimensions of nuclear culture even as its concerns may overlap with those of the earlier critics.

What then might be the justification for a second phase of nuclear criticism if it no longer needs to contest the hawkish postures of the Cold War United States and Soviet Union? The first is simply that of historical accuracy. A defining feature of the Cold War period was the nuclear context, and to ignore it is to fail to represent the period in full as surely as if one were to ignore Civil Rights struggles, debates about gender and sexuality or the rise of late capitalism. The Cold War nuclear standoff changed the sense of personal and collective peril, even if it often fell into the background in comparison with, say, protest about the Vietnam War in the late 1960s.

Redressing this imbalance can involve looking afresh at nuclear disaster fictions – the same texts tackled by earlier nuclear critics – as David Seed does in *American Science Fiction and the Cold War*.[10] In *States of Suspense* this means reading them through the issue of anxiety and considering them in terms less of the nuclear wars they describe, and more of the world on the brink of nuclear war out of which they come.

Alternatively, reassessing the period in the light of nuclear concerns might involve a broader analysis of the impact of nuclear issues on society, as it does in Margot Henriksen's *Dr. Strangelove's America*.[11] In *States of Suspense* this means moving out into texts closer to the cultural mainstream, where the nuclear seems to be a more peripheral concern, or even one that is not directly mentioned, to explore the shaping influence of nuclear contexts on their meaning. It can also mean the contrary motion, less important to, though not absent from, this book, of reading nuclear motifs as metaphors for other social concerns.

Finally, a new nuclear criticism might look to the ongoing representation of nuclear issues in the culture, a subject broached in the final chapter of this book. This might mean exploring the lasting legacies of nuclearism or analysing the transformations in the concepts of anxiety and terror since the Cold War.

Centrally for this book, though, the passing of the Cold War and the opportunity this gives us to focus on the literature of nuclear anxiety rather than disaster, means that we can reassess what constitutes the nuclear literature of the Cold War period. Just as, for Nadel, 'containment culture . . . was a product of large, unstable elements – nuclei radiating their detritus',[12] so, for *States of Suspense*, the traces of nuclear anxiety are more widely scattered than we might expect. Suspense and anxiety are definitive features of the Cold War cultural response to nuclear technology, and it is to the literary representation of these things that the chapter now turns, before moving on to contextualise them in relation to postmodern culture.

The literature of nuclear anxiety

It is useful to distinguish between nuclear disaster narratives (those texts concerned with the lead up to, or the experience or aftermath of, nuclear holocaust) and nuclear anxiety narratives (where the focus is less on the physical impact of nuclear war, than on the psychological and cultural consequences of living in anticipation of this event). To be sure there is overlap between the two. Disaster narratives, for instance, may originate in nuclear anxiety and frequently involve some representation of it. Nevertheless, the master trope of disaster will often, in these texts, subsume and resolve the potentially disruptive forces of anxiety. It may even cathartically exorcise them.

Closure is a key issue. Nuclear anxiety is, until at least the end of the Cold War, held in suspension, left unresolved either by disarmament or by conflict. Nuclear disaster narratives provide a fantasy of resolution to this anxious suspense and thus slide over the states of mind definitive of the period. Even nuclear thriller narratives, of the race-against-time-to-stop-the-bomb type, which we might expect to be more attuned to the depiction of suspense, actually are best understood as disaster texts, providing closure by the overt aversion of immediate nuclear crisis. They too distract from the signature Cold War experience: drawn out, unresolved suspense.

In contrast, nuclear anxiety literature represents not nuclear war *per se*, but anxiety produced in anticipation of it. There are a number of locations in which we might look for depictions of this anxiety. First, and most obviously, there are those rare texts that take nuclear anxiety (rather than nuclear disaster) as their main subject. Most prominent among these, and a frequent point of reference in this book because it is so central to the canon of anxiety fiction, is Tim O'Brien's *The Nuclear Age* (1985). The narrator-protagonist, William Cowling, is part of what Michael Mandelbaum calls the 'nuclear haunted' generation in the United States,[13] who as children experienced drills for atomic attack at school, whose first adolescent cognitions of death coincided with prominent public discussion of the possibility of nuclear war, and who would have been familiar with nuclear imagery from media photographs and newsreel footage of bomb tests. William is indeed haunted, recurrently suffering the psychological and physiological effects of his nuclear obsession: dreams and visions of nuclear destruction; generalised anxiety and insecurity; constipation. Although the scale of his fear is exceptional, he represents, in caricature, a more widely felt nuclear anxiety. Crucially, William's narrative gives the novel a focus less on nuclear war itself than on the long-term psychological impact of living with the possibility of this event. Even though he is revealed to be self-deceiving, with some of his anxieties rooted in traumas peculiar to him (as when the panic that leads to the digging of a bomb shelter is revealed to be induced by the discovery of his wife's infidelity), William is noteworthy, nevertheless, as a rare fictional depiction of someone whose psychological and personal life is acknowledged to be shaped by the existence of nuclear weapons.

Yet narratives making this their main subject are extremely rare and certainly considerably less numerous than disaster fictions. One reason for this is quite mundane: there are many more narrative possibilities in the event itself than there are in the definitively non-eventful dimensions of nuclear anxiety. Another reason is that people became habituated to nuclear peril. While nuclear war itself remained the subject of periodic comment or protest, the attendant anxiety was normalised, its most dramatic fears quelled by the year-on-year persistence of non-nuclear everyday life. A further reason stems from a 'psychic numbing' identified by Lifton.[14] While nuclear war could be represented in a relatively direct form, through an established, perhaps even cathartic, iconography of mushroom clouds and flattened cities, the nebulous and unresolved anxiety its possibility induced was harder to conceptualise and the mind might actively resist contemplating it. Finally, a 'containment culture' effectively connected microcosmic, domestic to macrocosmic, geopolitical realms such that preoccupations in one were metamorphosed into new forms in the other.[15] Nuclear anxieties were thus blurred, morphing into forms not immediately identifiable as nuclear and also functioning as metaphors for other social anxieties.

Although its *direct* expression is unusual, though, it can be found through attentive reading of texts where it might not immediately be apparent. Disaster fictions, for instance, can be read in ways that open up their anxious aspects. Conventional nuclear narratives, like Nevil Shute's *On the Beach* (1957) and Judith Merril's *Shadow on the Hearth* (1950), are about anxiety as much as they are about nuclear war, though the latter may be their more obvious subject.

Furthermore, there are 'anxious' moments, explicitly or metaphorically nuclear, in other texts not obviously nuclear at all. When the eponymous protagonist of Saul Bellow's *Herzog* (1964) opens a newspaper, a 'hostile broth of black print', and reads, '*MoonraceberlinKhrushchwarncommitteegalacticXrayPhouma*', the novel communicates not simply a cursory glance at the headlines, but an eruption of intermingled geopolitical and personal anxieties into the mundane reality of Grand Central station. Anxieties also haunt Esther Greenwood, the narrator of Sylvia Plath's *The Bell Jar* (1963), whose reality is similarly transformed by oppressive Cold War national and military contexts. Eisenhower not only 'beamed up at me' from *Time*, 'bald and blank as the face of a foetus in a bottle', but more disturbingly is encountered in the pictures of 'Eisenhower-faced babies' in the magazine, *Baby Talk*.[16] Tuberculosis is described as 'a bomb in your lung'; her oppressive boyfriend has a 'khaki' cap; 'red and blue and white jacketed skiers' fling themselves down a ski slope 'like fugitive bits of an American flag'; and her hotel in New York has a view out to where the 'UN balanced itself in the dark, like a weird, green, Martian honeycomb'.[17]

In heightened versions of these generalised Cold War anxieties, texts sometimes contain eruptions of the nuclear into the imagination. In Don DeLillo's *End Zone* (1972), Gary Harkness, a college footballer, has waking visions of nuclear holocaust and plays out a nuclear conflict in a war game. In the Canadian writer Douglas Coupland's *Generation X* (1991), a post-Cold War text that carries the markers of the earlier era and is drenched in apocalyptic images, Dag tells a story to his friends in which they are asked to imagine themselves in a supermarket when nuclear war starts. In Bellow's *Mr. Sammler's Planet* (1970), Artur Sammler is caught between the utopian dreams of Govinda Lal, who writes of fleeing the earth to establish colonies on the moon, and the possibility of the Earth being destroyed ('[t]o blow this great blue, white, green planet, or to be blown from it'),[18] an outcome which is linked in the novel to Sammler's first-hand experience of the Jewish holocaust of the Second World War.

Such instances are surfacings in the texts, and in the characters' mental lives, of psychological traces of anxiety about the end of the world specific to the Cold War context. They are sometimes unbidden, sometimes willed, sometimes moments of emotional and existential terror, and at others rationally analysed possibilities. While earlier literature was certainly not without eschatological dimensions, the Cold War context inflects these visions of the end in specific ways. Nuclear anxieties are tangible extrapolations about the future from the contemporary technological and geopolitical environment (or, in the case of *Generation X*, recent memories of such possible futures). The nuclear end is imagined as coming with little warning, as wreaking its effects with remarkable rapidity and as being largely arbitrary, rather than an expression of the divine apportioning of justice that accompanies conventional eschatological visions. The effect of these eruptions is widely varied. While, for instance, Gary Harkness finds himself increasingly isolated from others by his fascination with nuclear holocaust, Andy, Dag and Claire's sharing of end-of-the-world stories is a way of giving meaning to their lives and cementing their friendship.

Such explicit visions of nuclear war are not the only traces that reveal nuclear anxiety. An analogy might be made with the architectural legacy of the Cold War which, as Tom Vanderbilt writes, is both ubiquitous and obscure: 'The Cold War was – and is – everywhere in America, if one knows where to look for it. Underground, behind closed doors, classified, off the map, already crumbling beyond recognition, or right in plain view, it has left an imprint as widespread yet discreet as the tracings of radioactive particles that blew out of the Nevada Test Site in the 1950s.'[19] Literary markers of nearly half a century of nuclear standoff are similarly 'widespread yet discreet', only becoming apparent when we make ourselves alive to them so they are not passed, un-noted, in texts.

Sometimes these are, pace Vanderbilt, literally architectural, particularly in the United States where civil defence produced numerous physical changes to the built environment. Whereas British civil defence was largely a muted affair – revealingly, in John Wyndham's *The Midwich Cuckoos* (1957), a village meeting to discuss the strange events at Midwich only generates interest '[o]nce people had been convinced that it was not simply a matter of another Civil Defence drive'[20] – in the United States it had a greater manifest impact. In Jayne Anne Phillips' *Machine Dreams* (1984) Mitch proposes building 'an airtight shelter' about the time of the Cuban Missile Crisis,[21] bringing to a head a domestic crisis with Jean. In O'Brien's *Northern Lights* (1975), Perry and Harvey's dying father urges them to build a fallout shelter, described, in an image expressive of a broader concern with emasculation in the text, as protection against radiation that will rot 'a man's testicles'.[22]

In *Vineland* (1990), Pynchon re-imagines the country's highways in terms of a secret nuclear America. An ominous convoy of 'field-gray trucks, locked shut, unmarked' drives a 'little-known and only confidentially traveled FEER, or Federal Emergency Evacuation Route' that is shrouded in camouflage and was originally conceived, disturbingly, as 'a disposable freeway that would only be used, to full capacity, once'. Clearly part of contingency planning for nuclear war, the road leads to a secret valley 'intended as a holding area able to house up to half a million urban evacuees in the event of, well, say, some urban evacuation'.[23] While a characteristically Pynchoneseque paranoia underpins this other, unmapped America coexisting, palimpsest-like, with more public Americas, such re-imaginings of the landscape are not limited to the pages of fiction. In *Travels with Charley* (1962), his account of a road trip around the United States, John Steinbeck writes of getting lost in traffic. Finding himself between a cement mixer and 'what I judged to be an atomic cannon', he suddenly realises he is on an Evacuation Route, 'a road designed by fear'. Recalling turkeys on a farm ('[t]hey gather in vulnerable groups and then panic at rumours'), he imagines, in an interesting juxtaposition of images of movement and stasis, people fleeing nuclear attack: 'the roads clogged to a standstill and the stampede over a cliff of our own designing'.[24]

We can easily add other examples: the abandoned uranium mine in Leslie Marmon Silko's *Ceremony* (1977), or even the city streets down which Daniel and Susan, 'alone in the Cold War', run in E. L. Doctorow's *The Book of Daniel* (1971).[25] We need not, of course, limit ourselves to the physical environment, and might consider, for instance, the V-2 rockets that become nuclear at the end of Thomas Pynchon's *Gravity's Rainbow* (1973), the hysterical paranoia of the United States of Robert Coover's *The Public Burning* (1977), or the analogies between Fidel Castro's Cuba and 'Papa' Monzano's San Lorenzo, from where ice-nine destroys the world, in Kurt Vonnegut's *Cat's Cradle* (1963).

It is not, of course, profound to point out that these features are related to the Cold War environment, many of them unthinkable in literature before 1945. But when we start to take note of these markers we realise that, far from being insignificant details of individual texts, or significant only in terms of the particular texts within which they appear, they also have a broader collective significance. While the nuclear legacy does not crop up in most texts of the period, it certainly turns out to be more widely spread than we might otherwise have suspected. Compiling a glossary of motifs – of images of nuclear destruction; of 'nuclear' states of mind – allows us to identify the presence of a nuclear trace in literature where nuclear technology is not a direct referent.

The production of these motifs as nuclear may take place in either the writing of texts (through the conscious or unconscious impact of the nuclear context on the author) or in their reading (through the association made by the reader between the motifs and the nuclear context with which they are associated). Of course, such readings need to be conducted carefully. They are not falsifiable, in the sense invoked by the philosopher of science, Karl Popper, who argued that for statements to carry scientific validity they had, in principle, to be disprovable.[26] Consequently, there is a danger of constructing 'just so' stories to explain cultural manifestations of nuclear phenomena: x is a symptom of nuclear anxiety; x appears in a particular work of literature; therefore that work of literature is a product of nuclear anxiety.

I should, therefore, elaborate a little further on how certain motifs might justifiably be understood as nuclear. First, the presence of any one motif in a text does not, on its own, necessarily signify that the text is nuclear. It might mean, though, that there is a network of associations into which it plugs that is traceably nuclear. In this sense a nuclear anxiety fiction is as much a way of reading texts as it is a definitive body of literature. One way of thinking of these connections to the nuclear context is through a loose application of Wittgenstein's notion of 'family resemblances': 'a complicated network of similarities overlapping and criss-crossing: sometimes overall similarities, sometimes similarities of detail'.[27] A single feature need not denote a nuclear origin, but the more features that are present the more likely there is to be one, just as a series of similar facial features might lead us to read two faces as those belonging to sisters.

Of course, the traces I identify as nuclear can also have non-nuclear origins. For example, while the sense of the vulnerable city becomes established as a nuclear motif after the bombing of Hiroshima, it also has a more long-standing cultural background. The following discussion does not seek a complete and fully documented nuclear encyclopaedia (which would be a large volume indeed), but to identify the primary motifs of nuclear anxiety, alongside illustrative examples that establish a nuclear origin for these motifs in fiction, reportage on the bomb, nuclear criticism, or work in psychology on the impact of nuclear fear.

What, then, are the key motifs revealing of nuclear anxiety? Rather than simply being about personal mortality, *nuclear anxiety is about species death* or, at least, *about the end of civilisation*. Within days of the bomb falling on Hiroshima, and before the capacity existed for such an outcome, military nuclear technology was represented as capable of bringing the human race to its knees. Citing examples from early responses to Hiroshima, including the *Chicago Tribune*'s prediction that atomic war could produce 'a barren waste, in which the survivors of the race will hide in caves or live among ruins', Paul Boyer points out that '[w]ithin hours of Truman's announcement [of the attack on Hiroshima] . . . the prospect of global annihilation already filled the nation's consciousness.'[28] During the 1950s, this prospect became firmly established, partly because of the increasing power of the global nuclear arsenal, but also because fictions of the bomb entertained this possibility. Most dramatically influential in this respect, selling more copies than any other nuclear fiction and made into a Hollywood film, was British writer Nevil Shute's *On the Beach* (1957), with its vision of humans awaiting their deaths from radiation poisoning following a nuclear war. Even with the passing of the Cold War, and with the greater cultural currency of eco-catastrophes produced by climate change, the nuclear referent remains firmly associated with world-ending visions, as in Cormac McCarthy's *The Road* (2006). Certainly Cold War texts about end times almost inevitably get read within the context of nuclear war, even when they are not specifically about nuclear war and where such readings may be reductive, as in Paul Auster's *In the Country of Last Things* (1988), and the British writer Doris Lessing's *Memoirs of a Survivor* (1974).

Frequently conflated with this trope, and closely related to it, is another: *nuclear anxiety is about the imperilled planet and the end of the world*. Shute's vision is a proto-ecological one because it implies that the world is a set of interlocking ecosystems, mutually dependent for survival. The birth of the modern environmental movement, following the publication of Rachel Carson's *Silent Spring* (1962), gave much more sophisticated and self-conscious expression to this idea. Although never identical with nuclear concerns, and with ambivalent responses to nuclear technology (nuclear power has been represented both as a malign environmental contaminant, and as the answer to the ecological challenge posed by fossil fuels), environmentalism has produced a way of thinking influential on the cultural reception of nuclear technology. Sometimes the two have directly coincided, as in the 'nuclear winter' theory proposed in the 1980s and discussed in chapter five of this book.

If the planet, imperilled as never before, became nuclear after 1945, there are also two more specifically defined nuclear environments. *Nuclear anxiety is related to threatened cities*, imagined as either flattened by nuclear blast, or emptied by radiation. While the roots of this trope lie in the destruction by single atomic devices of Hiroshima and Nagasaki, it took a stronger hold as the Japanese experience was mapped onto American cities (Boyer points out that '[r]adio newscasters and newspaper articles and editorials compared Hiroshima with U.S. cities of similar size').[29] Spencer Weart writes that in the first years of the nuclear age, when atomic attack by a specific enemy was not an imminent possibility, people nevertheless 'felt that the ground had fallen away under them' because of the 'realization, which struck many people right from the first news, that at some point in the foreseeable future no city on earth would be safe'.[30] With the specific targeting of large numbers of cities during the Cold War, this sense of urban peril became well established and still persists in the nuclear imagination: the protagonist of McCarthy's *The Road* remembers the days following what we infer to have been a nuclear holocaust: 'They sat at the window and ate in their robes by candlelight a midnight supper and watched distant cities burn.'[31]

Yet, despite this focus on cities, the third nuclear environment is more commonly suburban than urban: *nuclear anxiety evokes external and internal threats to the home, in particular the detached middle-class home*. These threats are more frequently associated with suburbia than the inner-city because civil defence literature of the 1950s concentrated almost exclusively upon the former, partly because there was a strong ideological investment in making the middle-class environments of contemporary America seem secure, but also because defence against nuclear attack, always liable to seem absurd, was marginally more credible in areas at a slight remove from the main target areas. Yet the effects of civil defence campaigns were, as we will see in chapter four, always liable to make homes seem more, rather than less, vulnerable. The home was configured as both fragile, in the face of nuclear blast, and permeable to radioactive contamination. As we will see in relation to Judith Merril's *Shadow on the Hearth* (1950), the home becomes a particularly fraught environment in nuclear anxiety literature early in the Cold War, and this has a lasting association. In the (just) post-Cold War *Generation X*, for instance, Dag buys Claire a jar of, possibly radioactive, Trinitite beads, formed from the melted sand of nuclear tests. Giving her this present, he drops the jar, contaminating the house: 'countless green glass beads explode like a cluster of angry hornets, shooting everywhere, rattling down the floor, rolling into cracks, into the couch fabric, into the ficus soil – *everywhere*'.[32]

It is not surprising, given the centrality of the home to the nuclear imagination, that *nuclear anxiety is inflected in particular through the dynamics of family life*. The conceit linking nuclear family and nuclear war is a common one (used, for instance, by Paul Brians in his article, 'Nuclear Family / Nuclear War')[33] and the literature of nuclear anxiety is very frequently composed around family relations, as in *The Book of Daniel*, where the impact of the trial of the Rosenbergs, and its political fallout, is articulated through a series of threatened family groups: the Isaacsons (Doctorow's fictionalised Rosenbergs) and their children, exploding under the full force of the nuclear state; the fragile, angry foster relationship between Daniel and the Lewins; and Daniel's sadistic relations with his wife and son.

The three key nuclear environments – the planet; the city; the home – provide a structure for section two of this book because they epitomise the impact of nuclear anxiety at every level (it is everywhere), and thus provide a means of exploring its various other dimensions. For instance, because *nuclear anxiety is an anxiety about contamination*, it compromises the integrity of, and psychological security attached to, planet, city and home: all are potentially permeable to fallout. Worry about radiation became one of the defining anxieties about nuclear weapons because it was what seemed to make them categorically different to what had gone before: they did not simply cause larger explosions; they created entirely new, and frighteningly invisible, effects. They could get inside: inside houses and inside bodies. It is an ideologically powerful trope and ties nuclear weaponry into related discourses of infection, particularly those, as Andrew Grossman describes them, 'framing . . . Soviet communism as an ideological disease, where *ideas* can be understood as pathogens'.[34] So when enemy bomb tests are described in Coover's *The Public Burning* as erupting across the globe ('foreign A-bomb tests! Spreading over the earth like small-pox!'),[35] the simile of disease exploits Cold War anxiety about foreign influence on the United States and makes the familiar connection between nuclear technology and contamination (even though radiation is not a direct referent here).

Additionally, *nuclear anxiety is itself a contaminant* and, particularly in the early Cold War, there were worries that it might seed itself in ways destructive to national morale and social order. Hence, as Grossman puts it, one of the concerns for planners was that the public 'would overreact and become excessively fearful' of the Soviet bomb,[36] undermining the credibility of the United States' geopolitical strategy. Civil defence, designed to manage this fear, might therefore be understood as intending an inoculation against terror, preventing it from spreading from one person to another.

Nuclear anxiety is about the relation of the human to the sublime. The two key images of nuclear explosion, the blinding flash of light and the mushroom cloud, convey this. Spencer Weart has traced the meanings of the mushroom cloud and argues that a number of possible metaphors for the billowing clouds produced by atomic explosions ('cauliflower' and 'parasol' for instance) were used at the Trinity test, but that very swiftly the 'mushroom' cloud became the accepted designation. Arguing that mushrooms have a long cultural association with magic and transformation, he ties the mushroom cloud in with the mystical properties of transmutation with which nuclear power is associated.[37] The mushroom cloud is thus configured in the cultural imagination as the presence of a world-changing magic on earth.

Something similar happens in the frequently used metaphor of the flash of light from nuclear explosions as a sun, as in David Bodanis's description of the moment after the explosion over Hiroshima: 'An object resembling one of the giant suns from a distant part of our galaxy now appears.'[38] The image works its way into popular culture too: in Pink Floyd's song, 'Two Suns in the Sunset', the narrator looks in his rear view mirror and sees a second sun, a nuclear explosion alongside the setting sun.[39] The reference to the sun evokes the double meaning of nuclear energy as both life-giving (conjured up in a nice reversal of the image when David Lilienthal described the sun as 'a huge atomic-energy factory')[40] and life-destroying. The nuclear is presented as both a power of nature and a power beyond nature.

Michael Light's magnificent book of 100 photographs of bomb tests, titled *100 Suns* to evoke Robert Oppenheimer's famous comment on witnessing the Trinity test ('If the radiance of a thousand suns were to burst forth at once in the sky, that would be like the splendor of the Mighty One . . . I am become Death, the destroyer of worlds'),[41] is a dramatic articulation of the nuclear sublime. Framed in black throughout, and split into two sections, 'Desert' and 'Ocean', that evoke a sublime blankness and excessiveness in nature, the photographs turn nuclear explosions into terrible, beautiful incarnations of natural forces. In the face of this, the human perspective is overwhelmed by the magnitude of that it is trying to grasp.

Nuclear anxiety is about the potential for the world suddenly, and instantaneously, to be transformed. Nuclear attack is frequently imagined as coming with little or no warning. Hence, images of nuclear attack often encapsulate the sudden cessation of everyday life, not the scramble for cover of people fleeing a death of which they had forewarning. The silhouettes left on the ground of people vaporised as they went about their business at Hiroshima established the trope of the instantaneous transformation of the world, and entered the cultural mainstream, reappearing for instance in Ray Bradbury's short story, 'And There Will Come Soft Rains' (1951), in which the nuclear shadows of a family, enjoying their garden, are left burned onto the walls of their house.[42] In Philip Wylie's *Tomorrow!* (1954) war is visited on Green Prairie and River City without warning. In a *Life* article, as early in the nuclear age as November 1945, the next conflict was imagined as telescoping destruction into a '36-hour war'.[43] This trope of sudden and unexpected change persists into the post-Cold War era, both in retrospective imaginary depictions of US–Soviet nuclear war, like Stephen Frears' television film, *Fail Safe* (2000), in which the final images show General Black's wife with their daughter in New York, unaware that her husband has just released a bomb above the city as part of a deal to assuage Russian anger at a mistaken nuclear attack on the Soviet Union; and in depictions of the post-Cold War nuclear terrorist threat, like Tom Clancy's *The Sum of All Fears* (1991) where the Superbowl final is interrupted by a nuclear explosion. Such representations make nuclear anxiety evocative of the fragility and ephemerality of human life.

Nuclear anxiety is agoraphobic. As I noted in the introduction, with the United States exposed to surveillance, and potentially attack, from above, North American skies became threatening. Joanna Bourke quotes a child who, in the early

1950s, asked his mother: 'Please, Mother, can't we go someplace where there isn't any sky?'[44] Christopher Simpson describes an experiment in communications research, Project Revere, which included drops over the United States of, among other things, civil defence leaflets. On one side a newspaper article, 'U.S. Reported in Easy Reach of Red Planes', was overprinted with an ominous silhouette of a Russian bomber. On the reverse a call for volunteers to join the Aircraft Warning Service was headed by the title, 'This Could Have Been a Bomb! Invasion by Air is Possible!'[45] In this instance, leaflets designed to provoke fear of attack from above themselves fluttered down out of the sky onto United States soil. In Don DeLillo's retrospective novel about the Cold War era, *Underworld* (1997), Matt tells Janet about the system of government shelters constructed for nuclear war, a 'system predicated on death from the sky'.[46]

Consequently, nuclear fiction is full of images of people seeking safety in small spaces and *nuclear anxiety induces a desire to dig in and seek cover in shelters literal and metaphorical*. Matt, in *Underworld*, 'liked to duck and cover' in school bomb drills because, curled up on the floor, he felt 'snug and safe'; William, in *The Nuclear Age*, is only able to escape childhood fears of nuclear war by sleeping in a home-made bomb shelter where he feels '[c]osy and walled in and secure'; and the subway where Ben Cohen works in *The Book of Daniel* 'has barred windows and a heavy steel door. . . . If a bomb drops, you probably won't feel it.'[47] This digging in can, as chapter six details, also signal a disengagement from external realities indicative of an abnegation of political responsibility. Digging in can also, of course, evoke the opposite experience to agoraphobia, and the fear of being trapped means that *nuclear anxiety can be claustrophobic*, as in the British television film, *Threads* (1984), where local authority workers coordinating Sheffield's post-nuclear recovery are dug out from their shelter beneath the destroyed town hall too late to save them from suffocation.

Nuclear anxiety is paranoid. In his speech to the nation announcing the missile crisis in Cuba, President Kennedy said that 'American citizens have become adjusted to living daily on the bull's eye of Soviet missiles.'[48] Yet such an adjustment necessarily involved an acceptance that one was, over a sustained period of time, a target. Such an understanding was both realistic, as least if one lived in a city or near an army base, and potentially, were one to dwell on it, psychologically disabling. Slothrop's fear of the V-2 missiles in Thomas Pynchon's *Gravity's Rainbow* (1973) is, amongst other things, a potent metaphor for the latter. The complex geopolitical structures of Cold War engagement and espionage around the world, while conceptually distinct from this nuclear paranoia, were nevertheless analogous to it and similarly situated individuals as subject to forces they could neither control nor fully understand.

Nuclear anxiety is absurd in a loosely existentialist sense (and despite the fact that early existentialist thinking predates the nuclear age) in that the human drama is rendered as without any meaning beyond that provided by humans themselves. The 'double life',[49] identified by the psychologist Robert Lifton as characteristic of the Cold War (ordinary life is always shadowed by the nuclear alternative), puts us in a universe where meaning is always threatened by its negation. Although this is a specifically Cold War construction, related to the possibility of absolute and sudden global extinction, such a sense of the absurd can persist into the post-Cold War era, as in McCarthy's *The Road*. Two unnamed protagonists, 'the man' and 'the boy', travel the road south through the wreckage of unnamed towns to the ocean. Although clues in the text suggest the location is the west coast of North America, the generic designations (the man; the boy; the road; the ocean) signal that we are dealing with an abstracted (and savage) vision of the human condition. The road does not come to an end; it simply goes on. There is only the 'ponderous counterspectacle of things ceasing to be. The sweeping waste, hydroptic and coldly secular. The silence.' In such a godless, meaningless world, moral choices come down to a personally defined authenticity. So, although the man and boy talk of 'carrying the fire' and of 'being the good guys', this ethical framework is generated from within. In practice, starving and desperate, it boils down to the only moral choice available to them: 'We wouldnt ever eat anybody'[50] – a choice rejected by the bandits they meet on the road.

Because the possibility of a post-nuclear reality makes contemporary experience appear always pre-nuclear, *nuclear anxiety gives rise to a truncated sense of the future*. Not only is the future uncertain during the Cold War nuclear standoff, but the very concept of the future is problematized – there was, in Boyer's paraphrasing of Lifton, 'a "radical sense of futurelessness" that undercut people's hopes of living on through their work or their offspring'.[51] Not merely might one future for the human race play itself out rather than another, but there might be no future to be played out at all. Such a possibility is not necessarily considered to be imminent, but it is considered to be latent in contemporary reality as long as vast nuclear arsenals are poised in opposition to one another.

This is closely related to the final trope, and the guiding one for this book: *nuclear anxiety produces lives lived in suspension*. Without necessarily being obsessed with nuclear war, without it even being in the forefront of their minds most of the time, people had, nevertheless, to accommodate the new nuclear reality after 1945. This meant assimilating the possibility that they were living in the period preceding a world-ending nuclear war.

Increasingly, as the second half of the twentieth century progressed, this understanding of the contemporary moment had to be positioned in relation to an emergent and powerful postmodernist strain in Western and, to an extent, global culture. It is through postmodernist literature that one of the most powerful intrusions of the nuclear into 'mainstream' culture occurs, and it is therefore to the postmodern that the final section of this chapter turns.

Postmodernism and nuclear anxiety

Postmodern literature, and postmodern culture more broadly, has been explained as the product of a number of (not always compatible) phenomena: a continuation of the Modernist experimental tradition; a ludic reaction against the high Modernist tradition; a response to the growth of information and other technologies;

a consequence of the emergence of other cultural forms, challenging the status of 'Literature' and encouraging an experimentalism that contests traditional generic distinctions; a product of late capitalism; and a crisis of faith in Enlightenment 'metanarratives', among others. While nuclear influences have not been absent from these explanations, they have not been accorded much prominence.[52]

The various and competing definitions of postmodernism very frequently revolve around the sense in which it is 'post' what came before. For instance, Lyotard's definition of postmodernity situates it as a new era in the development of knowledge, grand narratives of modernity replaced by the micro-narratives of postmodernity, and for Brian McHale postmodernist literature is defined by virtue of its difference from Modernist literature, and a shift from predominantly epistemological preoccupations toward ontological ones. Such a focus on the relation to the past is hardly surprising: after all the term 'postmodern' presupposes that what is of interest is its distinction from a preceding 'modern'.

But even if the era is defined as 'post' modern, it is also worth asking what it imagines itself to precede. What is it 'pre'? The answer is, of course, all sorts of things: among others, a world very much the same, indeed stranded in the pastiche of endless cultural rehashing of what has gone before, a world defined by different geopolitical configurations, or a world become a technological utopia. Yet, among these projections of worlds-to-come, these continuations and developments of the present moment into limitless futures, is one possibility that forecloses all others.

During the Cold War, one of the things postmodernism had to be imagined as preceding was a post-nuclear nothingness. Even though this may not have seemed inevitable – one among a number of possibilities – it achieved a kind of primacy because it was a future that annihilated all others. Any other future, however terrible, at least contained the possibility of further futures beyond itself: continued existence promised the potential of transformation and the limitless possibilities of successive other futures. Yet, while the Cold War was ongoing, amidst each array of possible future developments one was always all-out nuclear conflict, shutting down all subsequent futures. The nuclear future thus seeded itself in the psychological and cultural matrix of the Cold War like a weed. Progress toward détente, and the distractions of other issues, might temporarily remove it from sight but, robust, it would always spring up again.

The potential futurelessness of the nuclear age therefore chimed with an emerging postmodern culture that had lost its confidence in teleological progression. Indeed, nuclear anxiety is surely one of the cultural contexts that provokes postmodernism into the forms that arose during the Cold War. While other causal influences on the emergence of postmodernism have been well documented, the anxious climate of the nuclear age has less frequently been acknowledged as influential on a mainstream culture increasingly identifiable as postmodern. This is not to say that the nuclear age *caused* postmodernism as such – a whole host of factors, including a crisis of legitimation in Western culture, the rise of late capitalism and the proliferation of information and media technologies, are surely more directly influential in this respect – but that the parallel presence of emerging postmodern forms and a Cold War nuclear standoff produced cross-fertilisations between the two that rooted nuclear anxiety in contemporary literature in particular ways.

Perhaps the most sustained attempt to connect the nuclear to the postmodern comes in Alan Nadel's *Containment Culture: American Narratives, Postmodernism, and the Atomic Age*, an innovative discussion of the atomic contexts of mainstream culture in the early and high Cold War periods. Arguing that 'containment', the umbrella term for the raft of strategies by which the United States sought to counter communist influence around the world, had surprising corollaries in a domestic culture and discourse favouring conformity, Nadel ranges through material as seemingly innocent of Cold War influences as the films *Pillow Talk, The Ten Commandments,* and *The Man Who Shot Liberty Valance.* In particular, he finds traces of constructions of self and other definitive of the United States' contradictory relationship to the Soviet Union. Underpinning these constructions is the defining technology of the period: 'Behind containment culture and in front of it lay nuclear power, with all its heft and threat.'[53]

Although some of the details of my readings of Cold War culture differ from Nadel's,[54] his work lays the foundation for the argument that there are fruitful connections to be made between postmodern culture and nuclear states of suspense. He focuses predominantly on culture predating that normally identified as postmodern, but claims it was the later fracturing of the containment narratives of this period that produced postmodern culture. In other words, in focusing on the high Cold War period he describes the nascent conditions for what came later in the century. For Nadel, postmodernism emerged from the failure of containment culture to resolve its inherent ideological contradictions: 'By the mid-1960s, the problems with the logic of containment – its blindness, its contradictions, and its duplicities – had started to be manifest in a public discourse displaying many traits that would later be associated with "postmodernism".'[55] Among others, these traits included challenges to authority, an explicit awareness of the ways in which narrative constructed historical knowledge, and self-referentiality.

This connection between high and later Cold War periods is one of the key justifications for moving, in the second section of this book, between more conventionally nuclear texts (normally located in the earlier era) and later postmodern texts, where the nuclear referent is neither always as obvious, nor so frequently discussed by critics. While Nadel's focus was on a mainstream culture of the first two decades of the Cold War, I take the more directly nuclear texts of this period and place them next to later postmodern texts.

Postmodern narratives are largely constitutive of the 'mainstream' culture in which this book is interested. Even though they are frequently experimental and challenging, and thus seek a subversive position on the margins, it makes sense to see them as increasingly central to late twentieth-century culture. Indeed, a cursory glance at intellectual, literary and cultural histories and anthologies of the United States confirms the cultural importance of postmodernism.[56] Furthermore, any general history of twentieth-century United States literature cannot ignore writers like Toni Morrison, Thomas Pynchon, Alice Walker, Kurt Vonnegut,

Don DeLillo, E. L. Doctorow and Paul Auster, who are closely associated with postmodernism.

Characteristic of the earlier Cold War period, for Nadel, is a containment culture in which a relatively few, largely unquestioned, discourses predominate. As the contradictions inherent in these inevitably work their way out, they explode into the later postmodern narratives that 'make legible the failure of containment'.[57] In my analysis, too, there are continuities between earlier and later Cold War texts, in particular between conventionally nuclear disaster fictions and those texts bearing traces of nuclear anxiety.

Why should postmodern texts, in particular, provide a rich source of these nuclear traces? First, the individual is shown in many postmodern texts to be in a remarkably fragile world. Unable to depend upon values and conceptions (of such basic things as the 'human', 'nature' and the 'real') strongly rooted in previous literature, the individual inhabits a universe that is arbitrary, possibly meaningless and above all textual. The Cold War nuclear standoff also carried this implication. Contemporary reality contained within itself the seeds of its own destruction, and had the potential suddenly to be shattered by an event that existed only in textual and other imaginary projections of the future.

Further, postmodern texts are particularly concerned with dislocations and slippages between language and reality. Language does not simply name a pre-existent set of concepts and categories, but actually constructs them; reality itself always remains out of reach. There is, in consequence, a self-consciousness, often a self-reflexivity, about postmodern texts. The very subject matter of nuclear war implies a similar excessiveness to reality, outstripping the power of language and imagination to make sense of it. Possibly minutes away, an alternative future threatens to negate everything that is 'normal' and meaningful on an individual level.

Finally, and it is this that ties in closely with my thesis about the suspenseful mindset, postmodern narratives frequently eschew conventional forms of closure. There is commonly, in fact, a deferral of closure in postmodern texts, either through suspension before a moment of revelation that we might more commonly expect to form the climax to a text, through the offering of multiple, not necessarily compatible, endings, or simply through an anticlimactic petering out of the narrative. In this sense I am following Jacqueline Foertsch, who implies a connection between the nuclear and the postmodern along these lines. Taking the postmodern as a 'theoretical and cultural concept' that 'fundamentally shapes our understanding of life (and time) itself ever since the bomb itself', she describes 'life in the postbomb era' as 'an endless counting down, an awareness of time and the momentousness of its movement toward midnight that bothers our dreams, diminishes our ability to care and love, and exacerbates our fears'.[58]

While the sense of being frozen before a nuclear moment that was potentially imminent hovered on the edges of consciousness throughout the Cold War, it does not on its own explain the refusal of closure in postmodern texts. It is, nevertheless, a significant characteristic of cultural expression in the period that resonates with both postmodern and nuclear contexts.

In the second section of the book this state of suspense will be examined through the literary representation of various nuclear environments. Before moving onto this analysis, however, it is worth taking a short detour to contextualise nuclear anxiety by examining the peculiar psychological and cultural characteristics of a profoundly vulnerable age.

Notes

1 Paul Brians, 'Farewell to the first atomic age', *Nuclear Texts and Contexts* 8 (1992), p. 3.
2 Brians, 'Farewell to the first atomic age', p. 1.
3 Brians, 'Farewell to the first atomic age', p. 2. Paul Brians, *Nuclear Holocausts: Atomic War in Fiction 1895–1984* (Kent: Kent State University Press, 1987).
4 Although there had previously been isolated critical works on nuclear issues, like I. F. Clarke's *Voices Prophesying War* (1966), the Summer 1984 edition of *Diacritics: A Review of Contemporary Criticism*, devoted to nuclear issues, was the first in a number of important critical works appearing from the mid-1980s to the early 1990s. This included a special edition of *Papers on Language and Literature: A Journal for Scholars and Critics of Language and Literature* 26:1 (1990), and some important monographs on the fiction and culture of the nuclear age: Paul Boyer, *By the Bomb's Early Light: American Thought and Culture at the Dawn of the Atomic Age*, new ed. (Chapel Hill: University of North Carolina Press, 1994); Brians, *Nuclear Holocausts;* Joseph Dewey, *In a Dark Time: The Apocalyptic Temper in the American Novel of the Nuclear Age* (Indiana: Purdue University Press, 1990); David Dowling, *Fictions of Nuclear Disaster* (London: Macmillan, 1987); Patrick Mannix, *The Rhetoric of Antinuclear Fiction: Persuasive Strategies in Novels and Films* (Lewisburg: Bucknell University Press, 1992); Stephen J. Whitfield, *The Culture of the Cold War* (Baltimore: Johns Hopkins University Press, 1991); and Spencer R. Weart, *Nuclear Fear: A History of Images* (Cambridge: Harvard University Press, 1988). There was also a second edition of Clarke's *Voices Prophesying War* (Oxford: Oxford University Press, 1992), and a collection of essays, edited by Nancy Anisfield, *The Nightmare Considered: Critical Essays on Nuclear War Literature* (Bowling Green: Bowling Green State University Popular Press, 1991).
5 Ken Ruthven, *Nuclear Criticism* (Melbourne: Melbourne University Press, 1993), p. 11.
6 Daniel Cordle, 'Cultures of terror: nuclear criticism during and since the cold war', *Literature Compass* 3:6 (2006), 1186–99.
7 Ruthven, *Nuclear Criticism*, p. 9.
8 Mannix, *Rhetoric of Antinuclear Fiction*, p. 172. Brians, *Nuclear Holocausts*, p. ix. Clarke, *Voices Prophesying War*, p. 209. Dowling, *Fictions of Nuclear Disaster*, p. 218.
9 Lifton defines nuclearism as the 'psychological, political, and military dependence on nuclear weapons, the embrace of the weapons as a solution to a wide variety of human dilemmas, most ironically that of "security"'. Robert Jay Lifton and Richard Falk, *Indefensible Weapons: The Political and Psychological Case Against Nuclearism* (New York: Basic Books, 1982), p. ix. I return to this definition of nuclearism in the next chapter.
10 David Seed, *American Science Fiction and the Cold War: Literature and Film* (Edinburgh: Edinburgh University Press, 1999).
11 Margot A. Henriksen, *Dr. Strangelove's America: Society and Culture in the Atomic Age* (Berkeley: University of California Press, 1997).
12 Alan Nadel, *Containment Culture: American Narratives, Postmodernism, and the Atomic Age* (Durham: Duke University Press, 1995), p. xi.

13 Michael Mandelbaum, *The Nuclear Revolution: International Politics Before and After Hiroshima* (Cambridge: Cambridge University Press, 1981), p. 212.

14 See my discussion of Lifton in the next chapter for more on the functioning of psychic numbing.

15 I return to the issue of a containment culture, a domestic corollary of a foreign policy of 'containment' of communism, in my discussion of Alan Nadel below, and in the discussion of Nadel and Elaine Tyler May in the next chapter.

16 Sylvia Plath, *The Bell Jar* (London: Faber, 1966), p. 85, p. 212.

17 Plath, *Bell Jar*, p. 84, p. 227, p. 90, p. 17.

18 Saul Bellow, *Mr. Sammler's Planet* (London: Weidenfeld and Nicolson, 1970), p. 51.

19 Tom Vanderbilt, *Survival City: Adventures Among the Ruins of Atomic America* (New York: Princeton Architectural Press, 2002), p. 19.

20 John Wyndham, *The Midwich Cuckoos* (London: Penguin, 1960), p. 67.

21 Jayne Anne Phillips, *Machine Dreams* (London: Faber, 1993), p. 163.

22 Tim O'Brien, *Northern Lights* (London: Flamingo, 1998), p. 20. This image also appears on p. 68 and p. 356.

23 Thomas Pynchon, *Vineland* (London: Minerva, 1991), pp. 248–9.

24 John Steinbeck, *Travels with Charley in Search of America* (London: Penguin, 1997), pp. 99–100.

25 E. L. Doctorow, *The Book of Daniel* (London: Picador, 1982), p. 179. The nuclear context is supplied by Doctorow's retelling of the story of the Rosenbergs, executed for passing atomic secrets to the Russians.

26 See, for instance, Karl Popper, *Unended Quest: An Intellectual Autobiography* (Illinois: Flamingo, 1986), pp. 41–5.

27 Ludwig Wittgenstein, *Philosophical Investigations*, trans. G. E. M. Anscombe (Oxford: Blackwell, 1974), p. 32.

28 Paul Boyer, *Fallout: A Historian Reflects on America's Half-Century Encounter with Nuclear Weapons* (Columbus: Ohio State University Press, 1998), pp. 7–8.

29 Boyer, *Fallout*, p. 32.

30 Weart, *Nuclear Fear*, p. 106.

31 Cormac McCarthy, *The Road* (London: Picador, 2006), p. 50.

32 Coupland, *Generation X* (London: Abacus, 1996), pp. 86–7. Coupland's emphasis.

33 Paul Brians, 'Nuclear Family / Nuclear War', *Papers on Language and Literature: A Journal for Scholars and Critics of Language and Literature* 26:1 (1990), 134–42.

34 Andrew D. Grossman, *Neither Dead Nor Red: Civilian Defense and American Political Development During the Early Cold War* (New York: Routledge, 2001), p. 23. Grossman's emphasis.

35 Robert Coover, *The Public Burning* (New York: Grove Press, 1998), p. 465.

36 Grossman, *Neither Dead Nor Red*, p. 30. See also the discussion of Grossman in chapter two.

37 Weart, *Nuclear Fear*, pp. 401–6. It could simply be, of course, that they look more like mushrooms than these other things. Nevertheless, the designation conjures up the associations Weart identifies.

38 David Bodanis, $E = mc^2$: *A Biography of the World's Most Famous Equation* (London: Pan, 2001), p. 167.

39 The song comes from the album, *The Final Cut* (EMI, 1983).

40 Boyer, *Fallout*, p. 29. Lilienthal was the first chairman of the Atomic Energy Commission.

41 Michael Light, *100 Suns: 1945–1962* (London: Jonathan Cape, 2000). Quotation from Oppenheimer on the dust jacket.

42 Bradbury's story appears in *The Martian Chronicles* (London: Flamingo, 1995). The collection was originally titled, *The Silver Locusts*.

43 Boyer, *Fallout*, p. 32.

44 Joanna Bourke, *Fear: A Cultural History* (London: Virago, 2006), p. 257.
45 Christopher Simpson, *Science of Coercion: Communication Research and Psychological Warfare 1945–1960* (New York: Oxford University Press, 1994), pp. 77–8.
46 Don DeLillo, *Underworld* (London: Macmillan, 1998), p. 458.
47 DeLillo, *Underworld*, p. 728. Tim O'Brien, *The Nuclear Age* (London: Flamingo, 1987), p. 15. Doctorow, *Book of Daniel*, p. 45.
48 Ernest R. May and Philip D. Zelikow (eds), *The Kennedy Tapes: Inside the White House During the Cuban Missile Crisis* (Cambridge: Harvard University Press, 1998), p. 278.
49 Lifton and Falk, *Indefensible Weapons*, p. 52. See my discussion of Lifton in the next chapter for more on the issue of the 'double life'.
50 McCarthy, *Road*, p. 231, p. 70, pp. 65–6, p. 108. Apostrophe absent from McCarthy's text in line with the minimalist grammar in his prose.
51 Boyer, *Fallout*, p. 236.
52 Tim Woods's excellent introduction to postmodernism, for instance, quotes Dick Hebdige's long list of things claimed as postmodern, including 'the dread engendered by the threat of nuclear self-destruction', but does not mention the issue again. Tim Woods, *Beginning Postmodernism* (Manchester: Manchester University Press, 1999), p. 2.
53 Nadel, *Containment Culture*, p. xi.
54 See, for instance, note 12 in the introduction for an example of an alternative reading of John Hersey's *Hiroshima*.
55 Nadel, *Containment Culture*, p. 3.
56 For example, Douglas Tallack ends his survey of the twentieth-century United States with a 'Conclusion: post-modernity'. *Twentieth-Century America: The Intellectual and Cultural Context* (Harlow: Longman, 1991), pp. 311–34. Paul Lauter et al. (eds) close *The Heath Anthology of American Literature* (Boston: Houghton-Mifflin, 2002) with a section on 'Postmodernity and difference: promises and threats', pp. 2821–67.
57 Nadel, *Containment Culture*, p. 34.
58 Jacqueline Foertsch, *Enemies Within: The Cold War and the AIDS Crisis in Literature, Film, and Culture* (Urbana: University of Illinois Press, 2001), p. 4, p. 3.

2

The sword of Damocles: the psychology and culture of vulnerability

Damocles, a sycophant of Dionysius the Elder, of Syracuse, was invited by the tyrant to try the felicity he so much envied. Accepting, he was set down to a sumptuous banquet, but overhead was a sword suspended by a hair. Damocles was afraid to stir, and the banquet was a tantalizing torment to him. (*Brewer's Dictionary of Phrase and Fable*)[1]

The story of Damocles is a fable about vulnerability pertinent to the Cold War. Just as Damocles felt himself frozen in the final moment before his death, so during the Cold War life was lived in suspension before an imagined end, although the magnitude and circumstances of this fear shifted and it was not always so present in people's consciousness as the sword was in Damocles'.

'Let this device hang over capitalists like the sword of Damocles',[2] Nikita Khrushchev, Soviet leader in a crucial period of the Cold War, is reported to have said when asked why the Soviet Union needed such 'cannibalistic' weapons. Khrushchev perceived accurately that the strategic value of nuclear weapons lay not so much in the devastation their explosion could wreak, as in the shaping influence the *threat* of their explosion would have on his enemies. Indeed, very early in the Cold War the build-up of armaments by both sides rendered almost redundant their strategic value in actual acts of war, because it would almost certainly have entailed the simultaneous annihilation of NATO and Warsaw Pact countries, and much else besides. It was, then, in the non-event of their threatened explosion that their significance to Cold War culture lay.

What Damocles is taught by Dionysius's harsh lesson is that the lives of the powerful are shadowed by threat. The banquet, the reward of power and riches, is tainted by the knowledge that the sword could strike at any moment. The sword, threatening Damocles only for the duration of the banquet, is, by implication, the condition of power, a symbol of the responsibility and peril hanging over Dionysius every day. The nuclear age offers us a democratised version of this fable: everyone, not just the powerful, is threatened.

'Every man, woman and child lives under a nuclear sword of Damocles, hanging by the slenderest of threads, capable of being cut at any moment by accident or miscalculation or by madness', observed Khrushchev's Western counterpart, President John F. Kennedy, in a speech to the United Nations in 1961.[3]

The sumptuous rewards of the post-War consumer boom promised the American middle classes unprecedented material wealth. Yet, like Dionysius's feast, this abundance came with the condition of suspense. Elaine Tyler May has charted the ways in which the post-war American dream, centred on middle-class aspirations to home ownership, material abundance and domesticity, far from being separate to geopolitics, was at the heart of the United States' Cold War ideology. It even, at times, supplied a rationale for foreign policy, as she observes in a powerful analysis of the famous 'kitchen debate' between Khrushchev and Richard Nixon: 'the [American] suburban home, complete with modern appliances and furnishings, continued to serve as a tangible symbol of the American Way of Life, and a powerful weapon in the Cold War propaganda arsenal'.[4] While worlds with consumer affluence but without the nuclear threat, and vice versa, were conceivable, the Cold War conditions in which both arose established a continuity between them, knitting macrocosmic struggles around the world to the microcosmic details of life at home and in the home.

This chapter theorises nuclear anxiety during the Cold War, which it sees as tying ordinary lives into the dynamics of geopolitical systems. Although nuclear anxiety consistently revolved around ideas of suspense and deferral (the threat of nuclear attack; the repeated postponement of possible resolution, by war or disarmament, of that threat), within these parameters its psychology varied widely. The chapter begins by considering nuclear strategy and the mind games of deterrence fundamental to the Cold War nuclear standoff. It then looks at psychological impacts, moving from a discussion of early Cold War concerns about the effect of the new era on children, to Robert Jay Lifton's concept of 'psychic numbing', which became paradigmatic for psychologists and psychiatrists working on nuclear issues in the 1980s. Next, the proposal by May and Alan Nadel that an ideologically powerful domestic 'containment' discourse was a corollary of foreign policy is picked up from the last chapter to establish the link to a culture of anxiety. Finally, Douglas Coupland's short story, 'The Wrong Sun', is used to take us back toward the literary context, providing a coda both to Cold War culture and to the discussion in this chapter of that culture's psychological roots.

War games

[Y]ou are the president of the United States. You have just learned that the Soviet Union has dropped an atomic bomb on New York. You know they will not attack again. . . .

You are about to press the [nuclear] button. The nation's policy is to retaliate in kind against a nuclear attack. The policy was designed to deter attackers; if you don't follow through the deterrent would have been a sham.

On the other hand . . . the damage has been done. Killing millions of Russians will not bring millions of dead Americans back to life. . . .

But then it is precisely this line of thinking that emboldened the Soviets to attack. . . . So you had better retaliate to show them it wasn't a bluff.

But then again, what's the point of proving *now* that you weren't bluffing *then*?. . . .

> But wait – the Soviets knew you would think it is pointless to prove you weren't bluffing after they tried to call your bluff. That's why they called your bluff. The very fact that you are thinking this way brought on the catastrophe – so you shouldn't think this way.
>
> But not thinking this way *now* is too late. . . . (Steven Pinker, *How the Mind Works*, 1997)[5]

In the absence of actual nuclear conflict between the superpowers, the kinds of mental gymnastics, here reproduced by Steven Pinker to illustrate an argument about the nature of human cognition, were fundamental to strategic military planning. With no history of warfare between nuclear states, strategists had to hypothesise about potential scenarios and the scales and dimensions of escalation they might produce. One way of working through these possibilities was to play war games, taking on the roles of East and West and modelling responses to various situations. Another closely related approach was to employ 'game theory', quantifying responses to abstract conflict problems in a seemingly rigorous scientific manner. I will return to these below because their 'virtuality' is a key feature of both military strategy and nuclear anxiety throughout the Cold War. However, it will be useful first to outline some of the shifting emphases in nuclear strategy against which these central features can be understood.[6]

One of the earliest impulses, formalised in, amongst other places, the Baruch Plan, presented to the United Nations in 1946, was to place atomic technology under international control. So revolutionary did atomic power seem that restraining its use would require a new world order. Radically unsettling as it was, in this respect atomic technology actually offered the hope of increased global security. Yet agreement proved hard to reach and plans foundered: the United States was reluctant to relinquish its monopoly and would not destroy its existing capability before agreeing international rules for developing the technology; and the Soviet Union saw this levelling of the playing field as a precondition for further talks.

In 1953, developments in United States military strategy were formulated in what became known as the 'new look' of the Eisenhower administration. Alongside the aspiration to 'contain' communism around the world, traceable at least as far back as George Kennan's 'long telegram' (1946) discussed below, there was a more explicit focus on atomic weapons within a broad strategy of deterrence (although toward the end of the 1950s there was a renewed emphasis, alongside this, on building up conventional forces). The hydrogen bomb, considerably more powerful than the atomic bomb (which had, after all, been developed in the expectation that it would be used, as it was against Japan) entrenched the strategy of deterrence. As Michael Mandelbaum comments, '[t]he decision to proceed with the hydrogen bomb provoked controversy because there was no apparent point to using it. . . . The fusion bomb was supremely, and perhaps exclusively, a weapon of deterrence.'[7]

For deterrence to operate, though, nuclear arsenals had to be able to withstand an initial assault and reliably provide a knock-out response, and it was not until the early 1960s, when the mobility, range and general invulnerability of medium and long-range missiles, and submarine-based systems, provided the technological guarantee that this could happen. In effect, the bipolar nature of geopolitics in the Cold War, the size of Soviet and United States nuclear arsenals, and the technology for delivering them to their targets, produced what was eventually conceived of in the West as Mutual Assured Destruction (MAD).[8]

Although attempts were made to find a strategy to limit any nuclear exchange – when Kennedy came to power a 'counterforce' or 'no cities' doctrine, targeting military assets before cities, was toyed with – they soon gave way to a more general strategy of all-out nuclear retaliation in the event of attack. This was in part because of the presumed difficulties of limiting any nuclear exchange, and the assumption that attacking military targets would, in any case, involve massive urban destruction.

One consequence of MAD was that nuclear capabilities had to be known and willingness to use the weapons had to be emphasised. These were not secret weapons to be sprung on an enemy only in time of war because their purpose was to prevent their own use; the moment they were fired they would have failed. As Mandelbaum comments, in reference to the Kennedy administration's relative openness about the United States' nuclear weapons programmes, '[p]ublicity fitted the logic of deterrence.'[9]

All this is relevant to nuclear anxiety, and a necessary precondition for our understanding of its cultural presence, because the 'publicity' of nuclear capability could not be filtered only to political and military elites; it also reached ordinary citizens, particularly in the more open societies of the West. Regardless of their real intentions, political leaders had publicly to affirm their willingness to press the proverbial button, destroying their own societies along with those of their antagonists.

Notwithstanding this public posture, a constant unknown was the reaction of political and military leaders to crisis situations. The strange parallel world of game theory, employed by strategists to work through scenarios deemed indicative of nuclear crises, provided a means to speculate, in a seemingly objective way, about actions in wartime. In some ways it challenged the MAD doctrine by making nuclear war conceivable. Herman Kahn, not exactly a game theorist but influential on military strategists in the 1960s and 1970s, and allegedly the model for Dr Strangelove in Stanley Kubrick's famous film, distinguished between 'two classes' of military thinkers: 'those who believe that any war would result in no less than mutual annihilation, and those who feel this is not necessarily so or even that it is in all likelihood wrong'.[10] Kahn sided strongly with the latter group and was part of a disturbing trend in military planning to 'think the unthinkable', presenting nuclear war as a viable, if unpleasant, trial of strength between the superpowers.

Game theory, while conceptually distinct from Kahn's approach, nevertheless also facilitated thinking the unthinkable. Its origins lay in the 1920s with John Von Neumann and, according to Lawrence Freedman, it 'provided a means of reducing strategic problems to a manageable form in which the dilemma and the paradoxes of the age could be bared and solutions explored'.[11] Crucial to well-known games like the Prisoner's Dilemma and Chicken, which were seen to bear on Cold War nuclear strategy, were two things: the 'interdependence of the adversaries' decisions' and the 'assumption . . . of rational behaviour, based on calculations aimed at maximizing values'.[12] Players were presented with a situation and had to choose a course of action to maximise their rewards at the end of the game. However, because outcomes depended on the strategy chosen by both parties, rewards could not easily be determined; a player had both to predict what his or her opponent would do and predict what their opponent thought they would do. Various outcomes could be quantified by plotting them on matrices which were 'until the mid-1960s . . . the *sine qua non* of a serious strategist'.[13]

Yet, rigorous though this approach seemed to be, it was beset by problems. As Freedman suggests, it assumed a strict adherence to rationalism, with little space to take into account the pressure of a real-life situation, the impact of domestic forces on a decision-maker, limits to their knowledge, and the possibility that they were not motivated purely by the best 'rational' outcome. Furthermore, however objective the process of compiling outcomes for any given game might be, the game remained a construct of the strategist: a model of real life, not real life itself.[14]

The problem, fundamental to the dynamic of nuclear anxiety more broadly during the Cold War, was that there was an uneasy relationship between what could happen in a war, and the hypothetical constructions (in game theory, in political discourse, in fiction and elsewhere) used to imagine that reality. There could be no direct access to nuclear war – it remained in the future conditional tense – so one was left only with competing constructions of it. Nuclear strategy more broadly was anxiety-inducing because it postulated a world of rational decisions in one that seemed otherwise absurd and unreal. Kahn, for instance, suggested it was necessary to talk seriously about nuclear policies that would produce only 50 million, rather than 100 million, dead Americans.[15] Clearly ignoring the subject, out of decorousness, was an abnegation of responsibility (saving 50 million lives was important, however obscene such large-scale rationalisations might seem) but the very process of working through this possibility seemed to make the unthinkable thinkable, and thus more likely.

The Cold War nuclear standoff had implications for diplomatic and military strategy, then, that challenged previous assumptions about international relations and conflicts. As the American political class was aware, the notion of war had entirely changed. Before the end of 1945, President Truman had declared that 'in international relations as in domestic affairs the release of atomic energy constitutes a new force too revolutionary to consider in the framework of old ideas'. His successor, Eisenhower, concurred: 'with nuclear missiles, it [war] is no longer a contest, it is complete destruction'. Two decades later, President Jimmy Carter reiterated the same point in front of the United Nations General Assembly: 'we can no longer think of war as merely the continuation of diplomacy by other means. Nuclear war cannot be measured by the standards of "victory" or "defeat."'[16]

The Cold War nuclear confrontation also challenged other established assumptions and categories, blurring boundaries between peace and war. An Army

Department field manual claimed in 1962 that peace was 'simply a period of less violent war in which non-military means are predominantly used to achieve certain political objectives',[17] and from a civilian point of view much the same point might be made. Peacetime was conceived of as low-level war rather than the absence of war; as Vanderbilt puts it, 'war went from a marked event to an underlying condition'.[18] Furthermore, the move to all-out war was frequently imagined to be sudden and almost without warning, a function of missile technology (by the 1980s Britons were expected to have only four minutes to take shelter once sirens signalled that missiles had been detected), nuclear strategy (a surprise attack was the best bet for limiting the nuclear response of the opposing side) and, possibly, unstable fail-safe systems. Consequently, a common motif in representations of nuclear attack was its sudden and unexpected transformation of the everyday, and nominally peacetime, into the extraordinary and cataclysmic.

The strategic situation, with large nuclear arsenals held by sides locked in bipolar confrontation, therefore introduced a fundamental insecurity into Cold War life. The strategic relationship between the two superpowers was, at heart, suspenseful. It involved the tacit, sometimes explicit, threat of nuclear destruction, perpetually deferred into hypothetical futures played out in war games and in the imagination. The juxtaposition between the mundane and its nuclear shadow, parallel tracks onto which reality could be jarred by deliberate or accidental nuclear confrontation, rendered existence absurd. Indeed, existential ideas like that of the absurd, although their roots were in Second World War experiences predating the atomic age, resonated with the insubstantiality of human lives framed by nuclear contexts (Todd Gitlin describes 'duck and cover' drills as events in which 'existentialists were made'), and it is no surprise that some key existential texts can be read as allegories for this new factor in the human condition.[19]

Deterrence made reality fragile. The way in which the everyday, which might otherwise be experienced as concrete and permanent, was thus rendered arbitrary and ephemeral is, if not exactly an untold story, certainly one which has been under-narrated.

Of course, as well as shifting along the developing contours of the struggle between East and West over four decades, the psychological impact of MAD also varied widely between individuals. People did not always feel insecure, nor were they permanently preoccupied with their nuclear fate. However, nuclear war was a potentiality for a sustained period of time and, one way or another, it had to be assimilated.

The next section explores some of these psychological consequences. It begins by looking at explicit fears, in the first decade and a half of the Cold War, about the impact on children of living in a world where their future was compromised. It then turns to a body of psychological and psychiatric studies, accompanying the resurrection of overt public interest in nuclear fears in the 1980s, that began to theorise in more complex ways the changes in outlook induced by nuclear deterrence.

Psychological considerations: from the 'defense decade' to psychic numbing

At the American Psychological Association's annual conference in 1953, a delegate, Douglas Courtney, warned, 'the atom bomb is a mysterious, frightening boogie man that creates terror in the youngster's mind and may affect his day-to-day living'.[20] He was not alone in worrying about the psychological health of children frightened by preparations for atomic war. In March 1952, the *New York Times* reported the formation of a Committee on War Tensions in Children by a group of parents, educators, psychiatrists and others. At their inaugural meeting, in Manhattan, they discussed the influence on children's development of living in a 'defense decade', and in particular the consequences of drills for atomic attack which were, by then, commonplace in United States schools. Anecdotes of terrified children (a small boy who carried a first aid kit with him; a teenage girl who always wore a headscarf because of the insistence in civil defence advice on covering the head and neck) were related. Various instances were reported of children forming superstitious attachments to dog tags distributed to help identify them (by implication their corpses) in the event of war, the tags taking on the qualities of 'talismans ensuring physical safety'.[21]

Eight months later, and now renamed the Committee for the Study of War Tensions in Children, the group contested the value of the widely distributed film, *Duck and Cover*, which had had its first showing in January and used a cartoon character, Bert the Turtle, to tell children what to do in the event of atomic attack. While advocates of the film argued that it gave a reassuring message, most members of the Committee claimed it was more likely to 'promote anxiety and tension in children'. Indeed they went further, stating that 'counteracting the contagion of fear and tension already being promulgated among children by TV, the movies, the radio and sections of the press', was an important responsibility for schools and communities.[22]

Two things are particularly noteworthy about the expression of these worries. The first is that children functioned to inflect adults' anxieties. While it is unsurprising that people were particularly worried about their children, this focus was also symptomatic of a decade of booming birth rates when the family was a central preoccupation (a preoccupation explored in more detail in chapter four). The family became the crucible in which broader social forces were forced together and, to a degree, in which their contradictions were contained or exposed. It is not therefore surprising that worries about the impact of nuclear fear found expression in discussions of the socialisation effects of the measures by which children were introduced to the idea that they were endangered.

Also noteworthy is that, instead of political agitation against atomic policies, concerned groups tended either to advocate shielding children from what were presented as inescapable realities, or to suggest ways of helping them adjust psychologically. For instance, Courtney, the psychologist warning that children were affected by their atomic fears, did not question the need for, or efficacy of, civil defence, but 'advocated "stepping up" regular school fire drills as a means of training children to act in the event of an atomic bombing'.[23] Similarly, the Committee for the Study of War Tensions in Children held that '[p]rotective and civil defense measures are essentially the responsibility of adults', and sought only to restrict children's involvement in them, rather than interrogating the country's warlike preparations.[24]

This was in keeping with a contemporary tendency to put faith in experts (psychologists or scientists, for instance) and thus adjust to the status quo rather than seek the political means by which it might be changed. May has written of a 'cult of expertise' in the 1950s which 'offered a distinctly apolitical means of solving problems that were often the result of larger societal restraints'. For instance, the popularisation of therapeutic approaches to sources of anxiety, 'called on individuals to cope and adapt to existing realities' and 'reinforced the political consensus by pointing to individual weaknesses, rather than to structural or institutional flaws, as the sources of problems'.[25] Early attempts to make sense of the psychological impact of the Cold War therefore tended to have conservative implications: they implied the atomic threat was a fact to which people had to adjust, not a political and technological fabrication they could contest.

Ellen Herman argues that the development of psychology as an academic discipline was closely tied to national defence. In the twenty years following 1945, the 'U.S. military was, by far, the country's major institutional sponsor of psychological research', and by the early 1960s the Department of Defense was spending 'almost all of its social science research budget on psychology, around $15 million annually, more than the *entire* budget for military research and development before World War II'. Many psychologists were, Herman claims, convinced 'that psychology was crucial to national security and that psychologists were obligated to serve their government, perspectives deeply rooted in World War II experience'.[26] Christopher Simpson has made a similar point about the related area of Communication Studies, arguing that 'U.S. military and intelligence agencies became instrumental in the systematic elaboration of an interlocking series of concepts about communication that have defined much of post-World War II communication research'.[27] While these areas of research were not (or only rarely) directly about the bomb, Herman's and Simpson's work uncovers some of the foundations of academic psychology in a conservative institutional relationship with national bureaucracies.

Psychology was even seen as serving directly the political management of nuclear terror. Andrew Grossman details the use of civil defence programmes to manage public responses to the prospect of atomic war and establishes clearly that their purpose was to create the illusion, rather than the actuality, of effective protection. Revealingly, techniques used by the United States military against enemy populations abroad were imported for use at home: 'Systematic dissimulation, in which the FCDA [Federal Civil Defense Administration] engaged, had more in common with psychological warfare methods employed against external enemies than with mainstream, government-run civic education programs for its own polity.'[28] Civil defence was intended to contain psychological reactions, preventing *nuclear terror* and producing in its stead the more socially useful *nuclear fear*.

The former could lead the public to withdraw consent for foreign policy and, in the event of war, collapse into civil anarchy, thus 'subvert[ing] the strategy of nuclear diplomacy and deterrence'.[29] The latter was conceived as a rationally controlled response, ensuring support for robust deterrence strategies and, if war came, maintaining social order: 'a successful defense program would achieve the goal of individual and group emotional control by *channelling* fear so that it would not become panic'.[30] (As I explain below, my preference for the term *nuclear anxiety* is in part to distinguish it from these concepts.)

Given these contexts, it is unsurprising that the concerns about traumatised children, discussed above, although probably absent of conscious bias and independent of government, remained unconnected to more searching interrogations of atomic policies in the high Cold War. There were simply few structures available in the 1950s to facilitate sustained critical thinking about the psychological impact of the atomic age. Only with a renewed interest in the impact of nuclear anxiety, after the period of détente, did a substantial body of more self-consciously politically implicated (and sometimes oppositional) work appear. Notably, Robert Jay Lifton's work in psychiatry, harnessing psychological terminology to an explicitly political context, constructed the basis for opposition to what he called 'nuclearism': the 'psychological, political, and military dependence on nuclear weapons, the embrace of the weapons as a solution to a wide variety of human dilemmas, most ironically that of "security"'.[31] His emphasis on politicising the interrogation of nuclearism is made explicit in the title of a landmark work, co-authored with Richard Falk: *Indefensible Weapons: The Political and Psychological Case Against Nuclearism*.

The origins of Lifton's thesis lay in work recorded in an earlier book, *Death in Life*, with the 'hibakusha', the survivors of the Hiroshima bombing who experienced what he termed psychic numbing: a chronic 'cessation of feeling' as a 'defense against death anxiety and death guilt'.[32] A survival mechanism, the numbing closed out stimuli, enabling people to do what they needed to to escape the immediate aftermath of the bombing and, longer term, to live without being overwhelmed by their memories of it. Yet, it became a disabling psychic injury: 'psychic numbing begins as a defense against exposure to death, but ends up inundating the organism with death imagery'.[33]

His insight, in *Indefensible Weapons*, was to make the jump from those who had direct experience of atomic warfare, to those who lived with it every day as a possibility. 'The central existential fact of the nuclear age', he wrote, 'is *vulnerability*.'[34] Much as the superpowers talked about security, it was guaranteed only by insecurity: the certainty that each could, with very little warning, entirely destroy the other.

For Lifton, nuclear weapons posed an unprecedented psychological challenge. Held in large numbers and likely to be used, if at all, en masse, they directly challenged the modes of 'symbolic immortality' by which death could normally be ameliorated or otherwise made sense of (genetic legacies; the memories of friends; at the very least, the cultural and societal continuity which, however quickly an individual is forgotten, promise some connection between past, present and future). They threatened a 'radical futurelessness': 'We are in doubt about the future of *any* group – of one's family, geographical or ethnic confreres, people, or nation. The image is that of human history and human culture simply terminating.'[35] Looking back, in a recent cultural history of fear, Joanna Bourke singles out precisely this characteristic as making nuclear war the 'greatest threat' of the twentieth century: 'The individual, community and nation: all would be destroyed. It was widely predicted that future historians ("if there were any") would call the 1950s and 1960s the "Age of Fear".'[36]

Jonathan Schell's *The Fate of the Earth* (1982) gives a flavour of the self-reflexive self-negation to which attempts to conceptualise such an absolute end gave rise. They had to deal with the impossibility of their own formulation: 'even the words "blankness" and "emptiness" are too expressive – too laden with human response – because, inevitably, they connote the *experience* of blankness and emptiness, whereas extinction is the end of human experience.'[37]

This is not to suggest that the possibility humanity was living in end times was unique to the nuclear age; it does, of course, go back a long way in the Western tradition. Indeed, biblical precedents, like Daniel's visions in the 'Book of Daniel' and the images of destruction in 'Revelation', conditioned some responses to nuclear war. Some even read it as literal biblical apocalypse. Disturbingly, Ronald Reagan is alleged to have said in 1971 that '[e]verything is falling into place. It can't be long now. Ezekiel says that fire and brimstone will be rained upon the enemies of God's people. That must mean that they'll be destroyed by nuclear weapons.'[38] Such reappropriations of Western eschatologies, nicely satirised in Robert Coover's novel, *The Origin of the Brunists* (1966), make nuclear war make sense by placing it within familiar psychological and cultural frameworks. They counter its essential absurdity with the comforting fiction that it is the enactment of divine justice.

However, even though 'apocalypse' and 'armageddon' became commonplace terms to describe nuclear war, such literal theological readings could hardly be creditable. Thus without cultural precedent, nuclear war posed a profound psychological challenge, its possibility not revealing the presence of God but the futility of human existence in a godless universe; the end of the human race could proceed from, in the large scheme of things, localised, trivial and ephemeral concerns. Both existentialist texts, and those nuclear disaster narratives in which war is triggered by accident or failure of 'fail-safe' systems, speak to this sense of the absurd.

For Lifton, just as the hibakusha had their ability to relate with feeling to the world around them damaged by the trauma they suffered in Hiroshima, so too, in the Cold War, was there a widely shared psychic numbing in the face of this overwhelming, and unprecedented, threat. To preserve some sense of self, the brain had to close out full consciousness of what nuclear war would mean, as is apparent in Lifton's definition of psychic numbing:

> What I am calling psychic numbing includes a number of classical psychoanalytical defense mechanisms: repression, suppression, isolation, denial, undoing, reaction formation, and projection, among others. But these defense mechanisms overlap greatly around the issue of feeling and not feeling. . . .
> Psychic numbing has to do with exclusion, most specifically exclusion of feeling.[39]

For Lifton, the broad numbing of emotions and sense of disassociation following from this psychological exclusion of nuclear reality has political consequences, most notably a generalised political disengagement. The effects of nuclear anxiety are not so much absent as driven beneath the surface, only to erupt elsewhere in disguised forms. The state of suspense, of being poised perpetually on the cusp just before a nuclear exchange, induces a tendency '[a]bove all . . . [to] live a double life': working, socialising and planning for the future on the one hand, yet on the other beset by a nagging awareness that all this is liable at any point to be rendered irrelevant by nuclear catastrophe.[40]

If Lifton is right, then there is an explanation for the seemingly muted cultural engagement with nuclear issues for large periods of the Cold War. If individuals were 'numbed', then the cultural artefacts they produced would have borne the traces of this numbing. Literature may not very frequently have been directly expressive of nuclear issues but, just as the individual's attitudes, feelings and behaviour were subtly transformed by the nuclear context, so too would the literature they produced have borne the coded markers of these transformations.

Surprisingly, although literary and cultural critics working on the nuclear age frequently invoke psychic numbing,[41] they do not tend explicitly to push through to these logical consequences following from it. We should distinguish between a relatively facile use of Lifton, as explanatory *within* texts (with psychic numbing deployed as, for example, a guide to characters' mentalities), and a more complex deployment of his ideas as explanatory *of* texts and cultural responses more generally. It is this latter use of Lifton that I want to suggest, although we should be wary of taking his ideas entirely for granted.

Certainly psychic numbing was an influential concept, becoming paradigmatic for a number of psychologists and psychiatrists working in the 1980s on the impact of nuclear weapons. Lowell Rubin, for instance, claimed that psychic numbing 'captures various dimensions of the denial people use' to cope with anxiety produced by nuclear weapons.[42] Ofer Zur, too, reviewing the psychological and psychiatric literature from the 1980s, acknowledged, though his article is critical of Lifton, that 'most scholars still explain the discrepancy [between people's opposition to nuclear armament and their lack of action to further this cause] in terms of psychic numbing or denial as it was originally formulated by Lifton.'[43]

It is easy to see why Lifton's thesis was appealing to professionals working on nuclear issues, especially emerging as it did, in the 1980s, when nuclear issues were beginning to dominate public agendas again. It explained the relative absence of nuclear issues from public discourse since the early 1960s and, for those convinced that people should be afraid of nuclear war, it explained the absence of overt evidence of widespread psychological trauma. But herein, of course, lay a problem: the very absence of evidence for nuclear fear became proof of its pervasiveness. As Zur rather witheringly puts it, the psychic numbing paradigm assumed people were 'worried, anxious and extremely concerned about nuclear war, regardless of their ability to report or experience it, or the researcher's ability to elicit or detect it'.[44]

It is certainly not this book's position that everyone was afraid of nuclear war but just did not know it. However, neither does it reject entirely the idea that there were widespread psychological and cultural adjustments necessary to live in the nuclear age. Zur's reading of Lifton is somewhat reductive. Lifton did not claim an entire absence of a traceable effect of nuclear anxiety, but rather that this effect was concealed and had to be uncovered. For instance, he cites a study in which adults, while not identifying nuclear issues as a predominant concern, nevertheless expressed fears that their or their children's lives could end suddenly or violently. Others in the study had a more nebulous feeling that they lived 'under a nuclear shadow, a sense that could not be equated with any particular life decision but just hung over one and would never quite go away'.[45]

Although the evidence is patchy (research was only carried out in any quantity during periods of explicit nuclear fear; it focused more on children and adolescents than adults; there were somewhat contradictory findings), studies nevertheless suggest a widespread impact of nuclear anxiety at various points in the Cold War, particularly during the 1950s to the early 1960s, and the 1980s. A study in the early 1960s asked 350 American children to think about the world in ten years' time: over 70% mentioned the bomb.[46] In 1983, a survey of teenagers in Britain revealed that over half thought they would experience nuclear war at some point in their lives.[47] Most convincing of all, an overview of the available research in 1986 found that 'quantitative studies concur in the finding that a significant number of youngsters report serious concern about the threat of nuclear war'.[48]

Even studies contesting conclusions like these reveal, on close inspection, some widespread impacts of the nuclear age. In 1965, J. H. Elder challenged the presumption that 'cold war tensions should produce a high incidence and large variety of emotional responses', claiming the evidence did not back this up.[49] He or she quotes approvingly a study of freshmen and high school students in Washington State that found less than 4% 'greatly affected by nuclear war' with another 7% 'moderately affected', and a survey of university students which found 7.6% raising the issue of war in response to a question about their fears for the future.[50] It is true that these numbers fall a long way short of the majority but they are surely not insignificant: in a class of thirty schoolchildren, we would expect one or two to be greatly affected, with two or three more moderately affected. Furthermore, such findings should be put in the context of another study, cited by Elder, in which 70% of parents said their children spoke spontaneously about nuclear war. Elder dismisses this latter study as too subjective, but does not note that, while the research of which he or she approves would have found only those subjects expressing fear of nuclear war on the day on which they were surveyed, the survey of parents would have picked up anxieties felt more sporadically.

Twenty years after Elder's paper, Jerome Frank made a similar claim for rather larger figures produced by a survey of adults: '*only* one fifth reported that they were considerably or greatly affected by [the nuclear threat].'[51] One in every five of the population is surely a significant figure, particularly if we add in the further 60% who, according to Frank, felt some impact of the threat even if only at the level of 'slightly or less affected'.[52] Certainly it is a level of response that could be expected to produce a measurable cultural impact.

In summary, although the evidence is not definitive, it does suggest that nuclear anxiety was a significant factor during the Cold War. The term 'anxiety' is used advisedly, for it suggests a more subtle and less obviously overwhelming response to Cold War nuclear contexts than the 'panic' or 'terror' early Cold War planners wished to avoid, or the 'fear' they wished to instil (although these emotions were apparent at various points too). It is more broadly expressive than are other terms of the drawn out impact of the nuclear context, sometimes explicitly present but more frequently hovering on the edges of consciousness or slipping into the background of everyday life. As Spencer Weart uses the term, in a discussion of the psychological impact of radiation, anxiety is 'something that rests upon helplessness and uncertainty, on the feeling that a threat cannot be escaped nor perhaps even comprehended before it is too late.'[53]

Two primary sites for the coded representation of this anxiety were a broad-based 'containment' culture in the early years of the Cold War, and the postmodern culture that superseded it. Containment therefore provides the final piece of contextualisation necessary for an understanding of the psychology and culture of Cold War nuclear anxiety.

Containment

[I]t is clear that the main element of any United States policy toward the Soviet Union must be that of long-term, patient but firm and vigilant containment of Russian expansive tendencies. (Mr X, 'The sources of Soviet conduct', *Foreign Affairs*, 1947)[54]

Published anonymously in 1947, though many knew the author was George Kennan, 'The sources of Soviet conduct' expanded on Kennan's 'long telegram' from Moscow of the previous year in developing a view of Soviet attitudes and policies that had far-reaching implications for United States foreign policy. Identifying its ideological antipathy toward capitalist cultures, Kennan portrayed the Soviet Union as seeking to spread communism around the world, both through force and through internal subversion within foreign countries: 'we have here a political force committed fanatically to the belief that with US there can be no permanent modus vivendi, that it is desirable and necessary that the internal harmony of our society be disrupted, our traditional way of life be destroyed, the international authority of our state be broken, if Soviet power is to be secure'.[55]

The logic of 'containment', the umbrella term for the portfolio of policies and initiatives through which the United States countered Soviet influence, meant abandoning long-standing isolationist traditions to meet the challenge posed by communism around the world. Military power played a key role in this: 'Impervious to logic of reason . . . it [Soviet power] is highly sensitive to logic of force. For this reason it can withdraw – and usually does – when strong resistance is encountered at any point. Thus, if the adversary has sufficient force and makes clear his readiness to use it, he rarely has to do so.'[56] It is easy to see the role nuclear threats could play in such a strategy.

Elaine Tyler May, in *Homeward Bound: American Families in the Cold War Era* (1988), and Alan Nadel, in *Containment Culture: American Narratives, Postmodernism, and the Atomic Age* (1995), have both argued that this foreign policy had parallels at home in powerful discourses of domestic containment. Although the ideology to which these gave rise was strongly questioned in the 1960s, the consequences of its early Cold War dominance continued to be felt, both in resistance to it, and efforts to resurrect it, until at least the 1980s.

In fact, although neither May nor Nadel discuss it directly, Kennan's long telegram did contain an overt reference to the domestic situation of the United States. In formulating how to deal with Russia, he wrote:

> Much depends on health and vigor of our own society. World communism is like malig-
> nant parasite which feeds only on diseased tissue. This is point at which domestic and
> foreign policies meet. Every courageous and incisive measure to solve internal problems
> of our own society, to improve self-confidence, discipline, morale and community spirit
> of our own people, is a diplomatic victory over Moscow worth a thousand diplomatic
> notes and joint communiqués.[57]

The metaphor of health – of society; of the body politic – was a significant one. Domestic threats, social, moral and ideological, were frequently constructed as diseases eating away at society from within. The simile likening communism to a parasite was prescient for it also underpinned the McCarthyite witch hunts, and was part of a wider discourse associating all forms of deviancy with communism. By extension, proper conduct in one's personal life – embracing normality – was thus to be healthy; to be a good American.

In *Homeward Bound* Elaine Tyler May discusses the centrality of the family in containment culture. Although this is the subject of chapter four, which focuses on domestic spaces, it is worth noting now some key features of this culture. It constructed the family, and the home, as sources of security in an insecure world. The end of the Second World War had not brought a sense of security for two reasons: people remembered the Depression that followed the boom after the First World War, and the world rapidly fractured along Cold War fault lines. Home and family were politically inflected precisely because they seemed to offer an escape from this frightening external world: the 'self-contained home held out the promise of security in an insecure world'.[58] The Americans of May's analysis were homeward bound because they embraced home life in unprecedented numbers (as statistics for marriages, births and home ownership indicate) and because their aspirations were tied to domestic ideals more than at any other point in the century.

Middle-class suburban life became the contemporary incarnation of the American dream. As such, it positioned the healthy society invoked by Kennan at very precise social coordinates: 'In the propaganda battles that permeated the cold war era, American leaders promoted the American way of life as the triumph of capitalism. . . . This way of life was characterized by affluence, located in subur-bia, and epitomized by white middle-class nuclear families.'[59] Although it was represented as an escape from a political realm, home life was therefore very much a product of it.

For May, then, containment was about much more than foreign policy. As she makes clear in a passage it is worth quoting at length, the suburban home became a container for contemporary ideals, a means of holding in check the contradictions of Cold War culture:

> In the domestic version of containment, the 'sphere of influence' was the home. Within its walls, potentially dangerous social forces of the new age might be tamed, where they could contribute to the secure and fulfilling life to which postwar women and men aspired. Domestic containment was bolstered by a powerful political culture that rewarded its adherents and marginalized its detractors. More than merely a metaphor for the cold war on the homefront, containment aptly describes the way in which public policy, personal behavior, and even political values were focused on the home.[60]

This reading of containment is important to my analysis of nuclear anxiety as a sustained state of suspense, because it views the quotidian as recourse from a threatening outside world. Turning inwards to the home was a way of shutting out insecurities beyond the front door; having children was an affirmation of the future in a world that possibly lacked one. But the outside could not be excluded: its influence might be disguised (as in the presentation as natural of culturally specific notions of the family, or as in the commitment to 'innate' capitalist values), but its contradictions were still present and likely, in time, to become apparent. Representations of ordinary life can, therefore, be as revealing of American responses to the nuclear age as direct and overt depictions of nuclear war; they may even be more typical. It was within ordinary life that anxieties about nuclear war had to be contained, and some accommodation had to be made to living in suspense before a threatened nuclear future.

Nadel's book, already discussed extensively in the preceding chapter, is an innovative discussion of mainstream containment culture. His central point, that Cold War policy generally, and containment specifically, had powerful domestic incarnations, is one that underpins the readings of texts in *States of Suspense*. Like May he argues that the narratives produced by containment 'attempted to reconcile the cult of domesticity with the demand for domestic security'.[61] It is the impossibility of effecting this reconciliation that leads to the collapse of containment in the 1960s, its dominant narratives gradually pulled apart by the more sceptical interrogations of the emerging postmodern culture.

Nadel's book also provides a useful methodological model for this study in its affirmation of the value of selective focus on a few key texts. Aspiring to 'anecdotal clarity' in his work, Nadel points out that '[o]f the thousands of films and novels produced between 1945 and 1965, I discuss only a handful'.[62] *States of Suspense* is similarly selective, even anecdotal. Whereas a discussion of explicitly nuclear fiction has a well defined object of study – the 'over a thousand' nuclear texts identified by Paul Brians for instance[63] – exploring the traces of nuclear culture as they move from these texts into a broader mainstream literature produces a much less clearly defined subject.

Rather than embark on the Sisyphean task of cataloguing all eruptions of the nuclear throughout Western culture, *States of Suspense* seeks instead a more modest target: a plausible abstraction from the study of a few significant texts. This abstraction does not account for every text, or every aspect of nuclear culture, in this period. Instead, a few disparate but carefully chosen texts and issues are studied for their value in provoking new ways of thinking about the nuclear context.

Coda: Douglas Coupland, 'The Wrong Sun'

A third recurring image, very simple: at my parents' house, in their living room looking out through the front window framed by pyrocanthus berries, out at the maple tree on the front lawn; The Flash flashes; I am awake. (Douglas Coupland, 'The Wrong Sun', 1994)[64]

Having outlined the parameters of Cold War nuclear anxiety in this chapter – the intrinsic insecurities of nuclear strategy; the tendency for early psychological analyses of nuclear fear to reproduce assumptions underpinning deterrence; the later formulation of psychic numbing as a means of engaging with the politics of fear; the effects of a containment culture that splintered into postmodern plurality; and above all this, and running through it, the drawn out experience of suspense – it is now possible to return more directly to the fiction and prose of the period. While the next section of the book explores this anxiety through representations of the key nuclear environments of city, home and planet, brief discussion, here, of a single short text will serve to bring into focus how the psychological and cultural dimensions outlined above can impact upon literary form.

'The Wrong Sun', a short story by the Canadian writer, Douglas Coupland, makes explicit what was largely implicit in literary representations of nuclear anxiety during the Cold War and provides a coda to the period. Although its author provides a perspective from outside the United States, the palpable sense of a fragile reality, viewed retrospectively from the relative safety of the post-Cold War period, gives an insight into a widely shared anxiety that transcends the Canadian setting. Encapsulating Cold War nuclear sensibilities, the story's two sections straddle the perilously thin line between competing realities: normal life and nuclear war.

Sudden presentiments of nuclear war, like that in the epigraph above, and observations about these recurring fears, comprise the first section, 'Thinking of the Sun'. The narrator's sporadic intimations of 'The Flash' are sparked either by heightened anxiety produced by public events (a bomb test; the Cuban crisis) or, more parochially, unexpected sounds or phenomena (a jet passing overhead; a siren sounding; a sudden, unexplained, rumble).

In this section nuclear war is forever about to happen. The text's fragmentary feel, heightened by numerous white line breaks, simple cartoons and the lack of narrative development (the plot, such as it is, is forever staggering across the cusp of moments imagined to be pre-nuclear into the anticlimax of realisation that nuclear war has not come), makes this a powerful representation of Cold War paralysis and suspense. Similarly effective is the deployment of the present tense throughout, even though the narrator is recalling events that have already happened. Cold War nuclear anxiety is presented as the experience of a perpetual present tense: causal developments connecting past to future are arrested by a stuttering inability to get beyond the present's repeated anxiety.

Although this anxiety is generalised into adolescent angst ('[w]hen you are young, you always expect that the world is going to end'),[65] it is also tied to historically specific contexts: the points of reference are all Cold War and the threat is clearly nuclear. Furthermore, it is stressed that the surfacings of nuclear fear which the section describes are not those of an unusually sensitive protagonist but shared broadly amongst the populace: 'these images are more common than I had realized before. . . . I have asked many of the people I know, and have interviewed many strangers.'[66]

In contrast, the second section, 'The Dead Speak', is about the experience of nuclear attack, as multiple narrators tell of the moments in which they died. Decontextualised fragments of personal experience, these narratives suggest the impossibility of finding a unifying perspective from which to make sense of nuclear war. We know nothing of the international events that might have led to these deaths. In a trope characteristic of the nuclear age, the attack is imagined as intruding suddenly on ordinary experience, heightening the impression of Cold War peacetime as fragile: 'I was by the fridge in the kitchen when it happened'; 'I was having my hair done when it happened'; 'I was in rush hour gridlock traffic . . . when it happened'; 'I was at the mall when it happened'; 'I was in the office . . . when it happened.'[67]

Hence the second section literalises Lifton's claim that Cold War experience is that of a 'double life': its narrators' experiences flip between peace and all-out war in seconds. Furthermore, it exists alongside the first section in which nuclear war does not happen at all. No commentary is made on the connection between the mutually exclusive realities of the two sections: they simply exist alongside each other.

'The Wrong Sun' is therefore both a nuclear disaster narrative and a nuclear anxiety narrative. Although awareness of nuclear threat is not presented as entirely disabling – indeed, at times it is even mundane, as when the sirens sound in a civil defence drill and 'nobody seemed to care'[68] – it is shown to be perennial. The eruption of the unusual into everyday life flips the narrator into the default expectation that this could be the moment of nuclear war. Cold War experience is here shown as that of living on the cusp between two different worlds. It is also represented as highly disruptive of narrative. 'The Wrong Sun' is more a collage of fragments than a story with a plot that develops over time: its episodes are not causally related, nuclear moments in the first section stall the narratives that comprise ordinary life, and in the second section, when they are made real, these moments are so sudden and devastating that there is no scope for plot or character development.

This shattering of narrative, and of a sense of a stable, lasting reality, is characteristic of both nuclear anxiety and postmodernism. Writing about the early atomic age, the historian Paul Boyer comments that '[f]ew grasped that the bomb had created its own categories, and that new metaphors were required to comprehend its meaning'.[69] A similar point is made by the critic, Joseph Dewey, writing at the very end of the Cold War: 'this force demands not only an entirely new vocabulary, but a new way of thinking'.[70] The connection both make between language and meaning, and the radical revision of the relations between these things and the world demanded by nuclear technology, is an important one. During the second half of the twentieth century, the emergence of a postmodern culture produced a similarly profound reorganisation of knowledge and narrative. While there is no simple causal relation between them, nuclear and postmodern cultures are connected in the changed conceptions of self and world they suggest.

Schell claims that nuclear holocaust assaults human life at three levels: 'the level of individual life, the level of human society, and the level of the natural environment – including the environment of the earth as a whole'.[71] Each nuclear environment explored in the chapters in the next section of this book resonates particularly closely with one of these levels. The city (chapter three) becomes a symbol of human society under threat, its civic and other public spaces evocative of the organising principles of civilisation. The home (chapter four) is where nuclear threats to the individual person are most keenly felt, although it will become clear that in Cold War discourses family structures link individuals up to the macro levels of social organisation. The planet (chapter five) becomes the conceptual category through which nuclear assaults upon nature are explored. It is in the altered relations between self and world, made manifest in the transformations of these environments, and their expression through language, that the human is produced as a nuclear subject after 1945.

Notes

1 Ebenezer Cobham Brewer, 'Damocles', in Betty Kirkpatrick (ed.), *Brewer's Concise Phrase and Fable*, ed. Betty Kirkpatrick (London: Cassell, 2000). 'Tyrant' is capitalised in the original to denote a cross-reference to a separate entry on the subject in the dictionary.

2 Andrei Sakharov, the Soviet nuclear physicist and humanitarian, reported this comment. Yu. N. Smirnov, 'This man has done more than all of us . . .', in B. L. Altshuler et al. (eds), *Andrei Sakharov: Facets of a Life* (Gif-sur-Yvette: Editions Frontières, 1991), p. 603. Ellipsis in Smirnov's title.

3 Address to the United Nations (25 September 1961). www.wagingpeace.org/articles/2003/11/17_carnegie_jfk-nuclear.htm (6 February 2006).

4 Elaine Tyler May, *Homeward Bound: American Families in the Cold War Era*, 2nd ed. (New York: Basic Books, 1999), p. 144.

5 Steven Pinker, *How the Mind Works* (Uxbridge: Softback Preview, 1998), p. 407.

6 A decade before the end of the Cold War, Michael Mandelbaum astutely charted developments in nuclear strategy since 1945. My brief run through of nuclear strategy is indebted

to this work, to which the reader is referred for more detailed information. Michael Mandelbaum, *The Nuclear Question: The United States and Nuclear Weapons 1946–1976* (Cambridge: Cambridge University Press, 1979). Michael Mandelbaum, *The Nuclear Revolution: International Politics Before and After Hiroshima* (Cambridge: Cambridge University Press, 1981).

7   Mandelbaum, *Nuclear Question*, p. 49.

8   Robert McNamara coined the phrase 'mutual assured destruction'. Paul Boyer, *Fallout: A Historian Reflects on America's Half-Century Encounter with Nuclear Weapons* (Columbus: Ohio State University Press, 1998), p. 118. Mandelbaum comments that the Soviets did not 'develop a comparable specialized vocabulary of nuclear terminology [to that of the Americans]' and did not have an equivalent concept to 'Mutual Assured Destruction'. Mandelbaum, *Nuclear Question*, p. 212.

9   Mandelbaum, *Nuclear Question*, p. 78. Mandelbaum cites a revealingly bellicose comment by Robert McNamara in 1963 to illustrate this: 'we have enough strategic nuclear power to absorb fully a Soviet strike and survive with sufficient power to destroy utterly the Soviet Union. We have made that statement. We wish them to believe it. They should believe it. It is true.'

10 Richard Schwartz suggests that Kahn is the model for the eponymous character in *Dr. Strangelove: Or, How I Learned to Stop Worrying and Love the Bomb* (GB, Stanley Kubrick 1964). Richard Schwartz, *Cold War Culture: Media and the Arts, 1945–1990* (New York: Facts on File, 1998), p. 80. Herman Kahn, *On Thermonuclear War*, 2nd ed. (Princeton: Princeton University Press, 1961), p. 11.

11 Lawrence Freedman, *The Evolution of Nuclear Strategy*, 2nd ed. (London: Macmillan, 1981), p. 182.

12 Freedman, *Evolution of Nuclear Strategy*, p. 182. The Prisoner's Dilemma was seen to model decisions made in the arms race; Chicken modelled a crisis situation in which nuclear war was threatened. For descriptions of the games see Freedman, p. 186.

13 Freedman, *Evolution of Nuclear Strategy*, p. 182. Freedman's italics.

14 See Freedman, *Evolution of Nuclear Strategy*, pp. 183–4.

15 Kahn, *On Thermonuclear War*, p. 12.

16 Mandelbaum, *Nuclear Revolution*, p. 1. John Lewes Gaddis, *We Now Know: Rethinking Cold War History* (Oxford: Oxford University Press, 1997), p. 226. Mandelbaum, *Nuclear Question*, p. 207.

17 Quoted in Ellen Herman, *The Romance of American Psychology: Political Culture in the Age of Experts* (Berkeley: University of California Press, 1996), p. 124.

18 Tom Vanderbilt, *Survival City: Adventures Among the Ruins of Atomic America* (New York: Princeton Architectural Press, 2002), p. 39.

19 Gitlin quoted in Margot A. Henriksen, *Dr. Strangelove's America: Society and Culture in the Atomic Age* (Berkeley: University of California Press, 1997). Samuel Beckett's plays, *Endgame* (1957) and *Happy Days* (1961), are evocative of nuclear anxiety and existentialism, although to interpret them purely in atomic terms is to close off the much broader readings of the human condition they suggest.

20 Murray Illson, 'Atomic neurosis feared for young', *New York Times* (5 September 1953), p. 12.

21 Dorothy Barclay, 'Group plans to study the effects of defense activities on children', *New York Times* (7 March 1952), p. 16. Dog tags were distributed in New York and in some other US cities in the 1950s.

22 Dorothy Barclay, 'Film on atom war bad for children', *New York Times* (21 November 1952), p. 29. *Duck and Cover* can be viewed online at the Prelinger Archives: www.archive.org/details/prelinger (17 November 2006). For a less critical response to the showing of the film, see 'New film to help in bomb training', *New York Times* (25 January 1952), p. 7.

23 Illson, 'Atomic neurosis feared', p. 12.

24 Barclay, 'Film on atom war bad for children', p. 29.

25 May, *Homeward Bound*, p. 167. The phrase 'cult of expertise' appears as an index entry in her book.

26 Herman, *Romance of American Psychology*, p. 126, pp. 128–9 (Herman's emphasis), p. 134.

27 Christopher Simpson, *Science of Coercion: Communication Research and Psychological Warfare 1945–1960* (New York: Oxford University Press, 1994), p. 8.

28 Andrew D. Grossman, *Neither Dead Nor Red: Civilian Defense and American Political Development During the Early Cold War* (New York: Routledge, 2001), p. 57. Grossman points out that the FCDA made links with the Psychological Strategy Board which was intended to run overseas propaganda campaigns.

29 Grossman, *Neither Dead Nor Red*, p. 44.

30 Grossman, *Neither Dead Nor Red*, pp. 59–60. Grossman's emphasis.

31 Robert Jay Lifton and Richard Falk, *Indefensible Weapons: The Political and Psychological Case Against Nuclearism* (New York: Basic Books, 1982), p. ix.

32 Robert Jay Lifton, *Death in Life: Survivors of Hiroshima*, rev. ed. (Chapel Hill: University of North Carolina Press, 1991), p. 500.

33 Lifton, *Death in Life*, p. 503.

34 Lifton and Falk, *Indefensible Weapons*, p. 23. Lifton's emphasis.

35 Lifton and Falk, *Indefensible Weapons*, p. 67. Lifton's emphasis.

36 Joanna Bourke, *Fear: A Cultural History* (London: Virago, 2006), p. 260.

37 Jonathan Schell, *The Fate of the Earth* and *The Abolition* (Stanford: Stanford University Press, 2000), p. 138. Schell's emphasis.

38 Quoted in Hanna M. Segal, 'Silence is the real crime', in Howard B. Levine, Daniel Jacobs and Lowell L. Rubins (eds), *Psychoanalysis and the Nuclear Threat: Clinical and Theoretical Studies* (Hillsdale: Analytic Press, 1988), p. 42. See also introduction, note 32.

39 Lifton and Falk, *Indefensible Weapons*, p. 103.

40 Lifton and Falk, *Indefensible Weapons*, p. 52.

41 The following list of references to Lifton, though not comprehensive, gives an idea of the extent to which he has become an important figure: Paul Boyer, *Fallout: A Historian Reflects on America's Half-Century Encounter with Nuclear Weapons* (Columbus: Ohio State University Press, 1998), pp. 83–5, pp. 189–93, pp. 232–6, p. 242, p. 243. David Dowling, *Fictions of Nuclear Disaster* (London: Macmillan, 1987), p. 48, p. 217. Jacqueline Foertsch, 'Not bombshells but basketcases: gendered illness in nuclear texts', *Studies in the Novel* 31:4 (1999), p. 481. Henriksen, *Dr. Strangelove's America*, pp. 110–11. David Lavery, *Late for the Sky: The Mentality of the Space Age* (Carbondale: Southern Illinois University Press, 1992), pp. 7–8. Spencer R. Weart, *Nuclear Fear: A History of Images* (Cambridge: Harvard University Press, 1988), pp. 133–4, pp. 266–7.

42 Lowell Rubin, 'Melancholia, mourning, and the nuclear threat', in Levine, Jacobs and Rubin (eds), *Psychoanalysis and the Nuclear Threat*, p. 246.

43 Ofer Zur, 'On nuclear attitudes and psychic numbing: overview and critique', *Contemporary Social Psychology* 14:2 (1990), 103.

44 Zur, 'On nuclear attitudes', 109.

45 Lifton and Falk, *Indefensible Weapons*, p. 50. The study is Michael Carey, 'Psychological fallout', *Bulletin of the Atomic Scientists* 38 (1982), 20–4.

46 Sibylle Escalona, 'Growing up with the threat of nuclear war: some indirect effects on personality development', *American Journal of Orthopsychiatry* 52 (1982), 602.

47 Bourke, *Fear*, p. 259.

48 William R. Bearslee, 'Perceptions of the threat of nuclear war: research and professional implications', *International Journal of Mental Health* 15:1–3 (1986), 244.

49 J. H. Elder, 'A summary of research on reactions of children to nuclear war', *American Journal of Orthopsychiatry* 35:1 (1965), 120.
50 Elder, 'Summary of research on reactions of children', p. 122.
51 Jerome D. Frank, 'Psychological responses to the threat of nuclear annihilation', *International Journal of Mental Health* 15:1–3 (1986), 65. My emphasis.
52 Frank, 'Psychological responses', 65.
53 Weart, *Nuclear Fear*, p. 206.
54 Mr X, 'The sources of Soviet conduct' (1947), in George F. Kennan, *American Diplomacy: 1900–1950* (New York: Mentor, 1951), p. 99. Mr X is, of course, George Kennan, who published his article anonymously in the journal *Foreign Affairs*, although it was widely known that he was the author.
55 George Kennan, 'The long telegram' (1946), www.ntanet.net/KENNAN.html (15 June 2006).
56 Kennan, 'Long telegram'.
57 Kennan, 'Long telegram'.
58 May, *Homeward Bound*, p. ix.
59 May, *Homeward Bound*, p. xviii.
60 May, *Homeward Bound*, pp. xxiv–xxv.
61 Alan Nadel, *Containment Culture: American Narratives, Postmodernism, and the Atomic Age* (Durham: Duke University Press, 1995), p. xi.
62 Nadel, *Containment Culture*, p. 8, p. xi.
63 Paul Brians, 'Nuclear family / nuclear war', in Nancy Anisfield (ed.), *The Nightmare Considered: Critical Essays on Nuclear War Literature* (Bowling Green: Bowling Green State University Press, 1991), p. 151.
64 Douglas Coupland, 'The Wrong Sun', *Life After God* (London: Simon and Schuster, 1999), p. 83.
65 Coupland, 'Wrong Sun', p. 84.
66 Coupland, 'Wrong Sun', p. 86.
67 Coupland, 'Wrong Sun', pp. 89–97.
68 Coupland, 'Wrong Sun', p. 79.
69 Boyer, *Fallout*, p. 54.
70 Joseph Dewey, *In a Dark Time: The Apocalyptic Temper in the American Novel of the Nuclear Age* (Indiana: Purdue University Press, 1990), p. 4.
71 Jonathan Schell, *The Fate of the Earth* and *The Abolition* (Stanford: Stanford University Press, 2000), p. 22.

II
Nuclear environments

3

Empty cities: nuclear war and the end of civilisation

This sample [of sand fused in the Trinity test] and the picture [of Nagasaki] . . . should remind the people of your city that in another war their city would probably be destroyed in the first few hours of the conflict by atomic explosives. (Willard Stout of the Association of Los Alamos Scientists, 1946)[1]

In January 1946 the Association of Los Alamos Scientists, campaigning for control of atomic weapons by a world organisation, sent sand, fused in the first manmade atomic explosion, and a photograph of Nagasaki to the mayors of forty-two cities. Their message was simple: American cities were vulnerable.

Seven years earlier, long before the bomb was built, Enrico Fermi, a physicist later responsible for the first controlled chain reaction, had imagined the coming atomic age through the destruction of New York: 'Fermi was standing at his panoramic office window high in the physics tower looking down the gray winter length of Manhattan Island, its streets alive as always with vendors and taxis and crowds. He cupped his hands as if he were holding a ball. "A little bomb like that", he said simply, for once not lightly mocking, "and it would all disappear".'[2] Within months of the end of World War Two, Bertrand Russell, later a prominent anti-nuclear campaigner, used London as his point of reference: 'As I go about the streets and see St. Paul's, the British Museum, the Houses of Parliament, and the other monuments of our civilization, in my mind's eye I see a nightmare vision of those buildings as heaps of rubble with corpses all round them.'[3] In the final decade of the Cold War, Jonathan Schell located his vision of nuclear holocaust in an unspecified city: 'Now we are on our way to work, walking through the city streets, but in a moment we may be standing on an empty plain under a darkened sky looking for the charred remnants of our children.'[4]

When nuclear war was imagined it was, most frequently, in terms of the destruction of cities. Cities thus became nuclear environments. No longer places of refuge protected by encircling walls – the new perspective was from above, not outside – they were places to flee from not to, and were the primary strategic targets for Soviet and United States war planners.[5] As Tom Vanderbilt points out, the nuclear threat was the culmination of a long-term development (its recent history included the mass bombings of World War Two), transforming the city from a protective to a perilous environment.[6]

The city as nuclear target had a number of characteristics. Strikingly, it was frequently normal city life, not the city anticipating attack, that was imagined to be under threat, and nuclear attack was envisaged as the instantaneous transformation of peaceful urban existence. The visions of Fermi, Russell and Schell, noted above, place the everyday next to the nuclear. It is as if the city has suddenly shifted into a parallel reality that has been shadowing it all along.

After Hiroshima, '[o]ver every city hovered the ghostly afterimage of the Dead City'.[7] The parameters of urban life were changed in the second half of the twentieth century. People did not, of course, abandon cities – quite the opposite – and nor did they constantly dread nuclear attack when they were in them, but the possibility of nuclear devastation had to be added to the stock of imaginative possibilities for the future of the world's cities. As Schell's vision of the urban space transformed as one travels to work shows, the city was suspended in the moment before disaster: we go to work every day; any day might be one interrupted by nuclear holocaust.

This fundamental insecurity was fed by a common iconographic depiction of nuclear vulnerability: the map of a city with concentric rings of nuclear destruction imposed on top, like a target. Used to postulate the impact of a nuclear explosion on a familiar city, such images remained familiar throughout the Cold War. The *Milwaukee Journal* published such an image two days after Hiroshima, and it was still in use in the late 1980s when it appeared, for example, in British campaigning leaflets like *Target North-West: Civil Defence and Nuclear War in Region 10* and *Nottingham After the Bomb*.[8]

Such mapping provides a double coding of the city. It reproduces it from the point of view of the military planner: the city from above, as a target; a problem for demolition. It also implies its opposite: the view from below. It is powerful because it makes citizens see the familiar city as an aggressor might see it. It asks not only that we look down on the mapped city, but that we look up from the real city to the threatening spaces above.

Vanderbilt has shown how the development of aerial photography in the twentieth century transformed the conceptualisation of city space, simultaneously removing its human dimension, enabling analysis and promoting both city planning and the idea of the city as target.[9] The advent of missile technology to deliver nuclear payloads, particularly ICBMs in the 1950s and early 1960s, exacerbated the sense of the city as target. No longer could rings of anti-aircraft defence, the contemporary equivalent of a Medieval city's thick walls, be imagined to protect the city. Nuclear missiles might simply drop from above, from space. Notably, American skies, traditionally invulnerable in their continental isolation, in a way European skies had not been since at least the 1937 bombing of Guernica, now had to be imagined as threatening.

If the city was important because it actually was vulnerable, it was also important because it was a symbol of the civilisation threatened by nuclear war. When Russell imagined St Paul's, the British Museum and the Houses of Parliament in ruins, he was using them both metonymically, to denote the destruction of the greater city of which they are a part, and metaphorically to evoke the threats to the civilising achievements of religion, learning and political culture.

This chapter applies itself to the idea of the city as an actual and a symbolic target. In its first part, the general sense of imperilled urban space is fleshed out with a specific case history, New York's drills for atomic attack during the high Cold War,[10] which show the transformations in the idea of the city by civil defence preparations. The second part looks at two key early Cold War representations of atomic war, John Hersey's *Hiroshima* (1946) and Nevil Shute's *On the Beach* (1957), to open up key tropes in the imagined destruction of the urban environment: the flattened city and the empty city. Finally, the impact of such notions on postmodern depictions of nuclear anxiety is developed through a discussion of Thomas Pynchon's *Gravity's Rainbow* (1973) and Paul Auster's *In the Country of Last Things* (1987).

Staging nuclear attack: bomb drills in New York, 1951–61

For about a decade from 1951 atomic attack was played out at least once a year on the streets of New York. No less important than novels or films in the imagination of nuclear futures, civil defence drills co-opted vast numbers of people in pieces of theatre, sometimes as observers (100,000 were estimated to have witnessed a drill for civil defence workers in September 1952) and frequently as actors (it was claimed that eight million New Yorkers sought shelter during the 1960 drill).[11]

Civil defence was important in establishing the concept of the city under threat early in the Cold War. The drills featured as front-page news in the nation's paper of record, the *New York Times*, in each of these years, and from 1954 onwards they were part of 'Operation Alert' exercises across the United States, also involving, in some cases, Canadian provinces. Legal sanction was used to enforce compliance in New York, where the State Defense Emergency Act made refusing to seek shelter, when asked to do so, a crime carrying a $500 fine or up to a year in prison.

This is not exactly a forgotten history. Photographs of the streets emptied for drills are well known, appearing for instance in Jeremy Isaacs and Taylor Downing's *Cold War*, and some of the excellent histories of civil defence either give the exercises a passing mention, like Andrew Grossman's *Neither Dead nor Red*, or, like Guy Oakes's *The Imaginary War*, have longer discussions of Operation Alert.[12] However, there has been no sustained focus on New York's preparations and what they reveal about atomic-age conceptions of city space. It would be wrong to write them off as a quirky footnote of history, amusing aberrations revealing atypical neuroses. Sustained attention to representations of these drills in the *New York Times* reveals that they were firmly embedded in a larger sense of national crisis, and that they were part of the developing narrative by which the idea of the atomic threat was culturally processed.

The drills emerged from an ongoing sense that war was coming. From May 1951 sirens were tested at noon every Saturday and the city's Civil Defense Director urged people to reflect, on hearing them, if they knew what to do.[13] Spaces across the city were identified as shelter areas: in 1952 there were 888 public shelters and 92,865 private buildings with designated shelter areas in New York. By the middle of the following decade a team of seventy inspectors had responsibility for a total of 230,000 officially recognised shelters.[14] Vast numbers of people were involved in civil defence. In 1955 it was claimed that there were half a million civil defence workers in New York alone and although, by default, this would have included many police and firemen, it nevertheless represents a large number of people who, as part of their jobs or as volunteers, played civil defence roles.[15]

Sometimes drills were only for civil defence workers, although these could have dramatic elements of public performance: smoke was generated to mimic burning buildings, mains were opened to simulate bursts, sending geysers of water several storeys into the air, and 'casualties' were evacuated.[16] More typically, they involved public participation: as hundreds of sirens sounded alerts, New Yorkers would abandon cars, vacate streets and seek shelter. Sometimes public transport, including planes and trains, was stopped.

Two main tropes of the city under attack dominate reports on the drills, the second swiftly usurping the first: the damaged or destroyed city and the empty city. The damaged or destroyed city draws on Second World War experience, but that of mass conventional bombing rather than of the atomic attacks on Japan, perhaps because the flattened cities of Hiroshima and Nagasaki implied the pointlessness of civil defence. Appearing early in the decade, the photographs of the destroyed city in these reports are all but indistinguishable from those of conventional bombing raids in World War Two: firemen remove a casualty from the rubble of a 'bombed' building in the January 1951 drill; a building burns in November 1951; fire hoses are trained on a 'blaze' on Forty-Second Street, and someone leaps into a net to escape a 'bombed' building, in September 1952; and firemen pour water onto smoking rubble, and volunteers evacuate a 'casualty' from a ruined building, in December 1952.[17]

Although the city is shown to be under attack, this iconography is ultimately comforting and it might even be said to dissolve the suspense in which this book is interested. The hypothetical threat is placed within the spectrum of familiar experience and its elimination by established procedures is demonstrated. So, for instance, one report explicitly establishes the realism of the exercise by reference to the blitz: an 'observer who had been in London during the German blitz termed the scene "quite realistic" as smoke from the flares and smokepots settled gloomily toward the street and bandaged figures leaned against the buildings or sat in doorways'.[18] There is, in these enacted fictions of an atomic future, an afterwards to nuclear war: thousands of trained, healthy personnel work to a plan to save lives and resurrect the city. Rather than leaving them in a moment of perpetual expectation of war, the drills place people in an imaginary future where attack has happened and life goes on.

The second genre of images, the empty city (concurrent with and then supplanting that of the damaged or destroyed city), is, though, much more ambiguous. While it too ostensibly shows robust preparation to survive attack, it becomes apparent that a further meaning, of nuclear war as the end of civilisation, is always bubbling under the surface.

The dominant iconography is of streets emptied of people as the sirens sound. For the report on the public drill of November 1951, there are photographs of places entirely emptied except for occasional members of the authorities (a highway, Pennsylvania Station, Times Square, the Stock Exchange, and Idlewild – now JFK – airport). Photographs of empty streets feature in subsequent reports for the drills of April 1952 (Times Square), September 1953 (7th Avenue and 38th Street, which is choked with abandoned trucks), June 1954 (Times Square and a street in Washington), July 1956 (Times Square), July 1957 (9th Avenue and Times Square), May 1958 (Broad Street), and April 1959 (the Lincoln Tunnel, Times Square, and also inside Macy's). An image of emptiness appears one final time, for the May 1960 drill, when a shot of children playing on swings is contrasted with the scene, two minutes later, when the playground is abandoned during the exercise.[19]

These images are powerful because they remind us of the central existential fact of the nuclear age: that a world teeming with people can suddenly be emptied of them. In the silence of the once bustling city is a space in which to imagine not only preparations for attack, but a world depopulated afterwards.

The fascination with the empty streets is apparent not only in the preponderance of these photographs but also in the written reports on the drills. Revealing phrases demonstrate that reporters found something intriguing and spooky about the silence of the emptied metropolis: '[t]he city's streets were oddly silent in scant minutes'; 'an eerie quiet settled on the streets'; 'nothing broke the blanket of silence lowered on the city'; and 'New York was quiet as a prairie'.[20] Another preoccupation was with the rapid transition between one reality (the teeming city) and another (the empty city), and back again: police and civil defence workers swiftly created 'a ghost city out of a buzzing metropolis'; 'within seconds the city bustled back to life and New Yorkers went about their affairs as if nothing unusual had happened'; and, within five minutes of the all-clear, '[m]en and women were once again rushing to the office, to the hair dresser, the dentist or to the homes or offices of friends'.[21] It is as if the swift movement between one reality and another brings home the precariousness of contemporary reality, always liable to slip into its nuclear alternative.

New Yorkers themselves were as fascinated by the empty streets as the reporters were. Although they were meant to go to the basements or centres of buildings during the drills, which were safer areas, what they actually did, to the frustration of the authorities, was dutifully desert the streets but then rush to the windows of buildings to peer out at their city transformed.

What the iconography and the reports of the empty city demonstrate is that, behind the bustle of everyday life, a nuclear city is waiting to burst through. Just as Russell and Schell gazed at familiar cities and imagined them transformed by nuclear attack, so the drills enlisted millions of people in the imaginative superimposition of a nuclear reality on the everyday life of the city. Instead of showing the city in the fullness of its life, prepared for attack, as was intended, the empty city streets became the 'Dead City' invoked by Vanderbilt, as the mention of ghost cities in the reports suggests.

Other features of the drills should be noted. One is their underlying absurdity: they were always likely to propose a reality of nuclear attack that did not seem credible. For instance, in 1956 the scenario for the drill assumed no serious radio-active fallout because, as civil defence authorities explained to the *New York Times*, 'if yesterday's exercise had assumed the possibility of serious fall-out, Civil Defense workers could not have ventured outside for training purposes'.[22] In other words, the drill is a preparation for a real attack but, in order for the drill to be staged, it has to assume that a fundamental aspect of the real attack is absent. This is a fraught dialogue between the real and imaginary worthy of the SIMUVAC exercises in Don DeLillo's novel, *White Noise* (1984). Another is that, as well as raising, inadvertently, the possibility of nuclear war as the end of civilisation, they also postulated an alternative post-holocaust world: the police state. The pictures of empty streets were not in fact entirely devoid of human life. They often had uniformed figures on them – police or civil defence workers – and one of the stories of the decade is of increasing numbers of people protesting the drills by occupying the streets during the exercises, openly courting arrest as they sought to seize back control of public space. By the late 1950s and early 1960s there were protests of many hundreds of people around the city, which can reasonably be seen as forerunners of later and much larger scale protests against the Vietnam War: key figures in the Vietnam protests, like Dorothy Day and Norman Mailer, participated, as did large numbers of students, another important constitutive element of counter-cultural activism.[23]

Damaged or destroyed cities, and empty cities, also feature in nuclear prose and fiction. It is predominantly an image of more dramatic destruction, of cities in fact levelled by atomic bombing, that is the legacy of Hiroshima to textual representations of nuclear blast, and which is a significant feature of John Hersey's influential representation of the attack. Nevil Shute's *On the Beach*, in contrast, eschews images of destruction for the gradual emptying of the world of people. It is to these texts that I now turn.

The literature of post-nuclear cities: flattened and empty urban spaces

[T]he center of the city [Hiroshima] was turned into a flat, rubble-strewn plain. (Jonathan Schell, *The Fate of the Earth*, 1982)[24]

John Hersey's *Hiroshima*, dramatically representing the atomic destruction of the city through the experiences of six survivors, was highly influential in the United States and elsewhere. Taking over a special edition of the *New Yorker* when it was first published in August 1946, it was widely reproduced, read out on the radio and published in book form.

The tendency, in approaching the text, has been to focus on it as a disaster narrative, addressing such issues as its fidelity to the experience of the bombing, the benefits and limitations of Hersey's reserved documentary style, and the way in which his choice of protagonists shapes the narrative.[25] These are entirely sensible preoccupations: Hersey's text is, after all, seeking to communicate and pay testament to the experience of this first atomic bombing. It is also, as Paul Boyer points out, and David Seed discusses in some detail, modelled on an account of a natural disaster, Thornton Wilder's *The Bridge of San Luis Rey*.[26] Taking on the formal characteristics of this earlier narrative, it portrays the bombing as a calamitous natural event, without discussing the political and military context that produced it (although, of course, it is not that Hersey deems this context insignificant).

Critics' focus on *Hiroshima* as a nuclear disaster narrative, paying attention to the adequacy or otherwise of its depiction of an actual atomic attack, certainly makes a lot of sense. However, we must also acknowledge that if, as Vanderbilt says, an image of the Dead City haunts other cities after Hiroshima, then a representation of the attack as influential as Hersey's speaks also to these other cities; to their possible futures. Hersey's text is pre-Cold War, or at most very early Cold War, but increasingly over the following decades it was read in the context of a sustained Cold War anticipation of nuclear attack. The second edition (1985), published in a decade of nuclear paranoia, and updating the first by adding a chapter counterpointing the ongoing stories of Hersey's protagonists with facts about nuclear tests and proliferation, contextualises Hiroshima in terms of contemporary experience.

We might reasonably ask, therefore, how the actual atomic experience described in *Hiroshima* speaks to the potential nuclear realities of the Cold War. Hiroshima became the essential reality to which people returned in thinking through the effects of atomic explosions (much more so, than, for instance, Nagasaki). Although it was in the past, it was used to imagine the future. Hersey's text therefore functions as an anxiety narrative as well as a disaster narrative.

Like the civil defence drills in New York, where people found themselves moving rapidly in and out of different realities, one mundane, one constructed as atomic, *Hiroshima* repeatedly emphasises the sudden shift from ordinary life to a level of experience that is entirely other. It is a text of transitions, of the fragility of everyday reality. The opening paragraph introduces this notion of transition, narrowing down the passage into the atomic age to a single minute, a moment when everything changed and after which nothing could be entirely secure again. In the first sentence, a clerk turns to speak to the woman next to her at 8:15 a.m. on 6 August, 1945. The second sentence introduces us to Hersey's other protagonists, all similarly engaged in ordinary activities: sitting down to read; looking out the window; reading a magazine in bed; walking a hospital corridor and pausing at a door. As a portrait of city life in the atomic age, it thus emphasizes the fragility of contemporary reality, its potential suddenly to metamorphose into something entirely different. (A subsidiary effect of the opening two sentences is to link previously disconnected people together in a common fate, and we will see in chapter five how shared nuclear threats became the basis for broader discourses establishing common interests of resistance across national and other boundaries.)

Unsurprisingly, the overwhelming emphasis in the description of the attack is on disorientation, nicely phrased by David Seed when he describes *Hiroshima* as a 'drama of bewilderment'.[27] There is, of course, a radical geographical bewilderment produced by the instantaneous rearrangement of the physical space of the city. Close to the blast, Mrs Nakamura finds that 'all the houses in her neighbourhood had collapsed'. Further out, two miles away in the suburbs, the Reverend Mr Tanimoto looks over Hiroshima and sees only a 'thick, dreadful miasma' rising from the city.[28] Crucially, different perspectives do not yield clearer understanding, the erasure of physical reference points by which Hersey's protagonists might orientate themselves mirroring the psychological confusion caused by events. Hersey is meticulous in pinpointing, down to the nearest yard, the distance of his various protagonists from ground zero. Yet, this pointedly does not allow us to triangulate anything more than their relative physical positions, and their geographical bewilderment is related to other kinds of confusion: about the fate of loved ones, for instance, and later, as rumours spread through the city in the following days, about what could have caused such unprecedented destruction.

The text exploits the gulf between its protagonists' ignorance of atomic bombs and the knowledge of its readers, who are aligned with the narrator in a position of privileged narrative authority. What is a source of puzzlement to the surviving staff of the Red Cross hospital (the exposure of all the stored X-ray plates), or is only a passing detail in a broad spectacle of horror for Dr Fuji (people vomiting as he makes his way out of the city), is inevitably interpreted by Hersey's readers as probable consequences of radiation.[29] Only just over a year after the bomb was dropped, atomic weapons had transformed people's sense of the potential horrors of war, and radiation and radiation sickness had been factored into the cultural consciousness.

The effect is to situate Hiroshima as qualitatively new. The 'epicentre of the nuclear age',[30] as Boyer describes the point above the Aioi Bridge where the bomb exploded, Hiroshima changes everything that follows. Although it was one of the final acts in a war characterised by the bombing of cities (in some cases involving greater loss of life), the world is presented as transformed. In places, it seems as though natural cycles have been disrupted. Mrs Nakamura's son keeps asking, '[w]hy is it night already?' Later, 'abnormally large' raindrops fall and a whirlwind tears through a park where people seek shelter from fires raging in the city.[31] An entirely new category of experience pertains. In a phrase noted as significant by Seed, Father Kleinsorge returns to his room after the bomb has dropped to find it in 'a state of weird and illogical confusion': a first aid kit and a suitcase are untouched while other things have been destroyed or have disappeared.[32]

So while *Hiroshima* is very much a disaster narrative in its presentation of a city destroyed by bombing, it also suggests that the world has changed fundamentally with the atomic attack. Established categories have been reformulated. In this respect it is far more challenging to the contemporary sense of reality than those civil defence drills in New York working the trope of the destroyed city, which sought to keep projected nuclear attack within the bounds of inherited experience of conventional bombing.

The way in which *Hiroshima* speaks to the fragility of Cold War city life is nowhere more apparent than in the striking description of the cityscape Father Kleinsorge encounters when he returns to Hiroshima. The landscape is flattened, the few standing structures 'only accentuating the horizontality of everything else'. The abiding impressions are of erasure – the city above ground level has simply been removed – and stasis, the freezing of life and motion. Father Kleinsorge finds 'a macabre traffic – hundreds of crumpled bicycles, shells of streetcars and automobiles all halted in mid-motion'.[33] This is not a description of a city destroyed as its inhabitants sheltered from an air raid; this is the abrupt curtailment of activity as the city awoke to the normal bustle of its morning routines.

Hiroshima here becomes both past and present, pre-nuclear and post-nuclear. The pre-nuclear city is frozen and preserved, projected in negative image on the flattened reality of the post-nuclear city. In the months before it is rebuilt (and Hersey notes the astonishing speed with which a new Hiroshima arises) the ruined city preserves the moment just before, and just after, the world passed across the cusp into the atomic age, as if the bombsite were a portal between the two.

Although Hersey's text is a disaster narrative, it also therefore represents the suspense – more accurately, here, the suspension – in which this book is interested. To this extent, it is not necessarily the 'closing of accounts on a troubling episode' Boyer proposes in his reading of the text.[34] By focusing attention so directly on the ease with which one reality is superseded by another, *Hiroshima* marks out the city as a fragile environment, suspended forever before a moment capable of shattering it into a post-nuclear world, just as the bomb drills in New York created a sense of that city as liable to dissolve into a post-attack reality.

Passing through this portal is to enter an entirely other world. Miss Sasaki returns to Hiroshima on 9 September. In contrast to the sterility of the world frozen in time found by Father Kleinsorge, what 'particularly gave her the creeps' was that an astonishing and unnaturally verdant plant growth had sprung up throughout the ruins (with dubious scientific legitimacy, Hersey claims that the bomb 'stimulated' growth).[35] The bomb is here a bringer of life, but of an alien life. This is a recurrent trope in representations of nuclear reality. Richard Rhodes notes the cable sent to report the detonation of the first atomic bomb at the Trinity test site in New Mexico: 'Doctor has just returned most enthusiastic and confident that the little boy is as husky as his big brother. The light in his eyes discernable from here to Highhold and I could have heard his screams from here to my farm.' In Martin Cruz Smith's thriller, *Stallion's Gate* (1986), set in and around the Los Alamos site where the Manhattan Project came to its conclusion, Joe Peña endures a terrifying ride along treacherous roads to deliver a canister of plutonium, suspended precariously behind him in the truck: 'the canister had a pregnant quality. The slug deep inside it seemed, in Joe's mind, alive. . . . [M]etal that was alive.' In Don DeLillo's novel *Underworld* (1997), Nick encounters some patients in a radiation clinic in the former Soviet Union, and the preponderance of the definite article in DeLillo's prose suggests that what he there encounters is somehow expected: 'It is the boy with skin where his eyes ought to be, a bolus of spongy flesh, oddly like a mushroom cap springing from each brow. It is the bald-headed children. . . . It is the man with the growth beneath his chin, a thing with a life of its own, embryonic and pulsing.'[36] In all these cases, life is disturbing: made other and terrible by mysterious nuclear agents.

Shute's *On the Beach* also presents a vision of post-nuclear urban life, though one strikingly different to Hersey's. Shute, a peripheral figure now, was in the 1950s, according to Julian Smith, 'one of England's two or three best-selling writers' and his novel had an enormous impact around the world (hence its inclusion in this project on US literature). Over forty newspapers serialized it when it came out in 1957 and it had sold four million copies by the 1980s. Churchill, when he read it, proposed sending a copy to Khrushchev. Across the Atlantic, Herman Kahn felt moved to complain that the novel ('interesting but badly researched') made nuclear war seem unnecessarily terminal.[37]

Certainly the novel struck a chord in the United States. The *New York Times* review of the book expressed serious reservations about the structure, the characterization and the 'remarkable degree of cheerfulness' in the tone, but acknowledged that Shute's description of fallout wiping out life across the globe was 'enough to chill one's blood.'[38] Undoubtedly the context in which the book was published played a part in its success. It came out in the same year that Sputnik orbited the United States, and in a period in which the permeability of the continent to Soviet intrusion was a cause for concern.

By the time Stanley Kramer's Hollywood film of the novel came out two years later, a crisis was well under way in Berlin on which both Khrushchev and Kennedy would later stake their reputations. The film, featuring stars like Gregory Peck, Ava Gardner and Fred Astaire, ensured Shute's story stayed in the spotlight. It was released in an international premiere of unprecedented complexity, opening simultaneously in eighteen cities around the world, including Moscow, and after the first Hollywood showing Kramer put on a midnight press conference at which scientists, including Nobel prize winner and antinuclear campaigner, Linus Pauling, and other intellectuals, including Aldous Huxley, endorsed the film's vision.[39] Concern about the possible impact of the film on public morale was enough for it to occasion discussion within the Eisenhower administration.[40]

Whereas destruction is the focus of *Hiroshima*, *On the Beach*, though it describes the end of human life on earth following a nuclear war (its protagonists are in Australia, awaiting a cloud of radiation from a conflict in the northern hemisphere), contains only one scene of urban devastation. Dwight and Moira go to see an exhibition of paintings, and the winning picture shows a 'sorrowing Christ on a background of the destruction of a great city'. Dwight hates it, describing the subject as 'phoney' and complaining that it is 'too dramatic'.[41] This is a key moment in the novel. How could a representation of nuclear attack be too dramatic? What this moment points up is Shute's self-consciousness about his artistic choice to eschew dramatic representation of nuclear attack.

It is not simply that the Melbourne setting precludes the description of doomed towns and cities. Indeed, Shute's novel is stuffed full of post-nuclear urban spaces, both those directly involved in the war, and those doomed by radioactive contamination afterwards. Some are visited by the last operational US submarine, which scouts out the dying world, and others are conjured up in conversations by those awaiting their end in southern Australia. Paris, London, Seattle, Cairns, Port Moresby, Darwin, Brisbane, Edmonds, New York, Rio de Janeiro, and Mystic, Connecticut are all named, but all are also described as being pristine, their buildings untouched by nuclear blast. All that distinguishes them from their pre-nuclear realities is that they are now empty of people.

The narrative returns repeatedly to these urban spaces. When Moira says to Dwight that she's angry she will never get to see Paris now, because Paris no longer exists, he replies: 'The Rue de Rivoli may still be there, with things in the shop windows and everything. I wouldn't know if Paris got a bomb or not. Maybe it's all there still just as it was, with the sun shining down the street the way you'd want to see it. . . . It's just that folks don't live there any more.'[42] The final detail is, of course, the crucial one, rendering the familiar scene eerie and unusual. As with Hersey's description of the flattened Hiroshima, the emphasis is on erasure, but in this case it is the erasure of people rather than buildings. Later, Moira asks Dwight if he can visualise 'those cities, all those fields and farms, with nobody, and nothing left alive. Just nothing there.'[43] What are strikingly absent, from both Dwight's and Moira's descriptions, are the corpses – which are an abiding image in Hersey's text. When Dwight's submarine views Cairns, all he can report is the 'purely negative information' that it looks exactly like it did before: 'The sun shone in the streets, the flame trees brightened the far hills, the deep verandahs shaded the shop windows of the town. A pleasant little place to live in in the tropics, though nobody lived there'.[44] The absence of bodies is at least remarked upon a little later. When the submarine finds the same scenes at Port Moresby and Port Darwin, the submariners infer that people had 'died tidily'. John Osborne guesses that people have probably gone to bed to die. Dwight's response – 'That's enough about that'[45] – is a refusal to engage with the reality of the death which is approaching him, his crew, and those awaiting their return in Melbourne. The tidiness of the deaths in these places – and they find the same at Edmonds ('so normal in the spring sunlight')[46] and Seattle ('there seemed to be nothing wrong with the city at all, except that there were no people there')[47] – is part of a contradictory impulse in the novel, which both decries the civilisation that produced the war and celebrates it. The novel asks us to admire the dignity with which everyone meets their end. Like the onetime inhabitants of the empty cities of the novel, Moira, Dwight, Peter, Mary and John die 'tidily', bidding each other farewell with firm handshakes ('Good luck, old man'), and resisting to the end any impropriety, particularly of a sexual nature.[48]

The emphasis on tidiness and cleanliness is important for situating this novel amongst other nuclear disaster and nuclear anxiety texts, and echoes the scrubbed but contaminated domestic environments that will be explored in the next chapter. The radiation in *On the Beach* is both a force of contamination and, because it leaves the streets tidy, a cleansing agent. Indeed, the only dirty city in the novel is Melbourne, where, just before death comes, some citizens neglect to keep the city clean. When Dwight walks through Melbourne, it is a city where the 'streets were dirty now and littered with paper and spoilt vegetables', it is 'becoming foul and beginning to smell' and it reminds him 'of an oriental city in the making'.[49] A married couple, Peter and Mary, have the same experience. When they go into Melbourne, Mary asks, 'what's the matter with everything? It's all so dirty, and it smells horrid.'[50] She is relieved to return home to 'the cleanness that was her pride, the carefully tended garden, the clean wide view out over the bay'.[51]

Dwight reflects on what the city will be like in a few years' time: 'The human race was to be wiped out and the world made clean again for wiser occupants without undue delay.'[52] Radiation will contaminate the city, but it will also clean up the streets; it provides a radical solution to a world that has gone awry. The novel even renders deaths from radiation sickness less terrible than we might imagine. While an unpleasant period of vomiting and diarrhoea is mentioned, this is alleviated, almost as soon as it starts, by suicide pills.

George R. Stewart's seminal science fiction novel, *Earth Abides*, offers a similarly decorous vision of the demise of civilisation. Published in 1949, it deals with the death of most of humanity as the consequence of a plague, although its sporadic references to atomic weapons show an awareness of the threat of global war which gives its vision of the end a nuclear context.[53] As with *On the Beach*, there are repeated descriptions of empty cities, and there are very few bodies. Civilisation, the protagonist, Ish, observes, has 'gone down gallantly', and there was 'no disgraceful panic' in the cities.[54]

It is easy to mock the propriety of visions of the end of the world like those of Shute and Stewart, particularly when they are placed next to Hersey's brutal description of Hiroshima, where the landscape is littered not just with fallen buildings, but with corpses and with people so terribly wounded that their skin slips off or they are otherwise unrecognisable. However, such a criticism misunderstands the difference between the two types of text. *On the Beach* deliberately eschews the actual physical horror of nuclear war in order to communicate the 'purely negative information' of an empty world. Whereas *Hiroshima* seeks to show us what an atomic explosion *is*, *On the Beach* tries to shows what *is not*, following nuclear war. Even the sugary sentimentality of the storyline, and the ridiculous propriety, even priggishness, of the major characters as they face the end, function effectively as counterpoint not only to the absence of people from the world, but also of the value judgments by which the loss might be estimated or mourned once everyone is dead.

The unsettlingly empty city streets therefore function in a way contiguous with that in which, inadvertently, they carried meaning during the civil defence drills in New York. During the drills they ostensibly represented a city prepared for war and ready to take whatever was thrown at it, but they evoked an encounter with the sublime (of infinite nothingness) that provoked an unsettling response amongst those who witnessed them. The novel exploits this other meaning. The streets are a symbol of a lost civilisation; ordinary buildings become monumental, signifiers of a reality that has disappeared.

The focus on the empty silence of the world's streets allows Shute's novel, even though it is about the aftermath of nuclear disaster, to evoke the experience of waiting for an anticipated and dreaded end of the Cold War. After all, *On the Beach*'s protagonists are engaged, above all, in waiting. Although they go off and do various things – sail the world, in Dwight's case; take a secretarial course in Moira's; plan a future for their child in Peter and Mary's – these are simply distractions from the repressed knowledge of the death that awaits everyone. Their experience encapsulates a heightened version of the 'double life' Lifton claims is more widely led during the Cold War.[55] Hence the beginning of the novel, with Peter waking up, looking forward to a trip to Melbourne for work, and discussing plans to go to the beach with his wife, and knowing despite all this that death is coming to them all, is, for a novel criticised for its sentimentality, a remarkably subtle evocation of nuclear anxiety. The war, which has changed everything, only intrudes as a sub-clause of a sentence on the third page of the book ('They had a small car in the garage, but since the short war had ended a year previously it remained unused').[56] It is this tiny marker of nuclear reality, of course, that changes everything else, just as it is more generally the small markers of nuclear reality in everyday life that transform culture and consciousness during the Cold War.

Moving from such conventional nuclear texts to postmodern ones, as I am about to do, may seem a surprising leap to make, but it is not a wholly novel one. Notably, Alan Nadel has discussed *Hiroshima* in terms of a postmodern assault on the possibility of meaning. Arguing that 'substitution [of unrecorded activity by the historical record Hersey constructs] claims to capture or represent events, but instead replaces them with language', Nadel reads *Hiroshima* as a text that makes apparent the omissions, evasions and distortions inherent in discourse; as a text that is, essentially, postmodern. Hersey's history has 'performed the replacement of that event with its representation'.[57] Despite its highly conventional, indeed hackneyed form, *On the Beach* might similarly, because of its subject matter, be read as taking us to the point where narrative fails to represent experience. In this case its 'postmodern' concern manifests itself in a cessation of narrative rather than a replacement of the experience with narrative.

The novel ends with Moira committing suicide. Yet, as the discussion of the novel's empty town and city streets will have already made apparent, the true subject of the text is not Moira or Dwight (whose submarine has just 'vanished in the mist' on its way to being scuppered along with its crew) but the absence that follows all these deaths.[58] 'This was the end of it, the very, very end' muses the narrator, slipping into Moira's perspective as she watches Dwight's submarine disappear, yet in fact the end is only the beginning of the novel's subject matter: the absence of human experience and perspectives once everyone is dead.[59] The narrative must stop when Moira dies, just as it gets to the point where the subject matter in which it is interested is about to come into being: the absence of people from the world. Because any perspective on a post-human world implies the continuing presence of a human point of view from which to describe it, the novel has to collapse into silence: the text disappears as she does. Signification stops because signifiers imply the presence not only of signifieds but also of someone

to whom they signify. Hence the novel can only enact the impossibility of representing an entirely depopulated world.

It is in the encounter with such failures of discourse that postmodernism finds
much of its subject matter. Formally, of course, it develops a much more sophisticated response to this material but the texts I am about to discuss should be seen
as developments from, not entirely antithetical to, the more conventional nuclear
texts with which I have just dealt.

Postmodern nuclear cities

A screaming comes across the sky. (Thomas Pynchon, *Gravity's Rainbow*)[60]

Gravity's Rainbow opens with a sense of urban crisis that, though lodged in German
attacks on London during the Second World War, resonates with meanings produced by the nuclear states of suspense permeating the early 1970s culture in
which the novel was produced. Published in the middle of the Cold War, such a
novel could not fail to bear the traces of the discourses and modes of knowing
definitive of nuclear realities. The nuclear state (indeed, the Nuclear State) is
fundamental to the novel and is conjured up in its central image, the V-2 rockets
that deliver conventional explosives to London's streets and symbolically prefigure
the nuclear missiles of the Cold War. Rocket technology structures consciousness
in *Gravity's Rainbow*.

Pirate Prentice's dream, with which the novel opens, is a 'drama of bewilderment' which, plunged in without explanation, the reader must share.[61] It begins
with the sky transfigured into a source of terror. This is not temporary; it is an
ongoing state of affairs: '[s]creaming holds across the sky' we are told, just before
Pirate awakes. What he wakes to is not reprieve from the fear but a continuation
of it: looking out across London he sees in the early dawn the vapour trail of a
newly launched V-2, heading for the city. Just as his sleeping thoughts are driven
by the screaming in the sky, so too then are his first waking thoughts preoccupied
with expectation of death delivered from above. Even though, when the missile
arrives, it lands elsewhere, Pirate realises that there will be no relief from the state
of suspense in which he is held, and that the sky is now permanently threatening,
a reconfiguring of the space above that is consistent with the nuclear transformations of the sky noted in chapter one: 'There will indeed be others [other missiles],
each as likely to land on top of him [. . .]. Will we have to stop watching the
sky?'[62]

Pirate's dream is revealing. It is a dream of evacuation but not of escape. Rather
than a 'disentanglement from' it is a 'progressive *knotting into*'.[63] Marshalled by
ominous figures who wear 'cockades the color of lead, and do not speak', the
evacuees hear voices in their heads telling them they will not be saved. Underfoot,
'crunches the oldest of city dirt, last crystallizations of all the city had denied,
threatened, lied to its children'.[64]

It is a dream of betrayal. The personification of the city (it denies, threatens
and lies) turns it into a representation of malignant authority; a symbol of a mili-

tarised society. It thus conjures up other facets of the nuclear society that are a recurring preoccupation in discourse about the bomb: the military-industrial complex of the nuclear state, and the potential for fascistic forms of social organisation after nuclear war. A powerful image from the BBC's drama, *Threads* (1984), reproduced on the cover of the British listings magazine, the *Radio Times*, is of a traffic warden carrying a gun, a chilling symbol of inappropriately deployed authority.[65] In Judith Merril's *Shadow on the Hearth* (1950), discussed in more detail in the next chapter, one of Gladys's key realisations is that sources of authority are not to be trusted and sometimes have malign intent.

A different sort of nuclear city, combining military and manufacturing organisation on a massive scale, can be used to express this, as in Philip K. Dick's *The Penultimate Truth* (1964), where people toil in vast underground industrial works, unaware that their leaders live in luxury on the surface. From the beginning atomic technology required the construction of enormous military-industrial systems. The Manhattan Project necessitated that industrial levels of research and production be combined with secrecy and control. Oak Ridge, the Tennessee plant that enriched uranium for the Hiroshima bomb, was built from nothing in 1943, as 75,000 people were drafted in: 'they were building houses, one every 30 minutes', remembers one inhabitant, 'hauling them in, half-built, on trucks down the street'. Tens of thousands worked at Oak Ridge, unaware of the significance of the project on which they were working. As Jessica Taylor points out, by 1945 'Oak Ridge would contain the world's first nuclear reactor, the biggest building in the world, and would use one-sixth of all the electricity generated in the US', a forerunner of later excessive drains on the nation's power supply by its nuclear programmes.[66] (Energy is also a preoccupation in *Gravity's Rainbow*, where secret agencies make the clocks run at different speeds to disguise the war's tremendous power consumption.)[67]

Oak Ridge was one of a number of secret cities (it did not appear on maps at the time) necessary to the Manhattan Project. Such secrecy and such large scales of production were of course necessary in the context of the Second World War. In fact, the day after the bomb was dropped on Hiroshima, the *New York Times* ran a front-page piece celebrating the project, which began with the revelation of its scale ('The War Department revealed today how three "hidden cities" with a total population of 100,000 inhabitants sprang into being as a result of the $2,000,000,000 atomic bomb project, how they did their work without knowing what it was all about, and how they kept the biggest secret of the war'), and included statistics and graphics showing the power of the new weapon and the industrial levels of organisation required to produce it.[68]

In *Gravity's Rainbow*, the threatening city through which people are taken in Pirate's dream stands in for the secret cities of the nuclear state (although the link is one of analogy, rather than direct reference). The paranoia of Pirate's dream is not necessarily shown to be irrational in a novel in which malign systems shape and control individuals.

The novel evokes the collapse of the distinction between peace and war, a notable feature of the Cold War standoff. Looking at the various kinds of military and civilian police, Slothrop is moved to wonder, in passing, 'whatever civilian means nowadays', and Roger and Jessica find that the 'Home Front' is not simply a reality of wartime Britain, but a means of co-opting their lives to the military state, so that it becomes a 'fiction designed, not too subtly, to draw them apart, to subvert love in favor of work, abstraction, required pain, bitter death'.[69] Rather than an aberration, war becomes the norm and peace is not conceived of as an opposite and entirely other state. Both are unfoldings from the same logic, so that when Pointsman conceives that 'war is to be adjourned and reconstituted as a peace', we should note both that this is to be a temporary state of affairs (an adjournment, not a termination) and that it is to be a realignment of the same elements (a reconstitution, not a new thing entire).[70] One of the novel's paranoid fantasies is that wartime is a cover for, and stimulus to, the governing reality of capitalism; that 'the real business of War is buying and selling', and that mass death in wartime 'serves as spectacle, as diversion from the real movements of the War. It provides raw material to be recorded into History, so that children may be taught History as sequences of violence, battle after battle, and be more prepared for the adult world [. . .]. The true war is a celebration of markets.'[71]

By suggesting that peace and war are not truly opposite things, the novel is very much in keeping with the spirit of a Cold War nuclear confrontation where the world existed in the infinitesimal spaces between and across peace and war, not entirely in one state or the other. Peacetime became shaped – in terms of economy, social organisation and cultural production – by the increasingly powerful military-industrial complex. While the Cold War did not involve a conventional military conflict with the Soviet Union, neither, due in large part to the stasis of Mutual Assured Destruction, was it a conventional peace. It was a drawn out experience of nearly-war, or virtually-war, that continually threatened, without delivering, an apocalyptic resolution.

A text like *Gravity's Rainbow*, which finds in the Second World War the coordinates from which the post-war psychological and cultural landscape was mapped, is able, by rejecting realism for postmodern experimentation, and rejecting trust in authority for paranoia, to explore these strange and contradictory states of mind. The vision of the rockets, 'hanging the measureless instant over the black North Sea', poised before plummeting from the tops of their parabolas to their targets, is the vision which hangs over the world during the Cold War, although, as in the rocket which is suspended in the immeasurably small fraction of a moment before detonation at the end of the novel, they are nuclear, rather than conventional.[72]

It is, notably, the city which is shown to be an endangered environment. To Pirate's visions of cities threatened both by rockets and by malign, shadowy authorities, we can add other depictions of London in danger in the novel. Like Pirate, Jessica dreams of the city ('[s]omething's stalking through the city of Smoke – gathering up slender girls fair and smooth as dolls, by the handful') and awakes from her nightmare to the sound of a rocket bomb exploding.[73] Pointsman also dreams of a 'sacrificial city' that, though not directly linked with V-2s, has apocalyptic dimensions: it has a shelter 'lying steel-clad miles below' to which he cannot escape; outside the city, he looks back to 'pillars of smoke', and hears voices relaying news of 'South America burned to cinders, the sky over New York glowing purple with the new all-sovereign death-ray'.[74] Most crucially, in the novel, there are the actual V-2 strikes on London, Slothrop's paranoia that all the missiles have 'his name written on' given credence by the novel in its central conceit: the map of his sexual conquests that reproduces exactly the map of rocket strikes across the city.[75] (The mapping of attacks on London reproduces, of course, the conceptualisations of the city as target discussed earlier in this chapter.) The novel is nuclear not only in its use of the rocket bombs as a symbol of terror, but also in its presentation of a danger conceived as perpetually present and focused through images of a threatened city.

This might lead us to ask whether there are broader connections from nuclear anxiety and postmodern literature to postmodern conceptions of the city. Arguably, the city is the quintessential *modernist* environment, the industrial, commercial and personal spaces of the booming urban centres embodying the new impulses of the late nineteenth and early twentieth centuries, and demanding an entirely new cultural response. Yet cities remained central, and indeed grew in their influence, during the postmodern period, although they were shaped in different ways by the societies and cultures of the second half of the twentieth century than by those of the first. Edward Soja identifies six themes through which geographers have approached the postmodern city, and these give a flavour of the ways in which urban spaces developed in the second half of the twentieth century: '[g]lobalization of capital, labor, culture, and information flows'; '[p]ost-Fordist economic restructuring'; '[r]estructuring of urban form' (the growth of enormous cities; the more heterogenous spatial organisation of these cities, as multiple centres, suburban and non-urban ways of life, became mixed); '[r]estructuring the social order' (a shattering of simple divides between different social strata, though certainly not a move toward greater equality); '[c]arceral cities' (a more developed observation and control of space by city and other authorities); and 'Simcities' (a confusion of real and imaginary categories of identity and interaction within the city).[76]

There is certainly not a direct correlation between these postmodern cities and the nuclear context. The reorganisations of capital and social order producing these cities – most notably the rise of late capitalism, the shift in emphasis from manufacturing to service industries and greater and swifter movement of data, goods and people around the globe – are not equivalent to the anxious cultural forces shaping the idea of the nuclear-imperilled city. However, there are significant overlaps, largely analogous rather than causal in nature but, nevertheless, suggesting important continuities. For instance, the 'carceral' city is a postmodern incarnation of the very carefully controlled and demarcated environment of urban space pertaining during the New York bomb drills, and of the militarised city apparent in Pirate's dream.

Rather more directly, as well as the economic and social drives dictating the spread of the contemporary city, there was, at least in the early years of the Cold War, an emphasis, if more frequently apparent in discourse than in practical urban planning, on dispersing cities to make them less easy targets for atomic attack. Nan Ellin acknowledges this in discussing the rise of different conceptions of space in the postmodern city, and the trend toward suburbanization: 'new defense technologies (atomic energy) employed during the Second World War motivated and justified the dispersal of settlements. Combined with the extended power of the state, mass media, and transnational corporation, the enclosed space of older cities was transformed into . . . "abstract space", where place has become inconsequential, generalized, undifferentiated, indefinite, and undefined'.[77]

A more subtle impact on the trend toward suburbanization, leading in extremis to the development of commuter-belt communities beyond the suburbs, may have been the attractive security they seemed to offer in a world that seemed shaky and insecure, very largely because of the atomic threat. Elaine Tyler May points out that rural sales of properties increased markedly in the 1950s, and that these were often advertised as 'country properties for this Atomic Age' or 'protected country settings'.[78] Feeding on, and contributing to, this trend toward dispersal was, in the United States, the building of the network of interstate highways in the 1950s, as Vanderbilt points out: 'the system of coast-to-coast roads inaugurated by Dwight D. Eisenhower was, if not a direct byproduct of Cold War military contingency, at least touted by its proponents for its importance in national defense, reflected for many years in its very name: The National System of Interstate and Defense Highways.'[79]

Clifford Simak's science-fiction novel, *City* (1952), provides a nice précis of the theory that the solution to the atomic threat was the erasure of the idea of the city. Set in a future where urban environments have been abandoned, the novel has one of its characters, John J. Webster, bring city counsellors, and the reader, up to speed with the necessity of the city's demise:

> if the cities of the world had not been deserted, they would have been destroyed. There would have been a war, gentlemen, an atomic war. Have you forgotten the 1950s and the 60s? Have you forgotten waking up at night and listening for the bomb to come, knowing that you would not hear it when it came, knowing that you would never hear again, if it did come?
>
> But the cities were deserted and industry was dispersed and there were no targets and there was no war.[80]

City is not, of course, a postmodern text. However, it articulates neatly the early Cold War sense of cities as threatened, and potentially therefore anachronistic, environments. Such sentiments played only one small role in a much larger confluence of forces driving decentralisation of the cities (and which resulted, of course, not in the end of cities, but in the creation of vast hinterlands of suburbia which effectively extended city limits).

However, perhaps the most important linkage between the postmodern city and the nuclear-threatened city is much less direct than this. It is gestured toward in the idea of the 'Simcity', the hyperreal confluence of sign and sign-systems that comprise ordinary experience of the postmodern city. Notwithstanding Hiroshima and Nagasaki, the post-nuclear city is primarily a set of ideas, a sequence of images and motifs deriving from conjecture and the cultural memory of the bombed Japanese cities. The threatened imminence of nuclear war overlays these images on the 'real' cities of the world, much as Fermi, Russell and Schell imagined the cities they saw around them in atomic ruin. Although the signs of the hyperreal city are conceptually distinct from those of the nuclear imagination, both call into question the category of the real. In the postmodern city, the proliferation of signs is not just a masking of the real, but its transformation, because the idea of the real to which it refers is already a representation. As Jean Baudrillard articulates postmodern experience more generally, the 'principle of simulation wins out over the reality principle'.[81] Similarly, the images of nuclear destruction that haunt the city of the atomic era call into question the real existence of the city. Obviously, the living city is around its citizens in concrete and steel but the possibility of its extinction is always present, even though people might become habituated to this potential future, consciousness of it lurking in the back of the mind rather than functioning as a constant preoccupation.

A later version of the postmodern city than *Gravity's Rainbow*, pertinent to this discussion, is Paul Auster's *In the Country of Last Things*. Here the connection to the nuclear context is more tenuous than in *Gravity's Rainbow*: there are no missiles; there is no hint of military threat. In fact, to read the unnamed city to which the narrator, Anna Blume, goes in search of her brother as nuclear, might seem to be reductionist, imposing a 1980s context of nuclear paranoia on the text in a heavy-handed fashion. It is, though, precisely because of this context that I want to insist that there is a nuclear dimension to the novel; as Paul Brians points out, although not in relation to Auster, '[s]o pervasive is the notion that atomic Armageddon is our destiny that any book portraying a societal collapse is liable to be interpreted as a post-nuclear holocaust novel'.[82] Published in 1987, the vision of a collapsing city and civilisation makes it impossible not to consider the nuclear dimension (indeed, for Jacqueline Foertsch it is one of a number of postmodern novels 'that deal, however indirectly, with the devastation of nuclear war'),[83] even if only to reject it in favour of a focus on broader qualities in the text, like its exploration of identity, place and language.

In the Country of Last Things is, as the title suggests, about the terminal phase of human society. It is a book about the collapse of civilisation, told through the story of a strange, disorientating, disintegrating city. This, alone, gives it a nuclear resonance, but other qualities in the text allow such a reading to be sustained and developed.

The physical environment of the city is hostile and changing. The 'rubble is a special problem', Anna writes, constantly threatening to trip up the unwary. The geography of the city has a disturbing tendency to shift, whole areas disappearing, as when Anna goes to find her brother's office: 'I had not realized that the street would be gone. It wasn't that the office was empty or that the building had been abandoned. There was no building, no street, no anything at all: nothing but stones and rubbish for acres around.'[84] The levelling of parts of the city, and the geographical and psychological confusion of its inhabitants, echoes the 'drama of bewilderment' of Hersey's *Hiroshima*.[85] Like that city, the unnamed city of Auster's novel is a gateway between two types of world. The unidentified recipient of

Anna's dispatches receives news of an entirely other category of experience from, as Anna puts it, 'your old friend from another world'.[86] Anna has slipped, after her brother, into a world echoing, but fundamentally different from, that she had hitherto experienced as real but, in a novelistic representation of entropy, there is no way back to the more ordered world she left behind, and all she can do is send her incomplete memoir (in the last sentence, on which the novel ominously ends, she promises to write again) back across the divide.

This disorientating slip into another reality is indicative of both the nuclear and the postmodern dimensions of the novel. Both provide a robust challenge to ingrained Enlightenment assumptions about progress and the power of reason, even if in different ways. The apocalyptic possibilities of nuclear destruction create a rupture in the quotidian, steadily advancing progress of human civilisation, out of which pour alternative histories and systems of interpretation. *In the Country of Last Things* is populated by numerous death-cults and systems of belief: Runners charge through the streets until they die of exhaustion; Assassination Clubs allow people to elect to be assassinated.[87] There are also numerous groups which claim to be able to explain and control the unpredictable weather of the city: the Smilers, the Crawlers, the Drummers, the End-of-Worlders and the Free Associationists.[88] All these have systems of logic that are internally coherent, but their proliferation indicates the impossibility of mapping these systems of logic onto the external world. No single worldview is any more capable of explaining reality than another, and so they multiply, unchecked by the possibility of falsification. Pushed to extremis, in its final, apocalyptic phases, human culture collapses into ever more extravagant and doomed attempts to find meaning in the world, to shore it against the negation and meaninglessness of its impending absence. *On the Beach* sought, through the empty town and city streets of the world, to convey the horror of absence of human life and civilisation, but it remained firmly committed, through the stoic response of its characters, to the values of civilisation, which offered a dignified way to accept the end. *In the Country of Last Things* offers a horrific alternative: there is no meaning at all; in the final throes of humanity, as it approaches the end, everything is in flux. A similar flux is felt in the British writer, Doris Lessing's, novel, *Memoirs of a Survivor* (1974), which offers a half-way position between Shute's and Auster's visions of the demise of civilisation. As the narrator watches the city gradually fall apart from her window, after some unnamed calamity in Western civilisation, she muses that 'it is as if two ways of life, two lives, two worlds, lay side by side and closely connected. But then, one life excluded the other, and I did not expect the two worlds ever to link up.'[89] There is a severing of one world from another here, an enactment of the doubled mental life identified by Lifton as characteristic of consciousness in the Cold War.

Postmodernism, too, is a collapse of established forms of authority. The demise of master narratives, identified by Jean-François Lyotard as definitive of postmodernity, opens up in *In the Country of Last Things* not into a liberating proliferation of micronarratives, but a horrific series of internally coherent and rational, but externally unverifiable and desperate, attempts to find an explanation for the world and reassert human control over it.[90] Established forms of social authority are absent in *In the Country of Last Things*. This is not a vision of people brought together by common interest, as in *Alas, Babylon*'s (1959) vision of a post-holocaust society, but of people atomised into mutually suspicious units. When Anna arrives, she soon discovers that others are not to be trusted: 'there is nothing that people will not do, and the sooner you learn that, the better off you will be'.[91] Nor do conventional forms of authority lend legitimacy to one worldview over another. The 'chief function of government' is simply to send in trucks to collect the corpses each morning.[92] Unable to impose an absolute authority on the situation, in the manner of Pirate's nightmare dreams of totalitarianism, government resigns itself to the existence of anarchy.

The city becomes, then, an environment in which Auster is able to depict the eruption of the irrational into the world. The crisis of rationalism which *In the Country of Last Things* explores is a product both of the nuclear dimension and of postmodern discourses. The nuclear context of the world in which it was published, and the collapse of narrative authority associated with postmodern discourses, provide a particularly fecund environment for the novel's exploration of a crisis of civilisation.

One of the most striking features of *In the Country of Last Things* is its depiction of rootlessness. Left without homes, people must take temporary accommodation, living always with the risk of dispossession by intruders. Bogus estate agents, renting properties that do not exist, are able to thrive because people are willing to queue for hours in order to sit for ten minutes, looking 'at photographs of buildings on tree-lined streets, of comfortable rooms, of apartments furnished with carpets and soft leather chairs – peaceful scenes to evoke the smell of coffee wafting in from the kitchen, the steam of a hot bath, the bright colors of potted plants snug on the sill'.[93] These fantasies of suburban life are about more than the buildings that no longer exist: they are about a psychological comfort, rooted in notions of home and family that are no longer attainable.

These notions of home are the subject of the next chapter. While cities were the targets of missiles, and symbols of the civilisation threatened by nuclear war, the detached suburban house was a central and frequently used image in civil defence materials, as well as in the culture at large, for what was threatened by nuclear war. Consequently, depictions of attempts to secure this environment against the dangers of the age inflected the idea of family in ways ideologically specific to the nuclear context.

Notes

1 Anon., 'Exhibit will warn cities of atom ruin', *New York Times* (19 January 1946), p. 1.
2 Richard Rhodes, *The Making of the Atomic Bomb* (London: Penguin, 1988), p. 275.
3 Jonathan Schell, *The Fate of the Earth* and *The Abolition* (Stanford: Stanford University Press, 2000), p. 183.
4 Schell, *Fate of the Earth*, p. 182.
5 See discussion of nuclear strategy in chapter two.

6 Tom Vanderbilt, *Survival City: Adventures Among the Ruins of Atomic America* (New York: Princeton, 2002), p. 39.
7 Vanderbilt, *Survival City*, p. 74.
8 Paul Boyer, *By the Bomb's Early Light: American Thought and Culture at the Dawn of the Atomic Age*, new ed. (Chapel Hill: North Carolina University Press, 1994), p. 14. Robert Poole and Steve Wright, *Target North-West: Civil Defence and Nuclear War in Region 10* (Lancaster: Richardson Institute for Peace and Conflict Research, 1982). Anon., *Nottingham After the Bomb* (Nottingham: Nottingham Medical Campaign Against Nuclear Weapons, 1983).
9 See especially chapter 1, 'Dead city: the metropolis targeted', of Vanderbilt, *Survival City*, pp. 48–67.
10 See Appendix for a full list of the drills.
11 Alexander Feinberg, 'Civil defense tests disaster technique as city is "bombed"', *New York Times* (1 October 1952), p. 18. Peter Kihss, 'Nation takes cover in air-raid alert', *New York Times* (4 May 1960), p. 1.
12 Jeremy Isaacs and Taylor Downing, *Cold War* (London: Bantam, 1998), pp. 152–3. Andrew D. Grossman, *Neither Dead Nor Red: Civilian Defense and American Political Development During the Early Cold War* (New York: Routledge, 2001), p. ix, pp. 85–6, p. 158. Guy Oakes, *The Imaginary War: Civil Defense and American Cold War Culture* (New York: Oxford University Press, 1994), pp. 84–104.
13 'The sound of sirens', *New York Times* (26 May 1951), p. 12. It is not possible to determine how long these weekly tests continued.
14 Anon., 'Raid shelters increase', *New York Times* (4 June 1952), p. 18. Kevin L. Goodman, 'Out of the past: fallout shelters', *New York Times* (21 November 1976), p. 268. Most shelters would have been strong areas of buildings or subways designated as shelter areas, rather than purpose-built structures. They were likely to have been marked as shelters and possibly stocked with provisions. The inspectors were part of a 250-strong team of people in the New York City civil defense office.
15 Peter Kihss, 'City raid alert termed a success,' *New York Times* (16 June 1955), p. 17. Robert Condon, New York's Civil Defense Director, made this claim (the precise number was 543,517) and called for a few hundred thousand more to join them.
16 See, for example, Thomas P. Ronan, 'City civil defense mobilized in drill for "atom bombing"', *New York Times* (15 November 1951), p. 1, p. 16, and Alexander Feinberg, 'Civil defense tests disaster technique', p. 1, p. 18.
17 Anon., 'Civil defense practice drills held here', *New York Times* (22 January 1951), p. 12. Ronan, 'City civil defense mobilized', p. 1, p. 16. Feinberg, 'Civil defense tests disaster technique', p. 1, p. 18. Kalman Seigel, 'Biggest raid test turns New York into a "ghost city"', *New York Times* (14 December 1952), p. 1, p. 72.
18 Ronan, 'City civil defense mobilized', p. 16.
19 Thomas P. Ronan, 'Raid test silences city in 2 minutes; officials pleased', *New York Times* (29 November 1951), p. 1, p. 24. Feinberg, 'Civil defense tests disaster technique', p. 1, p. 18. Frederick Graham, 'Biggest defense test here called best', *New York Times* (26 September 1953), p. 19. Milton Bracker, '54 cities "raided" in U.S. Bomb Drill', *New York Times* (15 June 1954), p. 1, p. 32. Russell Porter, 'City at standstill in U.S.-wide atom raid test', *New York Times* (21 July 1956), p. 1. Will Lissner, 'Streets cleared swiftly', *New York Times* (13 July 1957), p. 3. Philip Benjamin, 'Millions here take cover in raid drill', *New York Times* (7 May 1958), p. 1. Philip Benjamin, 'H-bomb test raid stills bustling city', *New York Times* (18 April 1959), p. 1, p. 3. Peter Kihss, 'Nation takes cover in air-raid alert', *New York Times* (4 May 1960), p. 48.
20 Benjamin, 'Millions here take cover', p. 30. Ronan, 'Raid test silences city', p. 1. Seigel, 'Biggest raid test', p. 72. Graham, 'Biggest defense test here called best', p. 1.

21 Seigel, 'Biggest raid test', p. 1. Ronan, 'Raid test silences city', p. 1. Graham, 'Biggest defense test here called best', p. 19.

22 Porter, 'City at standstill', p. 6.

23 See, for example, the report on the 1960 drill. Kihss, 'Nation takes cover', p. 1, p. 48.

24 Schell, *Fate of the Earth*, p. 37.

25 For a discussion of reactions to *Hiroshima* see, for example, Boyer, *By the Bomb's Early Light*, pp. 203–10. Spencer R. Weart, *Nuclear Fear: A History of Images* (Cambridge: Harvard University Press, 1988), p. 107.

26 Boyer, *By the Dawn's Early Light*, p. 204. David Seed, 'The dawn of the atomic age', in Seed (ed.), *Imagining Apocalypse: Studies in Cultural Crisis* (Hampshire: Palgrave, 2000), pp. 94–7.

27 Seed, 'Dawn of the atomic age', p. 97.

28 John Hersey, *Hiroshima*, new ed. (London: Penguin, 1986), p. 27, p. 25.

29 Hersey, *Hiroshima*, p. 74, p. 47.

30 Boyer, *Fallout: A Historian Reflects on America's Half-Century Encounter with Nuclear Weapons* (Columbus: Ohio State University Press, 1998), p. 245.

31 Hersey, *Hiroshima*, p. 27, p. 52.

32 Hersey, *Hiroshima*, p. 30. Seed, 'Dawn of the atomic age', p. 97.

33 Hersey, *Hiroshima*, p. 88.

34 Boyer, *Fallout*, p. 13.

35 Hersey, *Hiroshima*, p. 91.

36 Richard Rhodes, *The Making of the Atomic Bomb* (London: Penguin, 1988), p. 688. Martin Cruz Smith, *Stallion Gate* (London: Macmillan, 1996), p. 145. Don DeLillo, *Underworld* (London: Picador, 1998), p. 799.

37 Julian Smith, *Nevil Shute* (Boston: Twayne, 1976), p. 110. Weart, *Nuclear Fear*, p. 218. Peter Hennessy, *The Secret State: Whitehall and the Cold War* (London: Penguin, 2003), p. 30. Herman Kahn, *On Thermonuclear War* (Princeton: Princeton University Press, 1961), p. 9.

38 Orville Prescott, 'Books of the Times', *New York Times* (24 July 1957), p. 23.

39 Murray Schumach, '"On the Beach" includes Moscow in 18-city premiere on Dec. 17', *New York Times* (30 November 1959), p. 27. Bosley Crowther, 'Screen: "On the Beach"', *New York Times* (19 December 1959), p. 34.

40 Boyer, *Fallout*, p. 110.

41 Nevil Shute, *On the Beach* (North Yorkshire: House of Stratus, 2000), p. 159.

42 Shute, *On the Beach*, p. 38.

43 Shute, *On the Beach*, p. 59.

44 Shute, *On the Beach*, p. 75.

45 Shute, *On the Beach*, p. 75.

46 Shute, *On the Beach*, p. 174.

47 Shute, *On the Beach*, p. 178.

48 Shute, *On the Beach*, p. 279. The central relationship in the novel is between Moira, single and unattached, and Dwight, whose wife died in the war. They both agree not to let their attraction for each other get the better of them.

49 Shute, *On the Beach*, p. 244.

50 Shute, *On the Beach*, p. 247.

51 Shute, *On the Beach*, p. 249.

52 Shute, *On the Beach*, p. 253.

53 The novel mentions for instance that '[m]ankind had been trembling about destruction through war.' George R. Stewart, *Earth Abides* (London: Millennium, 1999), p. 15.

54 Stewart, *Earth Abides*, p. 14.

55 See discussion of Lifton in chapter two.

56 Shute, *On the Beach*, p. 3.

57 Nadel, *Containment Culture*, p. 38, p. 67. For Nadel's full argument see chapter two, 'History, science, and Hiroshima', of *Containment Culture*, pp. 38–67.

58 Shute, *On the Beach*, p. 295.

59 Shute, *On the Beach*, p. 295.

60 Thomas Pynchon, *Gravity's Rainbow* (London: Picador, 1975), p. 3.

61 The phrase, 'drama of bewilderment', is Seed's. See note 27.

62 Pynchon, p. 8. Because *Gravity's Rainbow* is full of ellipses, the use of square brackets, when quoting from the book, indicates that the ellipses are mine.

63 Pynchon, *Gravity's Rainbow*, p. 3. Pynchon's emphasis.

64 Pynchon, *Gravity's Rainbow*, p. 4.

65 *Radio Times* (22–28 September 1984), front cover.

66 Jessica Taylor, 'Let's build a bomb', *Guardian* (5 July 2006), Section G2, p. 15.

67 Pynchon, *Gravity's Rainbow*, p. 133.

68 Jay Walz, 'Atom bombs made in 3 hidden cities', *New York Times* (7 August 1945), p. 1, p. 3.

69 Pynchon, *Gravity's Rainbow*, p. 22, p. 41.

70 Pynchon, *Gravity's Rainbow*, p. 75.

71 Pynchon, *Gravity's Rainbow*, p. 105.

72 Pynchon, *Gravity's Rainbow*, p. 135.

73 Pynchon, *Gravity's Rainbow*, p. 53.

74 Pynchon, *Gravity's Rainbow*, pp. 142–3.

75 Pynchon, *Gravity's Rainbow*, p. 25.

76 Edward W. Soja, 'Exploring the postmetropolis', in Claudio Minca (ed.), *Postmodern Geography: Theory and Praxis* (Oxford: Blackwell, 2001), pp. 40–5.

77 Nan Ellin, *Postmodern Urbanism* (Oxford: Blackwell, 1996), p. 246.

78 Elaine Tyler May, *Homeward Bound: American Families in the Cold War Era*, new ed. (New York: Basic Books, 1999), p. 94.

79 Vanderbilt, *Survival City*, p. 192.

80 Clifford Simak, *City* (London: Weidenfeld and Nicolson, 1961), p. 27.

81 Jean Baudrillard, trans. P. Beitchman, 'The orders of simulacra', in Patricia Waugh (ed.), *Postmodernism: A Reader* (London: Edward Arnold, 1992), p. 188.

82 Paul Brians, *Nuclear Holocausts: Atomic War in Fiction, 1895–1984* (Kent: Kent State University Press, 1987), p. 55.

83 Jacqueline Foertsch, *Enemies Within: The Cold War and the AIDS Crisis in Literature, Film, and Culture* (Urbana: University of Illinois Press, 2001), p. 37.

84 Paul Auster, *In the Country of Last Things* (London: Faber, 1989), p. 5, p. 18.

85 The phrase, 'drama of bewilderment', is Seed's. See note 27.

86 Auster, *Country of Last Things*, p. 188.

87 Auster, *Country of Last Things*, pp. 11–13.

88 Auster, *Country of Last Things*, p. 15, pp. 25–7.

89 Doris Lessing, *Memoirs of a Survivor* (London: Picador, 1976), p. 26.

90 For a discussion of the distinction between Enlightenment grand narratives and postmodern micronarratives, see Jean-François Lyotard, trans. Geoff Bennington and Brian Massumi, *The Postmodern Condition: A Report on Knowledge* (Manchester: Manchester University Press, 1986).

91 Auster, *Country of Last Things*, p. 5.

92 Auster, *Country of Last Things*, p. 5.

93 Auster, *Country of Last Things*, pp. 8–9.

4

Shadows on the hearth: the threatened domestic spaces of nuclear literature

Mrs. Howard [the Acting Civil Defence Administrator] said it was not necessary for any one to delay getting started on these exercises [in preparation for atomic attack]. Any family can begin by eliminating the obvious fire-traps around the home, she added. . . .

Each family, Mrs. Howard declared, was supposed to conduct its own evacuation drills to its own scientifically stocked shelter, complete with a three-day supply of food and safe drinking water. ('Family Plan Urged for Civil Defense', New York Times, 1953)[1]

In the previous chapter we saw how civic spaces in the nation's cities, directly targeted by Soviet missiles and symbolic of the civilisation that would be lost in a global conflict, became charged with nuclear peril during the early Cold War, an association they carried until at least the end of the Cold War period. We also saw an example of large-scale preparations for nuclear attack in the sequence of civil defence drills in New York.

However, big civil defence projects, particularly public shelter-building pro-grammes, consistently failed to get off the ground. This was partly an issue of cost, but it was also a result of the rapid advances in military technology, which meant that nuclear attack would come with less warning and greater destructive impact. As a consequence, much of the public money available was spent on encouraging people to make their own preparations. In practice this translated into giving advice about preparing homes for attack.

Such measures had complex, and sometimes contradictory, effects. Ostensibly they were reassuring: with basic DIY, they implied, homes could be made robust enough to ride out nuclear attack. However, competing with this discourse sug-gesting that the effects of the atom could be contained was another one stressing the incredible power of nuclear technology. For the Soviet Union to appear a credible threat, for the economic, human and military investment in the policy of containment around the globe to appear worthwhile, and for United States military power to seem robust, the full destructive effects of nuclear weapons had to be emphasised. Civil defence therefore always ran the risk of looking ridiculous: needs-must DIY and housekeeping (constructing a crude shelter; tidying up flam-mable materials; drawing the curtains) was all that stood against the achievements of brilliant scientific minds, and massive engineering and industrial efforts.

If homes were at stake in these contradictory discourses, families were too. As Elaine Tyler May says, 'in virtually all civil defense publicity, safety was represented in the form of the family'.[2] The recurrent image in civil defence literature and discourse was that of the single house, usually suburban, usually middle class and usually containing the stereotypical 'nuclear' family.

During the high Cold War, a period in which, with more people marrying at a younger age and having more children sooner than in the past, the family was a notable cultural phenomenon, there was, therefore, a significant emphasis on the middle-class family as a source both of security and vulnerability. May has charted in admirable detail the ways in which the family functioned as a container for social fears but also as a crucible in which forces perceived as destructive came together. In short, the home could not, in the end, contain and suppress the ideological contradictions of United States society.

Something analogous happens in the cultural construction of the family, and the family home, in civil defence advice. The call by Katherine Graham Howard, the Acting Civil Defence Administrator, cited in the epigraph to this chapter, for families to prepare for atomic attack is revealing. Though buried on page thirty-six of the *New York Times* (and, frankly, unlikely to have had a nation of homeowners dutifully drilling for attack), it is typical of discourses invoking the family as a bastion of national defence. The call for families to have ready-stocked shelters implies that the United States is in danger of an imminent attack liable to arrive without warning. A large-scale campaign, 'Grandma's Pantry', made the same point ('Grandma's pantry was ready. Is your pantry ready in event of emergency?'), domesticating nuclear war by comparing it to the unexpected arrival of guests with mouths to feed.[3]

What calls like Katherine Howard's do is reconstitute the family unit, as the most basic and 'natural' social structure, within an ideology of national unity. In effect, the family is asked to carry out, in microcosm, the policies of the national government. Nominally at peace (at least with the Soviet Union – this was only months after the Korean War had ended), the family is expected to be preparing as if the country were at war. Responsibility for national defence is devolved down to the family who become agents for the defence of the state.

For reasons economic, practical and ideological civil defence discourse largely revolved around the middle-class suburban family, effectively constituting it as threatened by the nation's enemies and as a bastion against that threat. Braced for attack in magazine articles and official leaflets by careful preparation or even a specially constructed shelter, the family home was also the most vulnerable of spaces, blown to bits in film clips from the Nevada test sites and subject to the effects of blast and radiation. This double and contradictory cultural coding of the home, as both strong and dangerously fragile, produces significant instabilities in Cold War narratives about home and family.

It is the exploration of these instabilities that is the focus of this chapter. Its analysis is informed by both May's and Alan Nadel's investigations of containment cultures in the United States. Both critics link personal discourses to national ones. May, for instance, shows how concerns about inappropriate parenting were linked to fears of national weakness, an overly maternal influence on boys thought liable to produce '"sissies", who were allegedly likely to become homosexuals, "perverts", and dupes of the communists'.[4] Nadel's approach similarly traces the powerful connections between personal relations and national discourses, focusing particularly on the migration of narratives about gender between private and public spheres: 'In distributing the potentials for domination and submission, allegiance and disaffection, proliferation and containment, loyalty and subversion – all of which require clear, legible boundaries between Other and Same – the narrative of the American cold war takes the same form as the narratives that contain gender roles'.[5] It is particularly in idealised notions of male and female behaviour, and deviations from these ideals, both within and outside the family structure, that this chapter finds the entry of nuclear concerns into nuclear anxiety literature.

Its first two sections examine the cultural construction of domestic space as vulnerable to nuclear threat, focusing on the fragility of the home in the face of nuclear blast, and its permeability to radioactive contaminants in civil defence discourses. It then turns to a key early novel, Judith Merril's *Shadow on the Hearth* (1950), where the domestic security of family and nation are at issue. Finally it explores the later developments of these discourses in the post-nuclear family of a key postmodern text, Don DeLillo's *White Noise* (1984).

The fragile home: 'better, safer housekeeping'

If footage and photographs of Hiroshima established right at the beginning of the atomic age that the world was dealing with a weapon of unprecedented destructive power, the extensive coverage of bomb tests subsequent to the war furthered this sense. For instance, it was claimed that more cameras witnessed the Operation Crossroads tests at Bikini Atoll in 1946, in which a fleet of over 150 derelict ships were subjected to two atomic explosions, than had filmed any event before.[6] Throughout the 1950s, tests not only in the Pacific, but also at home in the Nevada desert, received widespread publicity, and these sometimes included images of test houses subjected to nuclear blast. Even where such films were intended to demonstrate that houses could survive atomic blast, though, the image of the lone house lost in the nuclear storm inevitably showed the home to be vulnerable.

In the face of the forces to which houses would be subjected, civil defence inevitably ran the risk of appearing futile. So, while the 1950 leaflet, *Survival Under Atomic Attack*,[7] seeks to 'kill the myths' ('atomic weapons will not destroy the earth'), the simple, practical measures it advises ('be sure to shut the doors and windows and pull down the shades') seem likely only to be effective on the outer boundaries of an atomic blast zone. The more the family home, at the heart of civil defence discourses, was shown to be robust, the more such discourses called attention to the sublime, civilisation-destroying power of the atom with which they were faced.

Within these solid-fragile homes were solid-fragile nuclear families: those outside traditional family structures were rarely shown preparing themselves for atomic attack. Indeed, it was with a division of labour amongst the family, replicating the gendered roles of conventional suburban life (the male breadwinner, the female homemaker and so on), that atomic attack was to be met. A full page spread in a 1961 edition of *Life* devoted to civil defence (and containing an open letter from President Kennedy urging readers to follow the magazine's advice) showed, in a sequence of captioned photographs, the Carlson family constructing a shelter and stocking it with provisions. In the main and final photograph, they pose in their new, secondary home ('Family in the Shelter, Snug, Equipped and Well Organized'). The photograph (reproduced, incidentally, in a cropped form on the cover of May's *Homeward Bound*) suggests a continuation of family roles in the post-atomic world, as the caption makes clear:

> Inside the Kelsey-Hayes shelter which he and his son have put together, Art Carlson and his family demonstrate how a family might divide the responsibility for making it safe and livable. Here Carlson shows a table full of equipment which he would care for. It includes emergency tools. . . . Mrs. Carlson sits next to the larder of canned foods. . . . Daughter Charlene is in charge of bedding for the folding cots. . . . Son Claude looks after the candles, flashlights, transistor radio. . . . Daughter Judy is the shelter librarian with a stock of books and games to help pass the time.[8]

Explicitly about surviving nuclear attack, this is implicitly about a different sort of survival: learning and reinforcing socially validated social roles, so as to fit into United States society. This is an image of life before, as much as after, attack. For instance, Claude's responsibility for candles, torch and radio, consistent with the masculine 'emergency tools' of his father, guarantees the continuation of a model of American manhood, not only by aiding the physical survival of the family during atomic attack, but also by keeping him from the dangerously feminised responsibilities of his sisters for bedding and books.

One of the games for which Judy is shown to have responsibility is, ironically, the well known board game, the *Game of Life*. War, in this presentation, would involve an atomic game of life, fought in large part by affirming family structures fundamental to contemporary society. The Carlsons provide a picture of middle-class family life to which readers of *Life* might aspire: more austere than they would be used to, to be sure, but in which the physical fabric of the home is looked after by the men of the family, and the cooking, bedding and reading are the responsibility of the women.

This is an intriguing vision of life during and immediately after nuclear war. Society is, in more senses than one, atomised in this view, each family imagined to be subsisting on tinned provisions in its own self-contained shelter. The only connection with the outside world is the radio, relaying government advice and information without the intrusion of subversive alternative perspectives. Literally sealed in, it is also ideologically insulated. This is markedly different to experience during the Second World War when there was a potentially revolutionary mixing of people from different social backgrounds, as they took on unfamiliar roles. Women, for instance, moved in large numbers into professions in which they had not worked in any significant numbers before (although, as May points out, there was a rapid reversal of this effect after the war: women's average pay dropped by 26%, compared to a 4% drop for men, and most found themselves limited to jobs rather than careers).[9] The shelter, a concentrated version of the family home, is presented, then, as a place in which social structures are hermetically sealed, safe from the chaos outside, and ready to re-emerge, intact, once the worst is over.

Yet such idealisations could easily be jeopardised. The atomisation of society appeared, in some cases, to undermine the integrity of the social fabric. Just a month before the Carlson family were featured in *Life*, *Time* carried a short column, 'Gun thy neighbor?', that gained some notoriety. Charles Davis, planning a shelter for his family, suggested extreme measures to deal with neighbours in need in time of war:

> 'When I get my shelter finished, I'm going to mount a machine gun at the hatch to keep the neighbors out if the bomb falls. I'm deadly serious about this. If the stupid American public will not do what they have to to save themselves, I'm not going to run the risk of not being able to use the shelter I've taken the trouble to provide to save my own family.'
> This kind of tough talk from a Chicago suburbanite last week had echoes all over the US, as the headlines spread uneasiness and the shelter business boomed.[10]

A similar stance had been noted by the *Saturday Evening Post* four years earlier, when a Midwesterner responded to the possibility of nuclear evacuees: 'We'll get machine guns if we have to, to keep those city people from using up our children's food and water.'[11] Society, here, is not composed of family units aligned in a common purpose to rebuild the United States after an atomic attack, but is torn apart by vicious competition for limited resources.

Such depressing visions of pre- and post-holocaust society are inevitably absent from civil defence material. In general, it marries ideals of social cohesion to effective preparation for the bomb, deploying what might best be termed a discourse of effective Americanism, scaling up from family-level activity to national readiness for attack. Instructive in this regard is a 1954 public information film, *The House in the Middle*,[12] sponsored by the 'National Clean Up – Paint Up – Fix Up Bureau'. At the heart of the film is footage from the Nevada test sites, showing the fate of three houses subjected to a nuclear explosion. Two of the houses, unkempt, with peeling paint, newspapers left lying around and so forth, quickly catch fire and are destroyed, but the third, the eponymous house in the middle, survives.

The film is revealing in the connection it makes between the home and national defence. Social cohesion, produced by acquiescence in the carrying out of domestic chores, is promoted as integral to national security. The 'house in the middle', it becomes apparent, is any number of houses across the United States. The film opens by cutting from footage of a nuclear explosion to an unnamed medium-sized US town filmed from the air. Its typicality is to be admired, and the image we get is of a nation of hardworking citizens, living in the affluent suburban environments aspired to at the time: 'One American town looks like any other when you see it from an airplane window: trees line the quiet residential streets, and there's usually a highway running through to an industrial area where many town people work.'

However, this vision of harmony is threatened by a lurking danger: 'But in every town you'll find houses like this: run down, neglected. Trash and litter disfigure the house and yard. . . . A house that's neglected is the house that may be doomed in the atomic age.' While it is true that unpainted houses with litter lying about were more flammable and thus more vulnerable, the connection of personal purity and cleanliness to the integrity of national character and security is an insidious one. At the end of the film the viewer is asked to scrutinise their own behaviour: 'Which of these is your house? This one? [showing one of the houses flattened in the nuclear test]. The house on the right? Dilapidated with paper, dead grass, litter everywhere? The house on the left? Unpainted, run down, neglected? Is this your house?' The repeated questions encourage self-scrutiny; the viewer is asked to check themselves against the values of atomic America. Alan Nadel argues that one feature of the United States Cold War narrative is that '[i]nternal security . . . becomes synonymous with external, universal scrutiny'.[13] Here, security internal not only to the country but to the individual family is guaranteed by scrutiny that is both external (from the nation state) but also, crucially, enacted by the homeowner; the homeowner acts as an agent of the state to scrutinise his or her own behaviour.

Finally, the film suggests solutions. Notably, it moves out from individuals ('what can I do?'), reconstituting them as part of local social collectives ('What can my community do?'), which are themselves represented as functioning entirely in harmony with the national will ('All over America'):

> 'Alright', you say, 'what can I do about it? What can my community do?' All over America towns and cities are organising local clean-up, paint-up, fix-up campaigns. . . . Do those long delayed repair jobs now. Trim your shrubbery and trees, weed and plant flowers. Keep your block cleaned up. Beauty, cleanliness, health and safety are the four basic doctrines that protect our homes, our cities.

The continuity this establishes between personal domestic space and larger civic environments ('our homes, our cities') is an important one, bringing together two symbolically significant environments in the iconography of nuclear peril, and reconstituting the individual so that he or she is defined by his or her existence within national structures.

In this final sequence, the film's practical rationalisations (fire prevention) dissolve into aesthetic ones. How, exactly, planting flowers would protect against the bomb is left unexplained. 'Beauty' is equated with a controlled and homogenous social order, and a moral purity is implied as somehow implicit in outward displays of practical housekeeping and aesthetic cleanliness.

Clifford Clark has charted the history of the family home in the United States, tracing its physical embodiment of 'moral purpose', and the way in which the single-family house was repeatedly invested with the potential to 'protect and strengthen the family, shoring up the foundations of society and instilling the proper virtues needed to preserve the republic'.[14] Just as the architecture of homes thus produced family values consistent with ideologies of Americanism, so was their maintenance and cleaning similarly invested with national preoccupations, as *The House in the Middle* demonstrates.

The focus on dirt is particularly important. The film tells us that the house that is 'spic and span' is not a threat to its inhabitants or to the nation because it has been tidied up with 'better, safer housekeeping'. While this is ostensibly about physical threats, it draws on powerful constructions of communism and deviancy as dirty diseases threatening the nation. The full significance of discourse like that found in *The House in the Middle* can be appreciated when we consider who would be responsible for 'better, safer housekeeping' at this period in history. Although the film does not say so, there is no doubt that, although the painting of the house would be expected to be man's work, responsibility for its internal tidiness and cleanliness would be that of a female homemaker. May points out that a 'major goal of . . . civil defense strategies was to infuse the traditional role of women with new meaning and importance, which would help fortify the home as a place of security amid the cold war',[15] and what we see in operation here is the coming together of powerful ideological forces that politicise the home in gendered terms. For women, leaving the domestic realm becomes even more difficult because the 'natural' order is reinforced by Cold War discourses that make their place in the home intrinsic to national security.

The House in the Middle is about protecting homes from the blast and heat produced immediately after a nuclear explosion. It is, though, in the longer-term protection against radiation that the ideological significance of the obsession with cleanliness becomes most apparent.

The permeable home: 'It can go right through'

Shelters and inner refuges were not only necessary protection for the period during which a nuclear explosion was likely, but also had to protect in the longer term against radioactive fallout. They therefore had to be imagined as impermeable boundaries (if really impermeable, they would of course have suffocated their inhabitants), preventing the outside from getting in, as well being rigidly braced against the immediate impacts of blast, heat and falling masonry. Sometimes, as Charles Davis' plans to mount a machine gun by his shelter show, it was also felt that they would have to keep out forces of social disorder in the chaos following an attack. The necessity of making shelters impermeable to outside threats over an extended period meant that they had to function as self-contained living spaces. This is central to the feature on the Carlson family in *Life*. Sealed in from the chaos outside, they are imagined to be living a recognisable, if restricted, version of suburban family life.

Like so much else in civil defence projections of a post-nuclear future, this reproduces contemporary social preoccupations. The suburbs were already seen as a shelter from, in Clark's analysis, 'the noise and insecurity of the urban metropolis', and, more pointedly, from the threatening ethnic and class otherness of alternate social groups: 'The middle-class image of the suburbs as a peaceful refuge was further reinforced by the use of restricted covenants to exclude blacks and other minorities who were identified . . . with urban crime and disorder.'[16] The bomb shelter simply performed, in more extreme terms, a role already inherent in the suburbs: it kept the outside out.

The threat of radioactivity was particularly unsettling. Although it was expected that the blast and heat of nuclear explosions would kill more than would radioactive fallout, it was the uncanny properties of radiation – invisible; liable to get inside – that really frightened people. In *Survival Under Atomic Attack* nine of the twenty questions the booklet seeks to provide reassurance on actually mention, and a further three are directly about, radioactivity. As with advice about bracing houses and shelters to withstand heat and blast, they convey a rather mixed message.

They try to bring it within the bounds of lived experience, as if exposure is no worse than being out in the sun too long: 'just a few moments in the midsummer sun will not give you a tan or sunburn. . . . In the same way, the harm that can come to you from radioactivity will depend on the power of the rays and particles that strike you, upon the length of time you are exposed to them, and on how much of your body is exposed.' Yet the booklet's preoccupation with radiation suggests that it is dealing with a fear that cannot properly be allayed by such analogies. While sunburn was perceived to impact on the outside of the body, the horror of radiation was that it got inside. Transgressing corporeal boundaries it made the body permeable.

This echoes, of course, Cold War discourses about communism that, while externalising the threat beyond national boundaries in the form of the Soviet Union, also found it, in the Red Scare for instance, to be lurking within. Contamination, the fear of disease, is politically inflected, as Jacqueline Foertsch claims in her book, *Enemies Within*, which discusses anxious responses to nuclear- and AIDS-related '"epidemics" of fear, hostility, and global threat that plague our postmodern times'.[17] Because 'Reds and gays have long been considered infectious',[18] any hint of contamination invokes powerful cultural antipathies toward political and sexual deviance.

Even as *Survival Under Atomic Attack* seeks to quell fears, it is destabilised by, and is chilling in, its representation of radioactivity penetrating houses and bodies: 'Naturally, the radioactivity that passes through the walls of your house won't be stopped by tin or glass. It can go right through canned and bottled foods. However, this will not make them dangerous, and it will not cause them to spoil.'

When radiation is acknowledged to be dangerous, it is in an image of the body turning itself inside out: 'the first indication that you had been pierced by the rays . . . [would be when you] get sick at your stomach and begin to vomit.' The obsession with household cleanliness also appears:

> These totally invisible radioactive particles act much the same as ordinary, everyday dust. When present in any real quantity, they are scattered about in patches and contaminate, or pollute, everything they fall on, including people. . . . It is practically impossible to get absolutely all of them out of household corners and cracks.

This is a symbolic transformation of the everyday dirt of normal life, supposedly banished by the new consumer products flooding the markets of the 1950s, into something much more malignant. Radioactive fallout is not only literally threatening in the culture of the period, a terrifying force that would be unleashed in the event of atomic war, it also has a powerful symbolic role to play. The compromising of personal and domestic spaces connects fallout with household dirt, physical and psychological illness and the representation of deviancy.

The seemingly innocent act of cleaning the house, and the new and heavily advertised products which consumer society was trumpeting as available for this purpose, and which sought to make the home safe from infection, are therefore not politically innocent. Nadel writes of the response to Hiroshima, and of cold war narratives more generally, that they 'reveal repeatedly the need for and the inability to stabilize the distinctions between Other and Same',[19] and the process of cleaning, whether of ordinary domestic dirt or of the radioactive dust, might usefully be seen in a similar way. It is about transforming the domestic environment, so that it is clean in contrast to the dirt outside. Yet, in simple consumer terms, the home can never be clean enough; can never be entirely 'other' to the dirty world outside. The demands of consumerism require that new dirt be discovered, that whites be washed whiter, in order to drive demand for new products and distinguish further one's own clean home from the less clean homes of one's neighbours.

The cultural construction of radioactive fallout is not identical to that of household dirt in contemporary advertising (although the clean-up, paint-up, fix-up campaign of *The House in the Middle* might have been a point of sale for paint and other household products),[20] but there are powerful analogies between the two. In both a dangerous outside environment threatens the purity of the inner sanctum of the home. 'Practically impossible' to banish once it gets inside, radioactive fallout requires a careful attention to domestic hygiene like that advocated to keep the new suburban homes pristine. What is important about the dirt of various kinds threatening the suburban United States was that, although it had physical properties and physiological consequences, it was in its psychological role that it had the most profound effects. Fear of radioactive fallout, and of contamination more generally, expressed a broader cultural fear of otherness, particularly the sense that one might oneself become 'other'. More generally, as Andrew Grossman shows in *Neither Dead Nor Red*,[21] it was in part fear of the impact of fear of radioactive fallout (that Americans would panic in the face of the nuclear threat and remove consent for atomic and Cold War policies) that drove the production of leaflets like *Survival Under Atomic Attack*, designed to reassure the public that they could survive nuclear war.

This lengthy contextualisation is important for our understanding of nuclear anxiety literature because metaphors and images of dirt and cleanliness play a key role in it. Understanding nuclear anxiety is about tracing the cultural consequences that flow from certain states of mind. Judith Merril's *Shadow on the Hearth* is a prime example of the continuity between Cold War anxieties and seemingly more parochial domestic ones, with the fragile family home functioning symbolically to represent both the threat of the nuclear age and broader social concerns.

Judith Merril, *Shadow on the Hearth*

Shadow on the Hearth is an important book because it makes the suburban family home the crucible within which nuclear concerns and social concerns, including issues of family, gender and class, come together, and because the tensions at its heart are reproduced and developed in later nuclear anxiety fiction. Although nominally a nuclear disaster text – the United States is attacked with atomic weapons – it reads better as a novel of nuclear anxiety. After all, like *On the Beach* it is primarily about waiting. Isolated from the main attack on New York, in a suburb, Westchester, Gladys Mitchell barely notices the attack itself, sees no bomb damage and has to sit out the crisis with her two daughters. The reader, too, is stranded within this environment, leaving it for only a few pages, for a brief scene at the beginning featuring Gladys's maid, Veda, occasional updates on Gladys's husband, Jon, who is trying to get home from his office in Manhattan, and once when the family go to a hospital. The perspective of the novel is, then, very firmly within the home, looking out at the various dangers that threaten to come in and compromise it. Consequently, one of the recurrent motifs in the novel is the attempt to maintain, and the transgression of, boundaries.

The atomic attack on New York functions to precipitate a series of challenges to Gladys's worldview. Gladys is, it should be noted, a pointedly different figure to the novel's author. Although she is represented with sympathy in the text, she adheres to the aspirations of the upwardly mobile middle class in a way that Merril, politically active, artistically committed and firmly flouting convention in her personal life, never did.[22] The atomic attack serves to expose the fallacies on which Gladys's worldview is based, although she herself only becomes aware of some of these.

Before the bomb drops, Gladys's life seems successful. As white, a member of a newly affluent middle class, and having left the city for the suburbs after years of struggle, she represents a large demographic trend in the United States. Suburban growth increased by 50% in the 1950s, during which time the white population of the country's twelve largest cities fell by 3.6 million people.[23] In 1950 new housing builds reached an all-time high (1,692,000), and in the following two decades the suburban population more than doubled to 74 million.[24] With a husband in a professional job, financial security (an important consideration for those who remembered the Depression) and three children, Gladys lives the suburban life portrayed as desirable in the emerging domestic ideology of the period. As she does the dishes, she reflects that '[e]verything is almost too good. . . . How long could things go on, getting better all the time?'[25] Yet, even before the war comes, her life is revealed to the reader, if not to herself, to be fraught with problems and beset by anxiety and drudgery.

The seemingly idyllic suburban life turns out not to meet the promises of the advertising. Gladys notices the symptoms of this but does not diagnose the cause.

Despite her assertion that life keeps on getting better, when she looks up from doing the dishes she sees only unhappiness, although she barely registers the disjunction between this and her sense that 'everything is almost too good'. Outside the window, a young child is wrecking his parents' lawn, and, in a reflection of the era's preoccupation with parenting, Gladys muses disapprovingly about the long-term consequences on the boy of the excuses his mother will make for him to her husband. Next door, another woman has had a baby after years of trying but is laid up sick in bed while her husband, Jim, is on a 'business trip' (the implied sexual indiscretion is later first refuted, when Jim reveals he has been secretly training for civil defence, but then reinstated when he makes unwelcome sexual overtures toward Gladys). Seeing another neighbour, Edie, with whom she is meant to be going to luncheon, finally gaining access to a social circle from which she feels excluded, Gladys calls out a greeting but fears that it sounds like a 'fishwife's cry', revealing her origins in the working-class environment of the city.[26]

The suburban life that Gladys has been so eager to join is, then, like those of many of the women featuring in May's analysis, not a contented one: 'suburban life was not a life of fun and leisure but of exhausting work and isolation'.[27] When the bomb drops and radioactive fallout and other dangers confine Gladys and her daughters to their home, the isolation and misery they feel is a more extreme version of that they already feel, not something entirely new. Life after the bomb allows the text to explore the inadequacies of life before the bomb.

The novel goes into remarkable detail about the chores Gladys has to do, and the tiredness she constantly feels, filling, for example, six pages near the beginning with a long description of her trying to get all her housework done after the family have left for work and school. When she is finished she is able to put on a face for the world, but 'powder and lipstick hid the tired lines of her face'.[28] The life of the housewife, idealised in the culture of the period, is exposed as one of drudgery (although the novel is notably less sympathetic to the hardness of the labour undertaken by her much less affluent maid, who remains a comic figure throughout).

This focus on the domestic space, and the labour required to maintain it, remains a preoccupation throughout the book, and the counterpoint between preparing meals, keeping the house clean and so on, and the events of an atomic attack, does not serve only to emphasise the horror waiting to break in upon the banality of normal life, but also exposes problems already inherent within it. After the bomb explodes, the novel spends much of its time on the issue of radiation sickness. Yet, even before this, the home is shown to be contaminated with dirt. In her orgy of cleaning, near the beginning, Gladys is forced to cut corners, rushing through the living room, so that when she finishes, it 'looked clean, whether it really was or not'.[29] Just as Gladys, in her make-up, looks fresh and not tired, and just as the suburban street outside her house looks like an idyllic picture of family life, so too here there is a surface appearance that belies an underlying corruption. Later on, the house seems clear of radioactive fallout, but her daughter, Ginny, is sick with it, and the atomic reality cannot be covered up.

While, then, the ostensible shadow of the novel's title is the atomic threat to the United States, other shadows, produced by the limitations of contemporary domestic aspirations, are cast over the hearth. As May's research, 'locating the family within the larger political culture', suggests, these shadows are connected: 'cold war ideology and the domestic revival [are in the 1950s] . . . two sides of the same coin'.[30] Containment operates to circumscribe the influence of forces constructed as dangerous – nuclear power; communism; personal behaviour and aspiration beyond the bounds of 'normal' society – whether through the threat of military power against the Soviet Union, or by intense pressure to conform to the normative domestic ideology.

Containment culture functions rather like the 'psychic numbing' identified by Robert Jay Lifton as a psychological defence characteristic of the nuclear age (and discussed in chapter two as a manifestation of nuclear anxiety). May herself makes the direct link to Lifton's analysis when she positions the family in a broader political culture: 'Lifton attributed "nuclear numbing" to the powerful psychic hold that the fear of nuclear annihilation had on the nation's subconscious. . . . Americans were well poised to embrace domesticity in the midst of the terrors of the atomic age. A home filled with children would create a feeling of warmth and security against the cold forces of disruption and alienation.'[31]

Shadow on the Hearth suggests that home life provides a comforting refuge from uncomfortable geopolitical realities (though such a defence falls apart as soon as those realities work themselves into actual atomic conflict). Jon, reading the paper over breakfast at the beginning of the novel, finds the threat of war abstract compared with the reality of his family around him: 'The headlines jumped at him, bearing threats of war and disaster; in the shaded room the warnings were ludicrous. . . . The news the paper spoke of existed in another world, not in his home.'[32] The 'shaded' room here recalls the shadow of the novel's title, suggesting that the threat is very much present in the home, despite Jon's denial. He reflects that Gladys never reads the front page of the paper, and wonders if she has the right idea. Yet his characteristically masculine assumption that his wife is preoccupied with domestic matters, not public affairs, is later revealed to be false. She is as aware of the Bomb as he is, although she too has tried to contain her fears. Listening to the first radio reports of the atomic attack on New York, Gladys recalls her own suppression of atomic anxieties: 'Gladys remembered a description, read and shuddered over, and set aside, she had thought, even from memory . . . the description of an atomic bomb landing at Twentieth Street and Third Avenue.'[33] The image the article conjures up, of New York flattened, is reminiscent of the destroyed cities imagined by Enrico Fermi, Bertrand Russell and Jonathan Schell, discussed in the previous chapter. It is an imaginative superimposition of a nuclear future onto a familiar cityscape. Yet such overt fear is psychologically unsustainable over a long period of time, and it becomes an anxiety shadowing normal life, and the 'hearth', rather than a consciously acknowledged source of discontent.

Shadow on the Hearth's exploration of the linked anxieties of domestic and nuclear life is carried out largely through a concentration on boundaries, particularly those between private and public space (between the house and the world outside it), and the body and its environment. The novel begins not with Gladys, but with her maid, Veda, ringing in sick from her public rooming house (noticeably working class, and in the city, in contrast to the middle-class environment of Westchester). Ignoring Gladys's concerns that she'll 'suffocate . . . in that room of yours', Veda carefully inspects the windows and the weather stripping, blocks a crack with her stocking, checks the bolt on her door, uses another stocking to cover her ears and climbs under the covers of her bed.[34] We begin, therefore, with a careful closing off of boundaries, bodily and domestic, to a threatening outside environment.

This is developed in the novel's later careful attention to the boundaries of the Mitchells' home. Advice immediately following the attack is for people to stay indoors, and a curfew soon comes into operation. Effectively trapped within their home, the family have to face various threats that come from outside. The most immediate of these is radioactive fallout – Gladys's worry that the water supply will be contaminated showing that the outside can enter the home through subterranean routes that are hard to close off – but others soon follow.[35] Authority figures bring some relief, but are also themselves a source of threat, Jim trying to force his attentions upon Gladys in the absence of her husband. Broader forces of social disorder also appear, as when Gladys and Garson Levy, a blacklisted physicist to whom she provides refuge, have to fight off looters.

These outside threats explain the care with which the novel deals with the liminal spaces between inside and outside the house, particularly the doors and windows which are constantly being locked, checked or transgressed as Gladys attempts to maintain the integrity of the domestic environment. For example, there are the 'door and windows' bolted firm 'against invaders from outside'; the window to which Gladys is drawn 'against her will'; the 'soft drapes' outside which 'unknown danger' is poised; the window against which a tree ominously taps; the 'carefully' locked window of a bedroom; the 'glass panes of the door' outside which a man lurks and the window through which Gladys passes notes to him; the 'doors and windows' of the cellar Gladys goes to close; and the 'shatter of glass' as intruders try to break in.[36]

Yet, perfectly preserved boundaries are shown to be both intrinsically problematic and, ultimately, impossible to maintain. In a significant passage, Gladys and her daughter seek to secure the house in anticipation of an impending curfew: 'the two of them made the rounds, checking windows and doors. That didn't take long enough either; everything was all right, closed, tight, secure; danger was locked out and fear sealed in.'[37] Stranded within the home, Gladys can only construe the outside fearfully, and it is this fear, and her constant struggle to maintain her sanity, which actually threatens Gladys most directly. The locking of doors and windows is as much about psychological comfort – hence the complaint that it is over too quickly, leaving them to refocus on their fears – as it is about literal physical protection. This has a broader national significance, for, as Seed points out, in the novel 'the concept of home has been expanded into the whole nation to represent a collective state of vulnerability not security'.[38]

For Gladys, blocking off the outside world involves practical measures to keep the home safe, but it also signifies her unconscious psychological attempt to maintain the illusions by which she has lived her life. But the outside cannot be stopped from getting in; it is, indeed, already inside. In the climax to the novel, Gladys's youngest daughter, Ginny, falls sick with radiation poisoning. Significantly, the source of her illness is not direct exposure to the outside, but the toy horse, Pallo, which she had been given to cuddle in bed for comfort, but which had been left out earlier in the radioactive rain. Suddenly, it is not just domestic boundaries that are being compromised, but the even more fraught ones of the body, as is apparent in Dr Spinelli's diagnosis: 'inhalation of a fission product, with an alpha emitter lodged in the bones. . . . [T]he particles were deposited inside her body, in her bone marrow'.[39]

By the end of the novel, Gladys is forced to accept that her pre-attack view of United States society was flawed, and she embraces her older daughter, Barbara's, more cynical view, epitomised in a sarcastic reaction to the news that they have won the war: 'Hurray for the red, white, and blue!. . . . Red for courage and white for purity and blue for Pallo.'[40] Gladys realises that, although the war is over, everything is different, partly because of the atomic attack, which has revealed their vulnerability, but importantly also because United States society has itself been revealed as dangerous: 'There was a clear picture in her mind – the worn blue horse and the pink and white girl safe on the pillow together, night after night. *Isn't anything safe? Not the rain or the house? Not even a little blue horse?*'[41] The pink, white and blue of her daughter and Pallo echo the colours of the flag, recently sarcastically referenced by Barbara, suggesting the link between national and domestic crises. The image of domestic security rendered fragile – a child in bed with her toy – becomes the incarnation of national insecurities. The idea of the home as a safe place, sealed off from the outside world, has been exploded in a working out of latent domestic and atomic anxieties.

The novel reveals not only that vulnerability, rather than security, lies at the heart of United States society, but that government and other authorities are untrustworthy and dangerous. As well as the sexual indiscretions of Jim, the civil defence trooper, Gladys also has to cope with the realisation that the radio, a key source of outside information (as it was anticipated it would be for the Carlsons in the *Life* article) is spreading disinformation. The blacklisting and monitoring of Garson Levy, for his dissident views, also suggests a malign dimension to the United States political establishment. At the novel's close, Jon finally gets close to his home and is shot by the authorities, possibly by Jim. Although he is brought in wounded in the 1950 edition and survives, this ending was forced on Merril by her publishers: in the original manuscript his fate is left uncertain.[42] *Shadow on the Hearth* reveals that, if not quite totalitarian, the state is certainly capable of acting in ways that are totalitarian.

Merril's story deploys, then, its seemingly narrow domestic focus to open up disturbing trends in the Cold War United States. Gladys's anxieties, atomic and social, are intimately connected. They are not simple metaphors for each other; they produce each other. The legacy of these early and high Cold War nuclear connections between home and state lasts at least until the end of the Cold War. So when, for instance, in the otherwise disappointing television film, *The Day After* (1983), the action cuts between scenes of domestic life and preparations to launch Minuteman missiles, with one actually exploding out of a silo behind someone's house, this dramatically effective moment finds a military United States lurking within and beneath more mundane domestic realities.[43] Such instances in nuclear culture are moments of realisation. They reveal the nuclear state locked into the familiar contours of the nation, but they are also moments of conscious recognition of the nuclear anxiety lurking within, and now exploding out of, the intimate spaces of the psyche.

Postmodern nuclear anxiety texts explore the more extreme oscillations of this domestic-nuclear gyre. Largely contained in *Shadow on the Hearth*, though with an instability at their core which by the end of the novel is beginning to pull them apart, they are, by later texts, exploding into fractured family groups, disturbing forces within the home, and more strained relations between discourse and reality. In E. L. Doctorow's *The Book of Daniel* (1971), the volatile family experiences of the Rosenberg/Isaacson children are produced from anxieties of betrayal at the heart of atomic America. In Leslie Marmon Silko's *Ceremony* (1977), a home is lit up by a bright flash that is later traced to the first atomic bomb test at the Trinity site.[44] In Paul Auster's *In the Country of Last Things* (1987) it is, significantly, a broken family connection – a lost brother not a lover – that motivates Anna's journey to the disappearing city. In Tim O'Brien's *The Nuclear Age* (1985) William's shelter-digging is produced by the imminent break up of his family.

Don DeLillo's *White Noise*, a key text of the 1980s, provides a fine way into these postmodern dynamics of connections between apocalypse, anxiety and threatened domestic spaces. Although the novel is not 'about' nuclear war – it is not as obviously 'nuclear' as his earlier novel, *End Zone* (1972), for instance – it is (among many other things) about fear of mortality, and this is rendered in part through its depiction of disaster and recovery.

The airborne toxic event: Don DeLillo, *White Noise*

> Ever since I was in my twenties I've had the fear, the dread. Now it's been realized. I feel enmeshed, I feel deeply involved. It's no wonder they call this thing the airborne toxic event. It's an event all right. It marks the end of uneventful things. This is just the beginning. Wait and see. (Murray, in Don DeLillo, *White Noise*)[45]

At the heart of *White Noise* is Jack Gladney, a college lecturer, and his family, and the events that unfold after his son, Heinrich, spots a 'shapeless growing thing. A dark black breathing thing of smoke', that, in the official discourse, dispensed over the radio, transforms from a 'feathery plume', to a 'black billowing cloud', to, finally, an 'airborne toxic event'.[46] Forced to flee their home, the family become part of a mass evacuation, and Jack, exposed to Nyodene D, the source of the cloud, is left uncertain whether he faces an early death.

Jack's colleague Murray's description of the event as expected is revealing of a broader cultural preoccupation with disaster. In a decade, the 1980s, characterised in part by fear of nuclear holocaust, this preoccupation must have a nuclear dimension even though there is only one direct reference to such a context. Bob Pardee, biological father to one of Jack's stepchildren, mentions in passing his work raising funds for the Nuclear Accident Readiness Foundation, 'a legal defense fund for the industry. Just in case kind of thing.'[47] Characteristically of the book, and of nuclear anxiety, the actual threat here remains unstated ('in case kind of thing') – it is a threat which cannot be spoken about, partly because the industry is not keen to draw attention to culpabilities that will lay it open to lawsuits, and partly because it is uncomfortable to think about. It becomes one more in a long line of nebulous threats to Jack.

A key focus for the novel is the fear of death, and the experience of living in anticipation of death. In line with the more specific experience of Cold War nuclear fears, and resonant of the first section of Coupland's 'The Wrong Sun', discussed in chapter two, *White Noise* includes a sequence of expected moments of disaster that peter out into anticlimax, leaving the anxiety intact.

In one incident, Steffie, one of Jack's children, announces, apropos of nothing, that the radio has said they must boil their water. Nothing more is heard of this, and the family carry on as normal.[48] In another, the school has to be evacuated, and remains closed for a week, because children are suffering headaches and eye irritations. 'No one knew what was wrong' and there are a host of possible causes, including the ventilation system, paint, insulation, food, mysterious emanations from computers, or 'perhaps something deeper, finer-grained, more closely woven into the basic state of things'. The building is swept by men in Mylex suits with measuring equipment, but '[b]ecause Mylex is itself a suspect material, the results tended to be ambiguous.'[49]

Later, traumatised passengers, from a flight that nearly crashed, file through an airport where Jack is waiting to meet his daughter.[50] Elsewhere, the family watch television coverage of police digging at the site of a suspected mass grave. After seventy-two hours of searching for murder victims, nothing new is found and the 'sense of failed expectations was total'.[51] In yet another moment of anti-climax, SIMUVAC carries out an evacuation drill for a noxious odour, but three days later when there is an 'actual noxious odor', an 'irritating sting in the nostrils, a taste of copper on the tongue', nobody does anything at all.[52]

Most dramatically, there is the airborne toxic event itself, responses to which contain features characteristic of anxieties about nuclear disaster. Air-raid sirens sound. The family has to evacuate and is caught in a traffic jam of fellow evacuees that is at once desperate and absurd (when they arrive at their destination, everyone sits in their cars, uncertain whether it is safe to get out, until a family of five, who 'wore life jackets and carried flares', emerge from their car). At the evacuation centre Jack gets into conversation with a man who gives him a leaflet titled 'Twenty Common Mistakes About the End of the World', and who sees the disaster as part of a pattern of apocalyptic events signalling that 'God's kingdom is coming'. Nyodene D, as a contaminant that stays in the soil for forty years and the human body for thirty, evokes fears of radioactive fallout.[53]

The most important feature of the airborne toxic event, though, is that it is an anticlimax. It serves only to bring into the open a more general fear of disaster and death, which it cannot resolve and remove. Jack's exposure to contaminants leaves him knowing only that he has Nyodene D in his body, not what its effects will be. SIMUVAC experts tell him that if he lives fifteen years he'll know it will not have killed him in that time and he will be halfway to its disappearance from his body. As Jack, currently in his fifties puts it, 'I will have to make it to my eighties. Then I can begin to relax.'[54] Later he seeks further advice. He may or may not, he learns, have a 'nebulous mass' in his body. Reminiscent of the 'shapeless growing thing' of the cloud of Nyodene D when it first appeared, this evokes not only the possibility that corporeal boundaries might be penetrated by contaminants, but also Jack's more generalised fear of death.

These examples of deferred disaster exist in the text against a more general background of insecurity. Steffie, one of the children, regularly checks her chest for lumps. Heinrich, another child, already has a receding hairline that Jack speculates might be caused by toxins. Glorious sunsets, which become even more spectacular after the airborne toxic event, are rumoured to be the product of pollution. After the airborne toxic event, neighbours, the Stovers, always leave their car out of the garage, facing the street and with the keys in the ignition, ready for a swift evacuation.[55]

These things are not presented simply as disquieting evidence of the uncertainty of contemporary life in the novel. Disaster becomes a source of fascination, even as it unsettles people. There is a magnetic pull toward cataclysm even as it horrifies. The family gather, for instance, to watch television footage of disasters: 'We were otherwise silent, watching houses slide into the ocean, whole villages crackle and ignite in a mass of advancing lava. Every disaster made us wish for more, for something bigger, grander, more sweeping.'[56] Murray runs seminars at the university on car crashes, 'the suicide wish of technology. The drive to suicide, the hurtling rush to suicide.'[57]

This cultural obsession with disaster is brought into, and related to, the family. In contrast to the conventional nuclear family of Shadow on the Hearth, Jack and Babette's family is gloriously post-nuclear in its complexity: children from Jack's and Babette's previous marriages occupy the house, and there are complex arrangements with their various ex-partners.

Jack and Babette, both obsessed with death, talk about the family as a temporary guarantee against their personal mortality: '[Babette] thinks nothing can happen to us as long as there are dependent children in the house. The kids are a guarantee of our relative longevity. We're safe as long as they're around.'[58] Perhaps with this in mind, one of the things Babette most wishes is for 'Wilder [their youngest child] to stay the way he is forever'.[59] Yet, his failure to develop language skills is a cause for concern in the novel: he really is staying the way he is, and such stasis is as undesirable as the flux that threatens death. Conversely, just as Babette is threatened by her children's growth, Jack and Babette as parents seem unable to protect their children. Jack ruminates about the children misbehaving in order to annoy their parents and, running through the possibilities, wonders, '[w]ould they attack us for our status as protectors – protectors who must sooner or later fail?'[60]

It is in fact such a failure, rather than the more dramatic catastrophes with which they are all obsessed, that forms what climax there is to the novel.[61] Wilder pedals his tricycle across the expressway, missing death only by chance. It is with the possibility of this small-scale apocalypse – the death of a child – rather than the dramatic events of an airborne toxic event, that the novel moves toward its close. Yet, the novel has suggested a continuity between insecurity within the family and broader insecurities produced by a culture of catastrophe. The child peddling across the highway oblivious to his danger not only shows the horror waiting to erupt within every family, but also represents a broader lack of control in a society obsessed with disaster and prey to contingencies capable of producing it.

Like Gladys in *Shadow on the Hearth*, Jack and Babette seek security in the family. Yet there is never the sense of familial and social solidity Gladys invests in the concept of family. From the beginning of *White Noise* there is a pervasive sense of unease. The first brief section of the novel ends on an image of loss at the heart of the home: 'On telephone poles all over town there are homemade signs concerning dogs and cats, sometimes in the handwriting of a child.'[62] The second ends with a signifier of emergency within the home that no longer even evokes a response: 'The smoke alarm went off in the hallway upstairs, either to let us know the battery had just died or because the house was on fire. We finished our lunch in silence.'[63] DeLillo's characters, wandering through a postmodern superfluity of signs, struggle vainly to grasp concepts of death and nonbeing, but are instead only cast adrift amongst signs of these calamities. Even in narrating the incident that almost kills Wilder, Jack cannot eschew postmodern self-consciousness of his own construction of the event, resorting to irony in the denotation with which he labels the person who finally rescues Wilder: 'a passing motorist, as such people are called'.[64]

Jack's fear of mortality is, then, nuclear to the extent that it arises from a culture permeated by images of catastrophe, that it remains forever deferred into a threatening future, and that it connects broad cultural insecurities to those at the heart of the family. Not 'about' nuclear war, the novel carries the signifiers of a more subtly pervasive nuclear anxiety. The nuclear context is not, clearly, the overriding explanatory factor, the single keystone holding the text together – the novel is produced by numerous cultural currents – but reading it as a text that emerges from the Cold War nuclear environment allows us to open up other ways of thinking about its representation of anxiety.

In the next chapter, I turn to the final nuclear environment with which *States of Suspense* deals. This takes us from the microcosm of the home environment to the planetary context. As nuclear anxiety focused fear on the vulnerability of the home and the family, it also inflected concerns about the peril facing the world and suggested common interests that might unite the planet in common cause.

Notes

1 Anon., 'Family plan urged for civil defense', *New York Times* (30 August 1953), p. 36.
2 Elaine Tyler May, *Homeward Bound: American Families in the Cold War Era* (New York: Basic Books, 1999), p. 93.
3 May, *Homeward Bound*, pp. 91–2.
4 May, *Homeward Bound*, p. 130.
5 Alan Nadel, *Containment Culture: American Narratives, Postmodernism, and the Atomic Age* (Durham: Duke University Press, 1995), p. 29.
6 Newsreel of the tests, where this claim is made, is available online in the Prelinger Archives: http://www.archive.org/details/prelinger (28 December 2006).
7 The pamphlet, *Survival Under Atomic Attack*, is available online in a few places. For example: www.schouwer-online.de/technik/zivilschutz_atomicattack.htm (28 December 2006); http://honors.umd.edu/HONR269J/archive/SurvivalBooklet.html (28 December 2006). All quotations are from these sites.
8 Anon., 'Fallout shelters', *Life* (15 September 1961), pp. 104–5.
9 May, *Homeward Bound*, pp. 66–7.
10 Anon., 'Gun thy neighbor?', *Time* (18 August 1961), p. 58. The Russian state newspaper, *Pravda*, responded with predictable glee: 'If only we could open the eyes of these moles armed with machine guns . . . [t]hey would surely see that no-one threatens them with aggression and there is no sense hiding under ground. But moles, as we know, are unseeing creatures, and moles of bourgeois origin, moreover, suffer from class blindness.' Quoted in Theodore Shabad, 'Soviets twit U.S. on civil defense', *New York Times* (26 August 1961), p. 3.
11 Margot A. Henriksen, *Dr. Strangelove's America: Society and Culture in the Atomic Age* (Berkeley: University of California Press, 1997), p. 105.
12 *The House in the Middle* is accessible online through the Prelinger Archive. www.archive.org/details/Houseint1954 (28 December 2006).
13 Nadel, *Containment Culture*, p. 34.
14 Clifford Edward Clark, Jr., *The American Family Home 1800–1960* (Chapel Hill: University of North Carolina Press, 1986), p. 238.
15 May, *Homeward Bound*, p. 93.
16 Clark, *American Family Home*, p. 231. There were, of course, working-class suburbs too; importantly, though, the suburbs were imagined as middle class.
17 Jacqueline Foertsch, *Enemies Within: The Cold War and the AIDS Crisis in Literature, Film, and Culture* (Urbana: University of Illinois Press, 2001), p. 3.
18 Foertsch, *Enemies Within*, p. 17.
19 Nadel, *Containment Culture*, p. 20.
20 The claim that *The House in the Middle* was a point of sale for various household items was made in a 2004 exhibition at the Towner Art Gallery in Eastbourne in the United Kingdom. The text relating to the exhibition, of which the film formed a central part, is at the time of writing available on the web: www.hydropia.org/middle04.htm (28 December 2006).
21 Andrew D. Grossman, *Neither Dead Nor Red: Civilian Defense and American Political Development During the Early Cold War* (New York: Routledge, 2001). See discussion of Grossman in chapter two.
22 See Merril's autobiography, completed by her granddaughter after her death. Judith Merril and Emily Pohl Weary, *Better to Have Loved: The Life of Judith Merril* (Toronto: Between the Lines, 2002).
23 Clark, *American Family Home*, p. 228, p. 233. Conversely, the non-white population of the same cities grew by 4.5 million.
24 May, *Homeward Bound*, pp. 151–2.

25 Judith Merril, *Shadow on the Hearth* (New York: Doubleday, 1950), p. 8.

26 Merril, *Shadow on the Hearth*, pp. 7–8.

27 May, *Homeward Bound*, p. 155.

28 Merril, *Shadow on the Hearth*, p. 12.

29 Merril, *Shadow on the Hearth*, p. 6.

30 May, *Homeward Bound*, p. xxi.

31 May, *Homeward Bound*, p. 17.

32 Merril, *Shadow on the Hearth*, p. 5.

33 Merril, *Shadow on the Hearth*, p. 17. Merril's ellipses.

34 Merril, *Shadow on the Hearth*, pp. 1–2.

35 Merril, *Shadow on the Hearth*, p. 53.

36 Merril, *Shadow on the Hearth*, p. 39, p. 41, p. 57, p. 65, pp. 68–9, p. 139, p. 168.

37 Merril, *Shadow on the Hearth*, p. 218.

38 David Seed, *American Science Fiction and the Cold War: Literature and Film* (Edinburgh: Edinburgh University Press, 1999), p. 58.

39 Merril, *Shadow on the Hearth*, p. 255.

40 Merril, *Shadow on the Hearth*, p. 275.

41 Merril, *Shadow on the Hearth*, p. 275. Merril's emphasis.

42 Merril and Pohl-Weary, *Better to Have Loved*, pp. 99–100. See also Seed, *American Science Fiction*, p. 59.

43 *The Day After* (US, Nicholas Meyer 1983).

44 Leslie Marmon Silko, *Ceremony* (London: Penguin, 1986), p. 245.

45 Don DeLillo, *White Noise* (London: Picador, 1986), p. 151.

46 DeLillo, *White Noise*, pp. 109–17.

47 DeLillo, *White Noise*, p. 56.

48 DeLillo, *White Noise*, p. 34.

49 DeLillo, *White Noise*, p. 35.

50 DeLillo, *White Noise*, pp. 89–91.

51 DeLillo, *White Noise*, pp. 222–3.

52 DeLillo, *White Noise*, pp. 270–1.

53 DeLillo, *White Noise*, p. 113, p. 129, pp. 135–7, p. 141.

54 DeLillo, *White Noise*, p. 141.

55 DeLillo, *White Noise*, p. 257, p. 22, pp. 170–1, p. 302.

56 DeLillo, *White Noise*, p. 64.

57 DeLillo, *White Noise*, pp. 217–18.

58 DeLillo, *White Noise*, p. 100.

59 DeLillo, *White Noise*, p. 236.

60 DeLillo, *White Noise*, p. 235.

61 Mark Osteen has written perceptively about the way in which DeLillo's novels 'repudiate closure' in order to 'deconstruct the impulse towards apocalyptic closure as a tendency in human consciousness'. Mark Osteen, 'Against the end: asceticism and apocalypse in Don DeLillo's *End Zone*', *Papers on Language and Literature: A Journal for Scholars and Critics of Language and Literature* 26:1 (1990), pp. 144–5.

62 DeLillo, *White Noise*, p. 4.

63 DeLillo, *White Noise*, p. 4, p. 8.

64 DeLillo, *White Noise*, p. 324.

5

The fragile planet: articulating global anxieties

[I]n the Health and Safety Laboratory of the United States Atomic Energy Commission the bits of gummed film [from 169 cities around the world], with their twenty-four hour catch from an increasingly polluted sky, are analyzed and the data put together with evidence from some thirty other sampling systems to make up the atomic weather report. (Steven M. Spencer, 'Fallout: the silent killer', 1959)[1]

In the preceding two chapters we saw how cities and homes were established, early in the nuclear age, as vulnerable environments. Responses to the first use of the atomic bomb made the imaginative leap to see that every city was potentially another Hiroshima, and during the Cold War large numbers of cities in East and West had to be considered to be targets in any nuclear conflict. Facing this threat, the suburban home became, in civil defence materials, the location for national resistance to attack, the place in which the family took responsibility for United States security. Actually imperilled by nuclear war, these places also became thickly resonant with ideological significance. In particular, Mutual Assured Destruction placed the absolute vulnerability of all cities at the heart of a system reliant on radical insecurity to produce security, and the home became a robust-fragile buttress not only against the physical impact of nuclear explosion but also against social and political forces represented as threatening to normative notions of family, community and national life.

Despite the sense of a shared national peril, indeed in part because of it (because, for all the rhetoric of deterrence and preparedness, it was manifestly the case that national government could not protect its citizens against a determined nuclear attack), the primary dynamic associated with these threatened environments was one of division and alienation. Nation was pitted against nation, as the cities of the Eastern Bloc were threatened by the missiles of the West, and vice versa, and society was scattered, in imagined nuclear attacks, into isolated family units, who, if they emerged from their shelters at all, would find a devastated world where the social order had collapsed and in which they would be plunged into desperate competition for resources. The next chapter will explore how politically disabling this atomising dynamic could be.

However, even as the nuclear threat pulled societies apart, it also exerted a contradictory impulse. Broad-reaching anxieties about personal and global vulnerability suggested a commonality of interest to which one might appeal in order to resist nuclearism. It is to this counter-dynamic that this chapter turns, and it finds it in a third symbolically imperilled environment: the earth itself. If war could not be visited only on one country or region, and would threaten the whole planet, then a consequence was a shared peril implying a need for a concept of community transcending the divisive fault-lines of nation states and the Cold War.

As was earlier noted, almost as soon as news of Hiroshima got out the implications for the threat to the entire planet were realised. One early political response, although it did not last long in the face of Cold War *real politik*, was to seek international regulation of the new technology: in its most utopian manifestation this involved the fantasy of a world government; in a more moderate incarnation it sought to put atomic weapons under the control of the newly formed United Nations.

Another manifestation of this impulse toward collective identification, rather than atomistic isolation, was the development of a broad environmental consciousness, understood as a holistic appreciation of the interconnectedness of humans to and within a common environment. This was of long-lasting significance for the cultural representation of nuclear technology. Just as homes were shown, despite the best attempts to keep their boundaries secure, to be fragile in the face of atomic blast, and permeable to radiation, so too were national boundaries liable to be breached in the event of nuclear war. This was partly to do with Mutual Assured Destruction, which meant that nuclear states at war with one another were locked into a shared doom, but it was also, more importantly, to do with the impact on the broader environment of multiple nuclear explosions and the drift of radioactive fallout. Not only would participants in a war be affected; with the radical disruption of ecosystems, potentially the whole planet would.

In the late Cold War, the theory that a 'nuclear winter' would follow nuclear war, with temperatures on earth plunging catastrophically as dust from explosions blocked out the sun, gained both scientific credibility and popular currency, working its way into popular dramas like the BBC's *Threads* (1984). Carl Sagan, who jointly formulated the theory, put it in appropriately apocalyptic terms: 'It is the Halloween preceding 1984, and I deeply wish that what I am about to tell you were only a ghost story. . . . But, unfortunately, it is not just a story. Our recent research has uncovered the surprising fact that nuclear war may carry in its wake a climatic catastrophe, which we call "nuclear winter", unprecedented during the tenure of humans on Earth.'[2]

However, crucial to the environmental peril was that it was not just a possible consequence of a hypothetical future war: it could be happening now as a result of 'peaceful' uses of atomic technology. Bomb tests, in particular, were a source of concern in the 1950s. The contamination in 1954 of the Japanese fishing boat, the *Lucky Dragon*, following a nuclear test eighty-five miles away, did much to focus concern about the impact on those caught 'downwind' of nuclear tests. Moreover, with bomb tests taking place in the Nevada desert – 106 of the 216 atmospheric tests conducted by the United States before 1962, took place there[3] – this was also a concern that was very close to home for many Americans. Indeed, anxiety about the presence of strontium-90, a by-product of weapons testing that entered the food chain and accumulated in bones and teeth, gathered momentum throughout the 1950s, reaching a climax at the end of the decade. One study, published in *Science* in 1959, showed the level of strontium-90 to have doubled in young children during 1957; in 1962, a survey of 80,000 baby teeth sent in to scientists concluded that the level of strontium-90 was fourteen times higher for those born in 1957 than it was for those born in 1949.[4]

Nor were these concerns limited to the United States. The Russian physicist, Andrei Sakharov, a key member of the Soviet bomb team, was by the end of the 1950s anxious that his country would not resume nuclear tests, having 'calculated that every one-megaton atmospheric test would cost ten thousand human lives!'[5]

Steven Spencer's article for the *Saturday Evening Post*, quoted in the epigraph to this chapter, taps into these environmental concerns (although we should note that the term 'environmental' would not have been used in the 1950s in the way it is now). The story of the 'atomic weather report' demonstrates the United States to be connected in political and environmental systems that ring the planet. Protective observation against the effects of not-quite-wartime, not-quite-peacetime testing of nuclear weapons, takes place not simply within the United States but around the world. With the Atomic Energy Commission (AEC) based in New York, as the point for collection and analysis of the data, the United States becomes both guarantor of protection against radioactive fallout (the source of authority, able to act, through its designate, the AEC, on the data collected elsewhere), and, because of its involvement in weapons testing, one of the most significant contributors to it. Physical, political and scientific-bureaucratic systems (the air currents that carry the fallout around the world; the geopolitics of the Cold War responsible for the weapons tests; the AEC as a semi-autonomous organisation) enmesh the United States in complex planetary networks. Moreover, these networks function as vectors for radioactive contaminants (either literally, in the case of weather systems, or by creating the structures within which weapons testing can take place), shuttling them from the polluted globe to the most intimate spaces of the human body: '[Fallout] contaminates the air, the sea and the soil. It lies twice as thick over the Northern Hemisphere as the Southern, and is more heavily concentrated in the United States than anywhere on the earth's surface. And every living creature, man included, has in its bodies a few particles of radioactive strontium 90, some of which remain for life.'[6]

It is in these environmental concerns that civilian nuclear technology, often neglected in discussions of nuclear anxiety, comes to feature most strongly. It is, however, important not to oversimplify the relation between civilian and military nuclear technology. Opposition to nuclear bombs did not always and necessarily equate with opposition to nuclear power. Meredith Veldman observes, for instance, that a common tactic adopted by the British Campaign for Nuclear Disarmament (CND) in its early years was to contrast the debased military uses of nuclear technology with its purer applications in civilian energy projects: 'a frequent CND argument [before the 1970s] was to insist that the tremendous potential of nuclear energy was being wasted on military applications.'[7]

Yet events in the 1970s and 1980s did signal a shift against a nuclear energy industry seen as increasingly malign and dangerous. The controversy surrounding the death of Karen Silkwood in 1974, who had exposed lax safety standards in the United States nuclear industry, simultaneously called into question the safety of civilian nuclear facilities and tapped into a sense of powerful forces, operating to protect vested interests, that was resonant of broader Cold War conspiracy theories. The BBC's drama series *Edge of Darkness* (1985) mined these concerns to fine effect, connecting military and civilian nuclear industries in a common Cold War network of power relations, and contrasting them with a radical counter-movement that took its name, Gaia, from a popular environmental vision of the planet (discussed in more detail below). The Three Mile Island accident in 1979 (which coincided uncomfortably with the release of a Hollywood film, *The China Syndrome*, that echoed it uncomfortably), though not itself catastrophic, made the prospect of serious nuclear disaster coming from the energy industry, rather than military conflict, seem more probable. When such a catastrophe did take place, at Chernobyl in 1986, the image of the nuclear energy industry suffered lasting damage.

Alongside these specifically nuclear fears of radioactive pollution was the growth of the modern environmental movement. While the relation between the two was often complex, and sometimes tangential, they proceeded from a common mindset. Rachel Carson's book, *Silent Spring* (1962), arguably the founding text of modern Western environmentalism, is steeped in a Cold War, and specifically nuclear, conception of contamination, even though it is about pollution by pesticides, particularly DDT, rather than radioactive fallout. The analogy between chemical and nuclear contamination, inevitable for her readers given the year of publication, is explicitly made by Carson herself:

> Strontium 90, released through nuclear explosions into the air, comes to earth in rain or drifts down as fallout, lodges in soil, enters into the grass or corn or wheat grown there, and in time takes up its abode in the bones of a human being, there to remain until his death. Similarly, chemicals sprayed on croplands or forests or gardens lie long in the soil, entering into living organisms, passing from one to another in a chain of poisoning and death.[8]

Carson's new idea, pollution by pesticides, is explained by reference here to one with which her readers are assumed to be familiar: contamination by radioactive fallout.

The following discussion of the environmental consciousness of the nuclear age draws heavily on *Silent Spring*. It also draws on James Lovelock's 'Gaia' hypothesis that the earth functions as a single self-regulating organism. Although I argue that environmentalism facilitates a perspective opposing nuclear technology, this rela-tion between the two should not be taken as always and inevitably given. First, opposition to nuclear testing and nuclear power were as much a source for envi-ronmental activism as they were a consequence of it. Second, an environmental perspective does not necessarily presuppose an anti-nuclear perspective. James Lovelock himself, for instance, has dismayed some green campaigners by proposing that nuclear energy is the only viable answer to the problem of soaring carbon emissions.[9] Notwithstanding his personal advocacy of nuclear power, though, the Gaia theory embodies perspectives at the heart of modern environmentalism that were important to anti-nuclear campaigners.

One planet: environmental consciousness in the nuclear age

The real bonus [of space research] has been that for the first time in human history we have had a chance to look at the Earth from space, and the information gained from seeing from the outside our azure-green planet in all its global beauty has given rise to a whole new set of questions and answers. (James Lovelock, *Gaia: A New Look at Life on Earth*, 1979)[10]

There is, perhaps, some irony in the fact that one of the most potent images of environmentalism has its origin in the space race. The development of rocket technology, an urgent practical issue in the nuclear arms race, as well as in the battle for the prestige of being first to put humans into space and on the moon, was linked inextricably to the new technologies of destruction of the second half of the twentieth century. Yet this race also facilitated a wholly new perspective: the view from afar of the blue-green earth, small and fragile against the backdrop of space.

In the early 1990s David Lavery charted the 'mentality of the space age' in his book, *Late for the Sky*, arguing that our language and our modes of thinking were dominated by dangerous fantasies of transcendence. Escaping an earth we assumed to be beyond redemption had become a cultural obsession. Yet, in spite of the 'spaciness' identified by Lavery in late twentieth-century culture, one of the practical upshots of the technological realisation of this dream was a picture of the earth that encouraged a new relationship to it.[11] The technology of the brutal mastery of, and escape from, nature had, as one of its cultural spin-offs, a picture of our planet that encouraged us not to look outwards, but to turn inwards, re-evaluating our relations to the earth.

Lovelock first proposed Gaia, the theory with which he is most strongly associated, in 1969, the year of the first moon landing and therefore also of the most dramatic escape from earth.[12] Yet, looking back, he identifies the source of this theory with the glance backward to the earth that the space race made possible: 'The start of the Gaia hypothesis was the view of the Earth from space, revealing the planet as a whole but not in detail.'[13] This idea of the earth as a single entity is crucial to modern environmental consciousness. It is a view that looks not at the political map of the globe, but which sees the planet as a natural entity; indeed, for the Gaia hypothesis, it is treated as if it were a single living being. The focus is therefore not on difference but unity; we are asked to think not of what divides us but of what binds us, to our environment and to each other, in a shared fate.

Nuclear consciousness intersects with this perspective. Indeed, Jonathan Schell, even though he does not cite Lovelock directly, is surely thinking of Gaia, or something very similar, when he tries to convey the earth's nuclear peril in *The Fate of the Earth* (1982): 'This whole [the planet] is a mechanism in itself; indeed, it may be regarded as a single living being.'[14] Nuclear consciousness draws on this perspective partly because nuclear tests, and the potential for nuclear war, threaten the environment directly. More significantly, though, it is because they suggest that people are bound together in the face of destruction that cannot simply be delivered against one country or region, but that will impact upon, and potentially kill, people around the world. The political fractures across the surface of the earth, dividing one country from another, and the fault-lines dividing East from West in the Cold War, cannot therefore simply section off a threat which exists 'over there'. These boundaries are permeable and the rhetoric of anti-nuclear campaigning, as well as of environmental protest, often speaks to a shared human-ity. Where a safe realm is imagined it is in an imaginary space, coexisting with but outside and beyond the political boundaries that carve up the earth, as in Arundhati Roy's post-Cold War projection of a country beyond nationality in 'The end of imagination' (1998), her essay about the Indian and Pakistani bomb programmes: 'I hereby declare myself an independent, mobile republic. I am a citizen of earth. I own no territory. I have no flag. . . . Immigrants are welcome.'[15]

Such challenges to a politically conceived map of the world ask us to recon-ceptualise the danger, thinking not so much of one country threatening another, but of powerful elites, in various countries, threatening ordinary people around the globe. Although this did not, in the end, generate a politically successful global anti-nuclear movement during the Cold War, it did produce ways of speaking and thinking that challenged the idea of political division with that of shared humanity and global citizenship. The literary texts discussed later in this chapter can be seen as emerging alongside, and in parallel with, these new ways of con-ceptualising planetary peril.

If one powerful theme of environmental consciousness was the single planet, it also presupposed a vision of multiplicity within that single entity. Organisms are not isolated from one another, or separated out into discrete regions, but mapped into systems – environmental and (for humans) moral – of mutual dependency. It is a view of the planet as an ecology of shared interests, a confluence of inter-connected systems, in which contamination in one part is likely to transmit itself to all the others. In the introduction to the British edition of *Silent Spring*, Lord Shackleton identifies this perspective as the book's defining quality of vision: '[it] is not merely about poisons; it is about ecology or the relation of plants and animals to their environment and to one another'.[16] Horrific though they are, the many specific instances of contamination and sickness identified in Carson's book are not its most salient feature. Most striking of all is the new perspective it implies on the relations between people, organisms and the world.

Such a sense of interconnection also became increasingly fundamental to nuclear consciousness. Schell writes of the impact of nuclear war as unpredictable precisely because of these interlocking systems tying the local and the global together in complex relationships: 'When we proceed from the local effects of single explosions to the effects of thousands of them on societies and environments, the picture clouds considerably, because then we go beyond both the certainties of physics and our slender base of experience, and speculatively encounter the full complexity of human affairs and of the biosphere.'[17] What is crucial about this conception is that it does not see nuclear war as visited on particular nations or regions but on humanity and the environment more generally. The act of war is defined as anti-human in the broadest possible sense.

If environmental and nuclear consciousness asked us to re-imagine the world, they also asked us to reconstitute our sense of ourselves. Not only did they ask people to look outwards at the global picture, but also inwards at the physical impact on the world within themselves. This, in turn, implied a psychological reconstitution of the sense of self. Running through *Silent Spring* is not only the widespread impact of pesticides and poisons throughout the United States and the rest of the world, but also a preoccupation with what these things do when they get into what Carson describes as 'the ecology of the world within our bodies'.[18] It should be noted that this association – the body as a world with its own ecologies – forms the basis for a reconstitution of the idea of the human in this period. The human-as-world makes people not agents separately constituted from and outside of nature, but ecosystems that are microcosms of, and intimately connected to, larger ecosystems.

Carson's redirection of our attention to the penetration of the human by the contaminants accumulating in the natural world has a profound effect. As Frederick Buell comments, '[s]omething particularly anxiety-producing happens when one shifts attention from humanly caused damage to nature to environmentally caused danger to human health.' This 'expresses itself in the most fearfully intimate manner; it induces destructive change *inside* and not just around human beings'.[19] In other words the very viability of the human is challenged and rendered horrifically fragile. This is in part the horror of Spencer's article: the atomic weather gets inside, particles of the fallout from bomb tests infesting every living creature. Perhaps more significant than the physical effects – clearly the majority of people were not made ill by their intake of strontium-90, even though they carried it within them – was the psychological impact. Just as homes cannot be made safe, as we saw in the last chapter, so too are bodies imagined as frighteningly permeable to malign outside contaminants.

This is fundamental to the concept of anxiety I am proposing in this book. It implies a vague sense of unease, rather than a specifically experienced physical danger. Notwithstanding the actual and measurable physical impact of nuclear testing on some, relatively few, people, there was a much more broadly experienced, and much more generalised, sense of being imperilled. Very frequently this remained nebulous, even abstract. For many worried about the drift of residue from the bomb tests there may have been no malign physical impact at all. Even where there was a very likely impact, as in the appearance of increased instances of cancers amongst downwinders, individual cases could not be definitively tied to a nuclear or environmental origin. The presence of a nuclear origin for poor health was a question, largely, of probabilities, extrapolations and inferences.

This does, perhaps, sit a little strangely with the apocalyptic nature of some predictions of nuclear war or environmental collapse. They postulate an overwhelming transformation of everyday reality by dramatic change in the future, but very little of this potentially impending reality can yet be directly felt. This might explain in part the tendency of such horrific possibilities to fade into the background, exerting a subtle, periodically anxious impact, rather than an explicit and paralysing fear. Culture since the dawn of the nuclear age and, more recently, since environmental predictions of an imperilled earth have gained currency, is not overtly preoccupied with these things; nor, indeed, should we expect it to be because, much as people's lives are affected by consciousness of them, it is the mundane realities of life that are experienced most palpably. Rather, a more subtly felt anxiety permeates consciousness and culture, making itself felt unevenly and indirectly.

Perhaps the seeming abstraction and lack of immediacy of environmental issues explains why green politics was not, at least in the United Kingdom and the United States, overwhelmingly successful in the twentieth century, except in the form of pressure groups. Even less dramatic was the impact of anti-nuclear campaigning, except at specific moments of resistance on particular issues. Yet they are both important for the more subtle shifts in perspective they produced. As well as the sense of a shared fate for humanity, outlined above, there was one other key change. Carson suggests the need for a revised mindset in the face of the dangers she outlines; a new relation between humans and nature. At the end of *Silent Spring* she rejects the idea of 'control of nature'.[20] As Buell comments, the implication of *Silent Spring* was that, terrible though the situation was, a new mindset could produce a way out: 'Crisis was the result of a bad choice between two available mind-sets – between working with nature by thinking and acting ecologically and attempting to conquer and dominate nature.'[21] However, although there was no similar call to work 'with' nuclear technology (except in so far as there was hope for a benign nuclear power industry, though this did not involve the same rethinking of fundamental categories), there was an analogous appeal to a sense of connection between individual people, one to another, and the world around them. Resisting nuclear peril implied conceiving of the peoples of the world as commonly endangered by the worst outcomes of the Cold War, and commonly invested in the health of the earth as a whole; they suggested a common human peril that would be dangerously ignored if one were to think (as some admittedly did) of nuclear war as a viable means of promoting local national interests.

It is in this idea of humans embedded within planetary ecosystems, and sharing with them a common fate, that literature explores the global nuclear environment. This can be traced in a number of texts – for instance, despite its conservatism in so many matters, Nevil Shute's *On the Beach* (1957) was a powerful force in pushing the idea that everyone was imperilled by the bomb, and that a catastrophe in one place would work its way around the globe, even if the slow-

moving cloud of radioactive fallout it postulated was scientifically improbable –
but the remainder of this chapter will focus on just two novels to demonstrate
how this consciousness found a textual incarnation. Although its nuclear dimensions are those of analogy rather than direct reference, the first, Kurt Vonnegut's
Cat's Cradle (1963), sits most comfortably in the disaster genre. The second, Leslie
Marmon Silko's *Ceremony* (1977), is more in tune with *States of Suspense*'s sense of
nuclear anxiety as something inflected obliquely in texts. In both cases, this consciousness is precipitated by an anxiety that has nuclear dimensions, but it also
offers a countering and affirmative sense of connection. In some ways the stress
on shared human dimensions may seem unfashionably essentialist or even naïve
(although *Ceremony*, at least, is acutely aware of the divisive nature of constructions
of racialised identities), but this emphasis on what people have in common was
an important counter to the discourse of nuclearism during the Cold War, and
one which has, moreover, since been largely lost in the transformed geopolitical
discourses arising from the 'War on Terror'.

Kurt Vonnegut, *Cat's Cradle* and Leslie Marmon Silko, *Ceremony*

In Kurt Vonnegut's *Cat's Cradle*, ice-nine, a substance that turns water into ice on
contact, destroys the world following an accident. In Leslie Marmon Silko's *Ceremony*, Tayo, a Native-American Second World War veteran, suffers physical and
psychological illness on returning home to his people, who live near the New
Mexico atomic testing grounds.

The books have markedly different tones. While *Cat's Cradle* is comic, even
flippant, in its treatment of the subject matter (it is much closer to the satirical
black humour of the film, *Dr Strangelove*, than it is to the po-faced seriousness of
On the Beach), *Ceremony* is earnest and intense. Yet both are linked by the ways in
which they inflect nuclear issues as challenges to the environment and humanity.
While neither book is explicitly a nuclear text in the manner of, say, *On the Beach*,
Pat Frank's *Alas, Babylon* (1959) or Philip Wylie's *Tomorrow!* (1954), they are rep-
resentative of a pervasive environmental and nuclear consciousness.

Ice-nine makes *Cat's Cradle* the most explicitly nuclear of the two texts. It is
invented by a scientist, Felix Hoenikker, who worked on the Allied team to
produce the Hiroshima bomb, and it destroys the world. Furthermore, published
in 1963, the novel resonates with the Cuban crisis of the previous year with its
setting on San Lorenzo, a small republic ruled by a charismatic dictator, Miguel
'Papa' Monzano, who tries to get hold of ice-nine for his own purposes.

Particularly interesting in the novel's treatment of this issue is its presentation
of the threat to the world as an assault upon nature. Ice-nine is represented as
threatening the natural order. Fundamentally, it transforms water, the stuff of life,
into ice. Suddenly afflicted in this way, the world is presented as being in torment:
the sky darkens, the sun 'became a sickly yellow ball, tiny and cruel', and the 'sky
was filled with worms. The worms were tornadoes.'[22] Longer term, the effect is
resonant of Carson's spring, rendered unnaturally silent by the absence of bird-
song and used by Carson to depict the dangers of chemical pollution. When the
few survivors emerge from their shelter into the warm but frozen planet, where

the air is 'dry and hot and deathly still',[23] they find a world in which the flux of nature has been replaced by stasis and the seasons have been frozen:

> There were no smells. There was no movement. Every step I took made a gravelly squeak in blue-white frost. And every squeak was echoed loudly. The season of locking was over. The earth was locked up tight.
> It was winter now, now and forever.[24]

This is a representation of the stilling, and thus the end, of time. Forcing us into a perspective after the crisis point of environmental catastrophe – it is narrated retrospectively by Jonah – the novel constructs the period preceding the devastation wrought by ice-nine as one with a teleology. Anxiety texts more frequently focus on, or at least are expressive of, the point before the goal of human history, the final annihilation of the human, is reached. Here the horror of human destruction triggers narrative release from suspense that may, in some degree, help to explain the discharge of comic energies throughout the novel. Humans' destruction by ice-nine, or by its obvious real-world referent, nuclear war, is transformed into a comedy of the absurd. A world poised instead on the brink before, and in anticipation of, this catastrophe, though not without its possibilities for black comedy, would sit less obviously well with *Cat's Cradle*'s lightness of tone.

In Vonnegut's novel, then, there is release from the suspense in which this book is interested. It is nevertheless valuable to this study for the way in which it points up the connection between nuclear anxiety and a broader environmental consciousness. Vonnegut's later work picks up this theme. In *Breakfast of Champions* (1973) there are images of human pollution of the planet and in *Galapagos* (1985) a virus destroys everyone except a small group of survivors whose descendants eventually evolve into fish-eating creatures. The species-threatening catastrophe here again conjures up a nuclear dimension, particularly through this latter novel's preoccupation with a common nuclear theme, the presumptive overreaching of the human intellect.

Cat's Cradle casts the destruction of the environment in the form of a filial betrayal, humans destroying the mother nature from which they come. As Mona, an innocent figure of purity in the novel, says: 'Mother Earth – she isn't a very good mother any more.'[25] Tayo, in *Ceremony*, tries to make a similar point. He returns from war to a land ravaged by drought, and tries to explain to Harley the paucity of their existence on a seemingly dying earth: 'Look what is here for us. Look. Here's the Indians' mother earth! Old dried-up thing!'[26] The dominant image in *Ceremony* is one of sickness: the dying earth is linked, through the webs of imagery woven by the novel, to the mining and desecration of the land for uranium, and the testing and use of atomic weapons.

Although *Cat's Cradle* has very specifically Cold War points of reference (Hoenikker's son, Newt, for instance, has an affair with a Soviet spy, Zinka, who is after the ice-nine) – the novel more generally locates the source of the world's perils in human tragicomic frailty. Hoenikker is less an evil genius than a brilliant but childish mind, endlessly distracted by whatever problem he finds interesting, and monstrous in his amorality rather than his immorality. If the novel does find a more general source for the world's demise, it is, rather simplistically, articulated through a recurrent anti-science trope. Repeatedly, the novel asks us to side with people who reject science for art or for a more generally humanistic enterprise. Marvin Breed, a tombstone salesman, tells the story of his nephew who gives up science for sculpture after the invention of the atomic bomb: 'He was all set to be a heap-big re-search scientist, and then they dropped the bomb on Hiroshima and the kid quit, and he got drunk, and he came out here, and he told me he wanted to go to work cutting stone.'[27] Later, as 'Papa' Monzano is dying, his doctor, going through a religious ritual in which he does not believe, perceives this act of human mercy as antithetical to his scientific background: 'I am a very bad scientist. I will do anything to make a human being feel better, even if it's unscientific. No scientist worthy of the name could say such a thing.'[28]

Cat's Cradle makes the scientific impulse a treacherous human flaw. Like many of Vonnegut's novels, though, Cat's Cradle is also replete with an affectionate humanism that finds common ground between people in their attempts to make sense of an essentially meaningless world. Throughout the book we are treated to the insights of Bokanism, a religion that is shown to be knowingly false, but which is used to make sense of the existential horror of existence. The act of finding meaning is located as human, although the meaning itself may be a fabrication.

Like Cat's Cradle, Ceremony places itself in opposition to scientific explanations. For instance, Tayo remembers a science teacher at school mocking Native American myths of origin.[29] These alternative modes of knowing, the Native American mythic narrative structures through which people's relation to the land is understood, are posited as true. (Arguably, despite this opening up of alternative cultural perspectives, the novel rather problematically resorts to essentialism in this respect: closeness to the land and to myth is represented as authentic experience, in contrast to 'white' ways of knowing the world deemed to be wrong.)

Ceremony attempts to construct a much more complex set of associations between the sickness of the land and its destroyers than does Cat's Cradle. The building, testing and use of the atomic bomb is just one facet of a larger system of malevolent forces. In the myths of origin invoked by the novel, white settlers in North America are linked with the bringing of disease. Strikingly the experience of this sickness is rendered in ways which, because of the nuclear allusions in the novel, also conjure up images of radiation sickness:

> They will bring terrible diseases
> the people have never known.
> Entire tribes will die out
> covered with festered sores
> shitting blood
> vomiting blood.
> Corpses for our work.[30]

Although the novel focuses on the eradication of Native American peoples and culture, it makes a connection to a broader danger to all the peoples of the world, and resistance to this peril is shown as a binding force, bringing them together. Tayo understands that his people's land is connected with the development of the bomb: Trinity, the site of the first test, is only 300 miles southeast, and the laboratories where the bomb was created are at Los Alamos in the Jemez mountains, commandeered from Native Americans. From here, the bomb is understood as transgressing all boundaries, implicating the whole of the Earth: 'There was no end to it; it knew no boundaries; and he had arrived at the point of convergence where the fate of all living things, and even the earth, had been laid.'[31]

But being near the centre of things, here, connects Tayo to a planetary fate, rendered through a nuclear analogy: 'human beings were one clan again, united by the fate the destroyers planned for all of them, for all living things; united by a circle of death that devoured people in cities twelve thousand miles away'.[32] As soon as the threat to the Earth is articulated it implies the possibility of a resistance to this threat that conceptualises itself in global terms. As Rachel Stein puts it, in Ceremony the 'final threat of nuclear destruction reforms humans into a new collectivity that subsumes social differences into a new clan, united by shared danger'.[33]

Silko elevates the nuclear threat out of the realm of specific socio-political circumstances to a mythic level. The 'destroyers' emerge as bringers of death who must be defeated through the ceremony of the novel's title. Crucial to this mythology, and related to the environmental consciousness on which this chapter focuses, is an affirmation of a connection with the land which is strength-giving. Tayo observes near the end of the novel that 'we came out of the land and we are hers'.[34] In contrast with the forced extraction from the land, through mining, of uranium, which produces the destructive powers to which the novel is opposed, this is a more natural emergence from the land. It is presented as a birth, an act of creation, and connects the healing of the land with a broader psychological and cultural healing.

Silko's novel is informed by a culture of nuclear anxiety. Nuclear anxiety is not the main focus of the text (as section one of this book suggested, this is not surprising: characteristically, such anxiety tends not to be at the centre of attention), but it is vital to the set of associations created by the novel between forces destructive to nature, Native Americans and people more generally. Ambiguous in its outcome – the novel is affirmative but leaves the Earth's future uncertain – Ceremony is also caught in a moment of cultural suspense. Unlike Cat's Cradle, where destructive forces wreak their worst effects across the planet, it posits powerful challenges to the continued existence of people and of the world but sets up a countering movement that might resist these challenges.

While the text draws on nuclear anxiety, it is also indebted to an experimental tradition that later came to be characterised as postmodern (and which Cat's Cradle may be seen as anticipating), although it is also inflected through the Native American traditions, stories and ceremonies on which Silko draws. This coming together of postmodernist and Native American cultural traditions produces complex dynamics. When Tayo looks around him and '[e]verywhere he looked, he saw a world made of stories', we could be in a postmodernist text where narrative is itself constitutive of reality. Yet, these stories are the 'long ago, time immemorial stories' of his people, suggesting a mythic truth about which post-modernist texts are more commonly sceptical.

This intriguing confluence of cultural traditions does connect *Ceremony* with other, perhaps more obviously postmodern, texts because it establishes a prob-lematic relation between language and reality. With different worlds colliding – the rational 'white' world amenable to scientific explanation, and the Native American world, explicable through a mythic oral tradition and controllable through rites and ceremonies – we are placed in a moment of ontological uncer-tainty, like that identified by Brian McHale as characteristic of postmodernism.[35] Regardless of where we may stand in relation to these competing belief systems, in the novel's terms their collision produces a fracturing, and the novel ends in ambiguity rather than absolute affirmation of the success of Tayo's new insights.

More broadly, the focus on a common humanity, particularly prevalent in writers like Vonnegut, does run counter to the scepticism of many postmodern impulses which resist essentialist categories like those of the 'human' or 'nature'. Nevertheless, both Vonnegut and Silko contest the view of nature as something separate from the human. They imply a need to put humans back into nature, rather than seeing nature as a resource for control and exploitation by humans. It is in this sense that they are expressive of a generalised environmentalist impulse.

The third nuclear environment, the planet, tends to produce, then, a different category of cultural response to that of the environments discussed in the preced-ing two chapters. Whereas both the city and home environments, under nuclear threat, involve a paralysis of, or even a turning away from, political action, the idea of the imperilled planet produces leverage for political action, perhaps partly because it involves a shift away from a concentration on the notion of personal threat, and toward a generalised danger which can be contested. Such leverage may be neither powerful nor sophisticated – it may, simply, be an affirmation of a humanity shared around the globe by all those imperilled by the threatened conflict of World War Three – but it does at least offer a broader vision than that which concentrates simply on personal or national peril.

Yet, postmodern texts generally have an ambiguous relation to political action, exposing the fallacies of claims to truth or power, but frequently unable to posit any alternative. It is this ambiguity that is the focus of the following chapter.

Notes

1 Stephen M. Spencer, 'Fallout: the silent killer', *Saturday Evening Post* (29 August 1959). Full text available on the web at *It Seems Like Yesterday: The Atomic Age*: www.itseemslikeyesterday. com/Atomic/article_fallout.asp (29 December 2006).

2 Carl Sagan, 'The atmospheric and climatic consequences of nuclear war', in Paul R. Ehrlich et al. (eds), *The Nuclear Winter: The Cold and the Dark* (London: Sidgwick and Jackson, 1984), p. 3. The nuclear winter theory was first proposed in R. P. Turco et al., 'Nuclear winter: global consequences of multiple nuclear explosions', *Science* 222 (23 December 1983), pp. 1283–92.

3 Michael Light, 'A note on the photographs', in Light, *100 Suns: 1945–1962*. No page numbers are printed in Light's book.

4 Paul Boyer, *Fallout: A Historian Reflects on America's Half-Century Encounter with Nuclear Weapons* (Columbus: Ohio State University Press, 1998), pp. 82–4.

5 Andrei Sakharov, trans. Richard Lourie, *Memoirs* (London: Hutcheon, 1990), p. 208. Sakharov is writing about the political pressure to resume testing, following a voluntary moratorium, in 1958. As he comments, '[e]ven if my estimates were on the high side, the number of potential human casualties was still colossal.' p. 208

6 Spencer, 'Fallout'.

7 Meredith Veldman, *Fantasy, the Bomb, and the Greening of Britain: Romantic Protest, 1945–1980* (Cambridge: Cambridge University Press, 1994), p. 154.

8 Rachel Carson, *Silent Spring* (Middlesex: Penguin, 1965), p. 23.

9 'I believe nuclear power is the only source of energy that will satisfy our demands and yet not be a hazard to Gaia'. James Lovelock, *The Revenge of Gaia: Why the Earth is Fighting Back – And How We Can Still Save Humanity* (London: Penguin, 2007), p. 86.

10 J. E. Lovelock, *Gaia: A New Look at Life on Earth* (Oxford: Oxford University Press, 1979), p. 8.

11 David Lavery, *Late for the Sky: The Mentality of the Space Age* (Carbondale: Southern Illinois University Press, 1992). See pp. 31–48 for a discussion of the constitutive elements of 'spaciness'.

12 Lovelock, *Gaia*, p. 11.

13 Lovelock, *Gaia*, p. 126.

14 Jonathan Schell, *The Fate of the Earth* and *The Abolition* (Stanford: Stanford University Press, 2000), p. 77.

15 Arundhati Roy, *The Cost of Living*: 'The greater common good' *and* 'The end of imagination' (London: Flamingo, 1999), p. 140.

16 Lord Shackleton, introduction to Carson, *Silent Spring*, p. 11.

17 Schell, *Fate of the Earth*, p. 22.

18 Carson, *Silent Spring*, p. 169.

19 Frederick Buell, *From Apocalypse to Way of Life: Environmental Crisis in the American Century* (New York: Routledge, 2004), pp. 111–12. Buell's emphasis.

20 Carson, *Silent Spring*, p. 257.

21 Buell, *From Apocalypse to Way of Life*, p. 182.

22 Kurt Vonnegut, *Cat's Cradle* (London: Penguin, 1965), p. 163.

23 Vonnegut, *Cat's Cradle*, p. 167.

24 Vonnegut, *Cat's Cradle*, p. 168.

25 Vonnegut, *Cat's Cradle*, p. 168.

26 Leslie Marmon Silko, *Ceremony* (London: Penguin, 1986), p. 25.

27 Vonnegut, *Cat's Cradle*, p. 49. Vonnegut's emphasis.

28 Vonnegut, *Cat's Cradle*, p. 138.

29 Silko, *Ceremony*, p. 94.

30 Silko, *Ceremony*, p. 137. Silko's emphasis.

31 Silko, *Ceremony*, pp. 245–6.

32 Silko, *Ceremony*, p. 246.

33 Rachel Stein, 'Contested ground: nature, narrative and Native American identity in Leslie Marmon Silko's *Ceremony*', in Allan Chavkin (ed.), *Leslie Marmon Silko's* Ceremony: *A Casebook* (Oxford: Oxford University Press, 2002), p. 203.

34 Silko, *Ceremony*, p. 255.

35 Brian McHale, *Postmodernist Fiction* (New York: Methuen, 1987). See in particular chapter 1, 'From modernist to postmodernist fiction: change of dominant', pp. 5–25.

III
Nuclear reactions

6

Going underground and digging in: the politics of nuclear literature

The price of deviating for me turned out to be an awfully high one but, nevertheless, the aim was real only because the bomb really does exist and hangs over the suburbs. (Letter to Betty Friedan, 1963)[1]

The response of the unnamed woman, quoted above, to Betty Friedan's ground-breaking analysis of women's position in *The Feminine Mystique*, is revealing of the ways in which containment straddled foreign policy and domestic culture in the United States. Rejecting the apparent security of marriage when at college, by the time she was twenty-five she found herself frustrated by what she saw as the political and intellectual disengagement of her contemporaries, who already had children and were 'too busy mowing lawns and buying things to be much interested in existentialism or the political situation in Algeria'.[2] The 'price' to which she refers, and that she puts down to her refusal to conform to highly restrictive social expectations and her trust in psychoanalysis, the fashionable solution to personal dissatisfaction, was indeed a high one: a nervous breakdown, and residence in a mental hospital from whence she wrote her letter to Friedan.

The associations this woman makes between domesticity (marriage and children), consumer capitalism ('buying things') and acquiescence to the political status quo is indicative of the extent to which containment promised a security it could not deliver. In an age of insecurity – when a civilisation-ending war was discussed as a strategic option – the middle-class family, living in the controlled environment of the suburbs and with access to an unprecedented wealth of material and consumer goods, seemed to offer security precisely because it promised to take people out of an overtly political realm to a sphere where the 'natural' values of family could flourish. It apparently magicked the bomb, a real threat but also a symbol of the most destructive forces of Western civilisation, out of people's consciousness. Hence the insistence in this letter that 'the bomb is real'.

Yet in order to provide security, containment had not only to cope with the bomb but also to contain forces – political; social; sexual – that might otherwise have seemed to threaten the country from within. Dissent from the norm and frustration with its restrictions were, crucially, not channelled through political

structures which might produce them as dissatisfaction with an artificial and historically specific form of social organisation. Instead, dissent was frequently constructed as psychological failure, even sickness, in the face of a natural state of
affairs. Those who felt out of place frequently, as Elaine Tyler May puts it, 'buried
their discontent and sought therapeutic, rather than political, solutions to their
problems'.[3] Indeed, there was a 'reliance on professionals', a trust in expertise
that 'offered a distinctly apolitical means of solving problems that were often the
result of larger societal restraints'.[4]

Containment is an important context for our understanding of the politics of
nuclear disaster and nuclear anxiety texts. It means that domestic environments
and themes are likely to be highly charged with significance; more so, when we
consider how central to the rhetoric of civil defence the suburban home and the
family were. It is therefore not surprising that, when we do find texts engaged
politically with nuclear issues, it is very often through the context of the family.
Although the domestic consensus (or, more accurately, the illusion of domestic
consensus) collapsed in the 1960s, by this time the ideal of the nuclear family had
become so deeply ingrained in Cold War discourse that it is not surprising that
even later texts continued to return to it.

Interestingly, explicit engagement with strategic policy, which one might expect
to be central to the political dimensions of nuclear texts, was rare and, where it
did occur, tended toward clunky polemic, as in Philip Wylie's *Tomorrow!* (1954)
or Pat Frank's *Alas, Babylon* (1959), both of which overtly promoted civil defence
programmes. Even texts clearly written to raise consciousness about the possible
consequences of nuclear war could be disappointingly banal in their representation of the causal role of strategic policy and the geopolitical context. Nevil Shute's
On the Beach (1957), for instance, eschews proper engagement with the Cold War
arms race by blaming the world-ending holocaust it describes on the acquisition
of nuclear weapons by small, and by implication uncivilised, countries ('[e]very
little pipsqueak country like Albania'), or on a generalised human failing ('we were
all too silly').[5]

Where such texts are more interestingly political, although it is largely an
unconscious politics, is in their visions of a social order under pressure. Often,
particularly in disaster texts where the destruction, and sometimes rebuilding, of
civilisation is directly broached, this can produce a deeply conservative response.
For instance, despite its awareness of nuclear war, *On the Beach* perversely locates
the threat to the world not so much with Western civilisation (which is indeed
celebrated) as elsewhere. This threat is overtly present in the blaming of 'pipsqueak' countries, noted above, but it is also more generally felt in a first-world
contempt in the novel for all that is threateningly 'other' to the perceived values
of the West, as in Dwight's horror, quoted in my discussion of Shute in chapter
three, that in its final days Melbourne becomes dirty, an 'oriental city in the
making'.[6] Nuclear war is, in fact, configured as redemptive in some ways. Moira,
the only character to show any significant development in the course of the text,
is actually reformed by the impending disaster. She is brought back within the
bounds of a culture closely related to the containment ideal of domesticity pertain-

ing in the United States. Originally drunken, flirtatious and a threat to the family structure, by the end she is taking a secretarial course, sewing buttons onto Dwight's jumper and, through her peculiarly chaste affair with him, preserving the sanctity of his marriage to his deceased wife. Nuclear war functions similarly to resurrect supposedly lost social values in *Alas, Babylon*. At the end of the novel, with America cleansed by nuclear fire, the group of survivors all turn down the option of leaving for a new life elsewhere, choosing instead to continue building their lives in line with ideals of self-reliance, family and frontier justice.

In nuclear anxiety texts, however, the politics of such social and domestic concerns tend to be broached in more complex ways, largely because they are shown to be traces of larger irregularities in the supposedly smooth and uniform continuity between foreign and domestic areas of policy and organisation. Whereas nuclear disaster texts represent the worst consequences of the age, showing civilisation succumbing to them or cathartically emerging from them, there can be no such resolution in anxiety texts. Not forced into grand visions of the death or rebuilding of civilisation, they must instead work the fault-lines of Cold War culture without resolving and removing the central suspense of the era. Dealing often (although not always) tangentially with the nuclear context, they evoke the hovering dread of nuclear war and are forced to represent the pall it casts over everyday life and social relations.

Tim O'Brien's *The Nuclear Age* (1985) is, perhaps, the novel that most explicitly takes nuclear anxiety, rather than nuclear disaster, as its subject, and it demonstrates the politicisation of the family within the changing nuclear contexts of the Cold War. Like Betty Friedan's unnamed correspondent, the narrator-protagonist of the novel, William Cowling, is desperate to communicate the existence of an actual threat hanging over a complacent United States: 'THE BOMBS ARE REAL' reads a placard he holds up, as he begins a solo protest in a college canteen.[7] These are not directly equivalent to the bomb that Friedan's correspondent insisted was 'real': William is protesting against the Vietnam War. However, William's life-long preoccupation with atomic war gives it a nuclear dimension. The point he makes here – '[t]here was a war on – they didn't know' – although specifically about Vietnam, is also the point he makes throughout the novel about the nuclear threat.[8] It is also the same one Friedan's correspondent was making: behind the illusion of security – affluence; democracy; freedom – there is a fundamental insecurity.

The Nuclear Age is ambiguous about the possibilities of political commitment in a way that is characteristic of both the nuclear age and postmodernism. William has a recurring dilemma, epitomised in the choice between 'going underground' and 'digging in'. As a child of the fifties, his life parallels the Cold War and his life story to middle age is largely an attempt to come to terms with the threats of the era. He is torn between political action (going underground), charted through his association with college contemporaries who move from peaceful protest to terrorist action, and outright rejection of political engagement (digging in), expressed in the paralysis he feels at the thought of nuclear war and alluded to most directly in the scenes to which the novel returns of William, as a middle-aged man, digging a bomb shelter. The tensions between these alternatives illustrate the failures of containment culture; indeed, they show the dramatic psychological and political fallout of this culture's false promises of security as William is traumatized by his efforts to reconcile himself to terrors that cannot be quelled.

The novel is also, in its preoccupation with language and the elusiveness of reality, characteristically postmodern. Indeed, if Alan Nadel is right that the contradictions of the containment culture he identifies in the 1950s sowed the seeds for later postmodernist scepticism and interrogation of cultural norms, then *The Nuclear Age* perhaps illustrates more overtly than most texts the Cold War, and specifically nuclear, origins of postmodern interrogations of language and reality. The novel traces what happens to the culture of the 1950s discussed by Nadel, exploring the long-term consequences of its Cold War nuclear origins.

This does not mean that it has an intrinsically radical agenda. Postmodernism is of a mixed, even contradictory, political complexion: while it can mount a powerful challenge to established discourses, exposing their reliance on historically contingent conditions, it also often remains conservative, unable to formulate an alternative position from which to contest the 'grand narratives' it rejects.[9] Linda Hutcheon is probably closest to expressing the contradictory impulses of postmodernism when she says that it 'ultimately manages to install and reinforce as much as undermine and subvert the conventions and presuppositions it appears to challenge'.[10] Accordingly, *The Nuclear Age* exposes the political and cultural consequences of nuclear realities, but it does not necessarily offer a means to oppose them.

This chapter explores the politics of nuclear anxiety fiction through O'Brien's novel. It begins by making the case for a reevaluation of the importance of *The Nuclear Age* in O'Brien's oeuvre, and of its more general significance as an extended fictional exploration of the consequences of nuclear anxiety.[11] It then discusses each of the alternatives facing William, examining the consequences of digging in and going underground. Although *The Nuclear Age* remains at the centre of the discussion, the chapter briefly suggests, in its conclusion, some of the ways in which other characters in nuclear-inflected texts bear traces of political contexts similar to those shaping William's life.

The Nuclear Age

Tim O'Brien's *The Nuclear Age* occupies a slightly curious position. Published in the mid-1980s it missed, by some considerable time, the decade – the 1950s – in which nuclear fear was most acutely felt in literature. Although the 1980s was another nuclear-anxious decade, by 1985, when the novel came out, the Cold War was beginning to thaw, and only four years later was over. The novel's projection of 1995, then, as a year in which the Cold War is ongoing, very rapidly dates it. Although the book is noted approvingly by a number of nuclear critics, albeit with some reasonable reservations about, for instance, the two-dimensionality of O'Brien's female characters (Jacqueline Foertsch comments that Melinda is 'barely there – mere background concern' in comparison with the male pro-tagonist), it does not garner extensive critical attention from them.[12] There are some journal articles on the novel, but it is mostly mentioned in passing in larger works, perhaps partly because it does not deal with nuclear disaster as such, and perhaps also because its appearance late in the Cold War meant the brief flower-ing of nuclear criticism was largely over by the time the novel had a chance to become established.

Even studies of O'Brien's larger output, which are becoming more numerous as he gains recognition as an important voice in contemporary United States fiction, tend to neglect *The Nuclear Age*. O'Brien's focus on the legacies of the Vietnam War, in which he served a tour of duty, dominate both much of his fiction (although there has been a shift away from this in his latest novels, *Tomcat in Love* and *July, July*) and much of the criticism on his work. In particular, critics concentrate on the representation of the personal and national psychological scars of the Vietnam War; one critic, Mark Herbele, has even gone so far as to christen O'Brien a 'trauma artist' in the title of his monograph on O'Brien's work, arguing that his novels 'reflect the traumatic circumstances of American postwar [post-Vietnam] life more generally'.[13] *The Nuclear Age*, when it is discussed, tends to be seen in terms of this psychological perspective, William Cowling's confused and traumatised state of mind seen as a corollary to O'Brien's ongoing attempts to come to terms with the impact of the Vietnam War on his life.

In many ways, such readings make sense. O'Brien's fiction *is* largely dominated by the impact of Vietnam, and his general interest in the traumatic legacy of the past means that *The Nuclear Age* can be assimilated fairly comfortably into his oeuvre as a minor text that, while not directly about Vietnam, does cover the period of the Vietnam War and does deal with psychological concerns that are analogous to those dealt with in his other novels.

However, such readings inevitably fail to do justice to the novel's function within the different dynamics of a canon of nuclear texts. This is partly because of the way in which the psychoanalytic perspective appropriates the text. It either recoups it within a paradigm of personal trauma (the novel as an investigation of William's tortured psyche, read implicitly as a projection of O'Brien's own trauma), makes it part of a more general literature of war writing investigating the psychological legacies of combat (the novel as representation of a universalised experience of war), or relates it to the political contexts of the Vietnam War explored in more detail in O'Brien's other fiction (the novel as expressive of per-sonal and national psychological scars produced by specific events in the 1960s and 1970s; this reading further marginalizes the text because, dealing only indi-rectly with Vietnam, it is seen as less crucial to O'Brien's oeuvre). All these read-ings work and can be productive of valuable insights. However, like all readings they leave things out. What they specifically exclude is the larger cultural context of nuclear anxiety, which is read either as a metaphorical expression of William's broader failings, or turned into a distorted reflection of trauma supposedly origi-nating in the writer's experience in Vietnam. Such readings also run the risk of re-plicating the failure May identifies when she writes of a 'reliance on professionals' in the 1950s: dissatisfaction is assumed to arise from psychological maladjustment rather than from politically produced social dislocations.

I want to make a case here for considering *The Nuclear Age* in a different light and for reading it on the terms on which it is explicitly based: as about 'the nuclear age'. It is perhaps the quintessential nuclear anxiety text. It makes the connection between the geopolitics of the Cold War and domestic circumstances, seeing them as different points on a continuous spectrum rather than public and private realms opposed in absolute binary difference. For instance, while William's self-deception reveals to the reader that his nuclear anxiety is in part a metaphoric incarnation of fears about the fragility of his marriage, the text also shows how the family operates within a larger cultural discourse falsely promising that security will follow from conformity. Fundamentally, the novel is about the idea of security and it demonstrates that security in the home is intimately bound to security in the homeland.

Containment, at home and abroad, is shown to be riddled with problems. Cowling can only suppress his fears of nuclear war, and of domestic insecurity, temporarily. When they force themselves into his consciousness, he can do one of two things: he can dig in or he can go underground.

Digging in

The novel begins with William digging. It is 1995 (in the novel's terms, deep in the Cold War) and William has suffered a late night resurgence of a nuclear fear that blighted his earlier life. He has left his wife in bed and is digging a bomb shelter in the garden. He articulates this as a defensive strategy – digging in – involving a conscious rejection of political engagement: 'no more crusades,' he says; '[c]all it what you want – copping out, dropping out, numbness, the loss of outrage, simple fatigue. I've retired. Time to retrench. Time to dig in. Safety first.'[14]

Where it surfaces into conscious fear, then, nuclear anxiety is configured as paralysing. The desire for an alternative state – security – induces a rejection of political action in favour of a defensive retreat from engagement with the world. William's moment of choice, in this regard, is set up by the structure of the book as the culmination of a life blighted by nuclear and other anxieties: as William tells his story we return periodically to the developing episode of his shelter-digging and its impact on his relations with his wife, Bobbi, and daughter, Melinda.

Digging in, and the desire for security of which it is an expression, is closely linked by the novel to the concept of family: the shelter is a more robustly protected version of the domestic space, appropriate for an age in which reality 'tends to explode'.[15] Yet, disturbingly, it becomes apparent that a key function of the shelter is not so much to preserve the family by keeping a hostile environment out, but to do so by keeping his wife and daughter in. Bobbi has had an affair and William is trying to prevent her and Melinda from leaving. By the end of the novel his excessive demand for security has itself destroyed the family he was trying to save: he has imprisoned and drugged Bobbi and Melinda, and threatens to dynamite the whole family along with the shelter. This is a dramatisation of a central problem of the age: containment is the means by which the security of the family is guaranteed, but it is containment itself, the literal containment of the family in this case, which blows them apart.

The hole William digs for his shelter is an attempt to make real a desire for security imagined, throughout his life, in images of small, protected spaces: a 'tree house', a 'snow fort', the 'lion's instinct for the den', 'caves', the 'mole in his hole', the 'turtle in his shell', the 'Alamo', 'castles on the Rhine', 'moated villages', 'turrets', 'frontier stockades', 'storm cellars', 'foxholes', 'an attic in Amsterdam', a 'nice thick coffin to keep out the worms', a 'tree house made of steel', a 'concrete igloo in Alaska', and a 'snug spaceship heading for the stars'.[16] William's preoccupation with such spaces demonstrates the long-standing pull of his desire for disengagement from an outside environment configured as overwhelmingly hostile. However, incongruities in the images through, for instance, dissonance ('tree house made of steel'; 'concrete igloo') or evident vulnerability (the 'attic in Amsterdam' presumably alludes to Anne Frank) signal the fallacy undermining his attempts to find psychological security. The spaces William imagines will not keep out his fear; nor, ultimately, will they protect him.

Such disconnection from an outside environment is regressive. William is essentially longing for a retreat to the womb, a notion also seen in the way in which his narrative represents women as both sexualised and maternal. When as a child, fleeing ridicule of his nuclear fears, he goes to the library to research civil defence, his reaction to a sympathetic librarian is mediated through the nurturing and sexualised image of her breasts: one grazes his neck as she bends over to see what he is studying, and he hopes she will sit down, with her 'soft chest', to chat to him at length. When he collapses at school, he comes to to find Sarah Strouch, a classmate he desires and who later becomes his girlfriend, ministering to him. As an adult, in a moment of nuclear panic on an airplane, a stewardess (Bobbi, whom he later marries) is similarly represented as maternal, temporarily returning him to an infant state when she 'wiped my brow, and then held my hand for a while'.[17]

As May has shown, and as chapter four discussed, in the 1950s the ideology of domesticity was closely linked to the rhetoric and policies of containment through which the United States engaged with its communist antagonists around the world. In *The Nuclear Age* we are able to follow the consequences of these links between family and nation throughout the Cold War. Although William grows up in a family conforming to the domestic ideal in every way (except for his lack of siblings in a period when large families were the norm), his parents are unable to provide security. Symbolically, this is enacted through his father's playing of Custer in the town's annual staging of the Battle of the Little Big Horn. Each year William must watch his father die, an outcome he both fears and desires: 'I craved bloodshed, yet I craved the miracle of a happy ending',[18] William comments, prefiguring his later dangerous fascination with apocalypse. Practically, it is carried through in William's acute awareness that there is no defence against the bomb. The family, meant to offer security and a safe future, can provide neither. William's childhood attempt to build a bomb shelter under a table-tennis table exposes him to ridicule, and demonstrates his fragility in the face of outside threats. This pattern of the breaking of the promise of security is repeated in William's adult life in the family he tries to form with Bobbi and Melinda. Overwhelmed by the pressure of his excessive demand for security, it collapses.

Crucially, William's brutal mistreatment of his family complicates what would otherwise be a simplistic representation of the relation between individual and state. It reveals that he is not simply a victim of the state's political investment in a strategic policy based on terror. Instead, the radical insecurity and anxiety flowing from the global strategic situation are reproduced in microcosm by William's terrorising of Bobbi and Melinda. Impotent in public life, he acts out an excessive display of bellicose potency in his private life, seeking to 'contain' Bobbi and Melinda, and force them to stay with him, thus shattering the security to which he aspires through his family. This consequence of digging in (reproducing in a supposedly private space the insecurities that retreat from an exterior world was meant to eradicate) appears elsewhere in fiction with dimensions of nuclear anxiety. In *The Book of Daniel* (1971), for instance, Daniel feels effectively debarred from political engagement: as a son of the Rosenbergs / Isaacsons any involvement with radical resistance will be taken as confirmation of his parents' guilt; yet not to resist is to acquiesce to the status quo. Thus impotent, he terrorises his wife and son, threatening to burn the former with a car cigarette lighter, and taking a game with the latter to extremes, throwing him higher and higher into the air until he is terrified.[19]

Much as digging in promises safety, then, sealing off the 'natural' family unit from malign outside influences, it actually reinscribes contemporary social fractures *within* the domestic setting. It is significant that William's ambitions for his shelter are for a family space reproducing the idealised suburban family home:

> I'll line the walls with concrete, put on a roof of solid steel. . . . Install . . . wall-to-wall carpeting. A family room, a pine-paneled den, two bedrooms, lots of closet space, maybe a greenhouse bathed in artificial sunlight, maybe a Ping-Pong table and a piano, the latest appliances, track lighting and a microwave oven and all the little extras that make for comfort and domestic tranquillity. It'll be home.[20]

These shelter plans are reminiscent, in their emphasis on suburban family living, of the Carlson family shelter featured in *Life* in 1961, and discussed in chapter four. With one exception – the steel lining – William's idealised shelter is the 1950s suburban home, the source of many Americans' aspirations, updated for the 1980s. The steel lining makes all the difference. To William it makes the space safe, sealing the family from threatening physical and social forces. Yet, of course, it is actually the steel lining that makes it most insecure, destroying the family dynamic he is attempting to preserve. Far from resolving domestic problems, digging the shelter exacerbates them; indeed, it is the excessive demand for security that has produced them. The impossibility of creating this safe domestic space, impermeable to outside threats, is emphasised by the discrepancy between William's dreams and the reality of his efforts: far from the cosy family room he imagines, his shelter remains a muddy hole in the ground.

The novel therefore presents digging in as unsuccessful. It cannot save the family from nuclear war; it cannot prevent the family from breaking up. However, the alternative, going underground, has equally ambiguous outcomes in the novel.

Going underground

Political engagement is always problematic in nuclear-anxious literature. Opposition to nuclear armament was rendered particularly difficult through the normal channels of party politics in the United States, because neither Republicans nor Democrats argued for disarmament during the Cold War, leaving only pressure groups to make the case to mainstream politicians. For William, permanently anxious about nuclear war and convinced most people are unable fully to comprehend the threat it poses, there is no obvious outlet for his concerns.

What is available, instead, is a form of political dissidence located in the margins of society and coalescing, in William's case, in the group that forms around him during campus protests against the Vietnam War. Their increasing radicalisation, and their adoption of violent tactics, makes them reminiscent of the Weathermen, the splinter group from Students for a Democratic Society, who employed terrorist tactics as a means of resisting the state. Indeed, the analogy with the Weathermen is made clear in a rather circumlocutory fashion when Ebenezer, part of the resistance network to which William's comrades sign up, says, 'Hurricane season. . . . Stormy climate, kiddies, that's what the Weatherman tells me.'[21]

Unwilling to get involved in violent resistance, less for ethical reasons than for the terror he experiences in situations of personal jeopardy, William finds himself increasingly marginalized. His splitting off is represented in the novel as an embrace of domesticity, and another metaphorical digging in. While his comrades plan terrorist activities, he adopts a role socially defined as feminine, making sandwiches, cleaning and watching game shows on television.[22] In a damning statement that links his political cowardice to sexual failures, Sarah issues an 'Emancipation Proclamation' on him: 'you can't get it up – conscience-wise, pecker-wise – can't perform'.[23] In contrast, Sarah pledges herself to violent protest that, among other things, offers her a way to resist the strong pull of the domestic ideal: 'Part of me wants to run away. . . . Have babies and clip coupons.'[24]

Marrying Bobbi and fathering Melinda allow William to reclaim his masculinity in a way that reaffirms, rather than challenges, socially validated visions of normalcy. As May comments, with foreign policy articulated in sexualised terms as the assertion of masculine power, '[h]usbands, especially fathers, wore the badge of "family man" as a sign of virility and patriotism.'[25] Yet this is another self-deception, and the contradictions within the idealised nuclear family inevitably emerge, leaving William emasculated again. Forced physically to constrain his wife and daughter to prevent them leaving him, William has, as a consequence of this show of violent masculine strength, to take on the chores they would otherwise do, adopting a role socially defined as that of the female homemaker: 'I find comfort in vacuuming the living-room rug. I'm domestic. I have duties. I dust furniture, defrost the refrigerator, scrub the kitchen floor. Ajax, I think, the foaming cleanser . . . I sing it.'[26] The singing of the jingle from the commercial reveals the extent to which William is subject to ideals of domesticity which align with the broader consumerism of United States society during the second half of the twentieth century. As chapter four discussed, family life, material wealth and the increasing number of consumer products designed to clean and sterilise the home seemed to offer security from outside threat, yet were unable so to do. There are echoes here of the immunity Babette, in Don DeLillo's *White Noise* (1984), associates with the wealthy families whose children attend her husband, Jack's, college, and which she expresses when she says that she has 'trouble imagining death at that income level'.[27]

William's happy immersion in commodified and domestic culture is in stark contrast to the possibilities for revealing the true insecurities of Cold War life that his earlier protests seemed to offer. As he stood in the student canteen in 1964 with his sign asserting the reality of the bombs, he was soon joined by Sarah, whose comment, '[w]hat this brings to mind . . . is shit. . . . Such true shit' is in keeping with the novel's broader preoccupation with the symbolically loaded relations between cleanliness and dirt. The repetition of 'shit', and its association with truth, bring to mind the muddy hole William digs for his shelter ('[s]afety can be very messy') and his insistence that a dirty, threatening political reality is hidden by the seemingly spotless domestic environment.[28] When his daughter comes to see the shelter he is digging, she will not let him pick her up because he is dirty, and he has to lead her by the hand into the home which 'smells of Windex and wax'.[29] As a child, William's mother is similarly associated with clean domestic environments when she asks him to forget his nuclear terrors and concentrate on getting to college: 'My mother vacuumed the living-room rug, dusted furniture, washed windows, told me to buckle down to my schoolwork.'[30] In all these instances, the domestic ideal, commercialised by the consumer items flooding post-war United States markets and politicised by containment, becomes a psychological 'digging in', a retreat from a threatening external environment.

William's attempts to maintain a focus on the dirty realities of the Cold War nuclear threat, and to respond appropriately, are repeatedly frustrated. His friends, less compromised by fear than he is, also fail: they are eventually killed when security forces catch up with them.

The novel therefore poses a key political question: how do you resist a Cold War culture that brooks no resistance? It is not that peaceful resistance in the United States was impossible (quite the opposite; for all the nefarious means by which the status quo was maintained in the United States it allowed scope for a freedom of expression impossible in many other countries). Rather, it is that resistance to the Cold War nuclear standoff was difficult for four main reasons. First, as noted above, neither of the mainstream political parties offered a consistently articulated interrogation of the terms on which the Cold War was played out.

Second, there was a problem of abstraction (a problem that also affected the environmental movements discussed in the last chapter): real though the threat of nuclear war was, there was also a strange intangibility to it – its effects could not be directly experienced until it was too late. This is William's repeated frustration, apparent from his earliest protests that the 'BOMBS ARE REAL'.

Third, the scale not only of the destruction threatened by nuclear war, but also of the greater organisational architecture of the Cold War, were so overwhelming that they made resistance seem futile. The systems, bureaucracies and hardware of the Cold War were too powerful, too impenetrable, to appear malleable to change by individual action. Indeed, open resistance seemed likely only to bring crushing defeat. Thinking about the personal catastrophe of losing Sarah to someone else, William muses, '[n]ever underestimate the power of power. Never take chances. Because you end up getting smashed. Every time – crushed.'[31] This articulates a felt emasculation that applies equally to William's engagement with public life, as to the specifics of his personal relationships.

Finally, like most discourses those of the Cold War exercised their ideological power largely by becoming internalised – hence William's continual reappropriation by systems and concepts outside of which he tries to step. He tries, for instance, to challenge the definition of sanity and insanity in order to articulate an alternative position: 'If you're sane, you're scared; if you're scared, you dig; if you dig, you deviate.'[32] But his 'deviation' is really just a more extreme conformity. He might be dissenting from the widespread denial necessary to live with the nuclear threat, but he is not challenging meaningfully the system that produces that threat: he does not campaign for disarmament; he does not participate in constructive political action; he does not even follow the path of radical resistance; he simply throws himself into domestic 'containment' and digs in.

While William remains politically marginalized, the text itself does at least draw attention to the subtle operations of Cold War ideologies. As a nuclear anxiety text, it engages with, and draws attention to, the psychological and political compromises necessary to live life with the nuclear threat and therefore serves to make visible what otherwise runs the risk of being suppressed. Importantly, the resolution offered at the end, in which William retracts his threat to murder his family, and vows to ignore his fear and live an ordinary middle-class existence, is shown to be false. Bobbi and Melinda surely, given what has gone before, will not be with William for long and the family security he seeks cannot be regained. Furthermore, living an ordinary life ('I will firm up my golf game and invest wisely and adhere to the conventions of decency and good grace') seems, in the context of the nuclear realities to which William has drawn our attention, to be as much of a denial, as much of a hole in which to hide, as the shelter he was digging in the garden.[33]

The politics of the text are, therefore, not so much apparent in outright opposition to Cold War nuclear armament, nor in effective advocacy of specific political action. They are, rather, present in an exposure of the manifold social and psychological impacts of nuclear anxiety. William is a caricature, an exaggerated nuclear obsessive, but he serves to draw attention to a more broadly and subtly experienced nuclear anxiety.

While representation of nuclear anxiety as directly as that in *The Nuclear Age* is rare, in texts which have nuclear-anxious dimensions to them there is often a similar sense of impotence to that experienced by William. I have already noted how Daniel in *The Book of Daniel* is rendered impotent in the novel. His sister, Susan, takes another course, throwing herself more fully into radical protest, but finally committing suicide after being incarcerated in an insane asylum. Slothrop, in Thomas Pynchon's *Gravity's Rainbow* (1973), ends up purely passive. Actively running all over the 'Zone' of Western Europe, he is nevertheless always at the whim of larger forces. So profoundly do these forces challenge his subjectivity that he simply disappears from the novel, '[s]cattered all over the Zone'.[34] Although Tayo, in Leslie Marmon Silko's *Ceremony* (1977), finds redemption through his enactment of his people's ceremonies, he too suffers a breakdown, and the novel charts the disintegration of his people's identity in the face of a culture that is in part defined as nuclear. In Don DeLillo's *End Zone* (1972), it is never likely that Gary will resist, and he suffers a similar fate to other characters sucked into obsessive contemplation of the nuclear dimensions of Cold War politics: he suffers a psychological breakdown.

Frequently male (they are almost entirely, though not exclusively, male – hence the focus on 'impotence' as an expression of lack of power is appropriate), protagonists are in these texts asocial, alienated and outside the normalising boundaries of family. Nor are there often convincing alternative social structures of political resistance. The impact of the Cold War is figured in terms of fragmentation – fission not fusion. Rather than being brought together by the common threat, these protagonists remain isolated, the possibilities for resistance exploded into their constituent elements. Terrified, incapable of conceiving of effective struggle, complicit with the systems from which they dissent, and compensating for their political emasculation with sadistic actions against those near to them, they offer a starkly dispiriting outlook for the possibilities of political change. Although one does not directly produce the other, nuclear suspense, in these cases, has a corollary in political suspension. Instead of active resistance to neutralise the nuclear threat, individuals are shown to be paralysed, frozen within structures of power the scale of which they cannot fully comprehend and for which, indeed, they are themselves culpable.

The end of the Cold War, and with it the end (or at least deferment) of the long-sustained possibility of all-out global nuclear war, changed the political and cultural context in which nuclear technology functioned. Most notably, it brought the end of the suspense which has, throughout this book, been taken as a determining factor in the production and representation of nuclear anxiety. However, it did not of course remove nuclear technology, and nor did the anxieties this technology had engendered simply vanish. In the final chapter of this book, I turn to this post-Cold War environment and suggest ways in which we might understand the developing cultural impact of nuclear technology after the Cold War and into the twenty-first century.

Notes

1 Quoted in Elaine Tyler May, *Homeward Bound: American Families in the Cold War Era*, 2nd ed. (New York: Basic Books, 1999), p. 190. The letter is dated 13 November 1963.

2 May, *Homeward Bound*, p. 190.

3 May, *Homeward Bound*, p. 164.

4 May, *Homeward Bound*, p. 167.

5 Nevil Shute, *On the Beach* (Yorkshire: House of Stratus, 2000), p. 81, p. 285.

6 Shute, *On the Beach*, p. 244.

7 Tim O'Brien, *The Nuclear Age* (London: Flamingo, 1987), p. 74.

8 O'Brien, *Nuclear Age*, p. 74.

9 For the first, and most well known, formulation of postmodernism as 'incredulity toward grand narratives', see Jean-François Lyotard, trans. Geoff Bennington and Brian Massumi, *The Postmodern Condition: A Report on Knowledge* (Manchester: Manchester University Press, 1986).

10 Linda Hutcheon, *The Politics of Postmodernism* (London: Routledge, 1989), pp. 1–2.

11 I have dealt with this elsewhere and some of the following material appears, in other forms, in 'In Dreams, In Imagination: Suspense, Anxiety and the Cold War in Tim O'Brien's *The Nuclear Age*', *Critical Survey* 19:2 (2007), forthcoming; 'Beyond the Apocalypse of Closure: Nuclear Anxiety in Postmodern Literature of the United States', in Andrew Hammond (ed.), *Cold War Literature: Writing the Global Conflict, 1945–1989* (London: Routledge, 2006), pp. 63–77.

12 Jacqueline Foertsch, 'Not bombshells but basketcases: gendered illness in nuclear texts', *Studies in the Novel* 31:4 (1999), p. 477. See also Foertsch's discussion of O'Brien in her book, *The Cold War and the AIDS Crisis in Literature, Film, and Culture* (Urbana: University of Illinois Press, 2001), pp. 147–9. The humble status of *The Nuclear Age* in the first wave of nuclear criticism is indicated by the fact that it is noted only in passing by Weart and that Dowling only devotes a page of writing to it (although it should be noted that the foci of these studies would make the novel less obviously interesting to them than other texts). Spencer R. Weart, *Nuclear Fear: A History of Images* (Cambridge: Harvard University Press, 1988), p. 415. David Dowling, *Fictions of Nuclear Disaster* (London: Macmillan, 1987), p. 191.

13 Mark A. Herbele, *A Trauma Artist: Tim O'Brien and the Fiction of Vietnam* (Iowa: University of Iowa Press, 2001), p. 297.

14 O'Brien, *Nuclear Age*, p. 8.

15 O'Brien, *Nuclear Age*, p. 200.

16 O'Brien, *Nuclear Age*, p. 15, p. 38.

17 O'Brien, *Nuclear Age*, p. 23, p. 41, p. 33.

18 O'Brien, *Nuclear Age*, p. 11.

19 E. L. Doctorow, *The Book of Daniel* (London: Picador, 1982), p. 74, p. 62, pp. 135–6.

20 O'Brien, *Nuclear Age*, p. 7.

21 O'Brien, *Nuclear Age*, p. 214. The Weathermen took their name from a Bob Dylan lyric in 'Subterranean Homesick Blues' (1965): 'You don't need a weather man / To know which way the wind blows.'

22 O'Brien, *Nuclear Age*, pp. 214–15.

23 O'Brien, *Nuclear Age*, p. 213.

24 O'Brien, *Nuclear Age*, p. 172.

25 May, *Homeward Bound*, p. 86.
26 O'Brien, *Nuclear Age*, p. 130. O'Brien's ellipses.
27 Don DeLillo, *White Noise* (London: Picador, 1986), p. 6.
28 O'Brien, *Nuclear Age*, p. 75, p. 6.
29 O'Brien, *Nuclear Age*, p. 6.
30 O'Brien, *Nuclear Age*, p. 38.
31 O'Brien, *Nuclear Age*, p. 92.
32 O'Brien, *Nuclear Age*, p. 200.
33 O'Brien, *Nuclear Age*, p. 312.
34 Thomas Pynchon, *Gravity's Rainbow* (London: Picador, 1975), p. 712.

7

Conclusion and epilogue: the legacies of the first atomic age

[I]f you read the newspapers and the headlines in *Time* and *Newsweek*, it [the 1950s] looks like a really scary time, but in person it was very exciting. You were caught up in this consumer boom – maybe because it was too unthinkable – that the world would ever . . . I mean, I think this is more of a guy thing, but there was a feeling that the atomic bomb was really . . . neat. (Bill Bryson, interview, 2006)

I never thought of the atomic bomb as 'kind of neat'. I was terrified. . . . At nine, I was sure my days were numbered, and I resented all of adulthood for taking my future from me. (Gary Wilson, letter in response to Bryson's interview, 2006)[1]

Any attempt to discuss half a century's cultural response to something with such a broad-reaching impact as nuclear technology faces a number of pitfalls. As the viewpoints quoted above demonstrate, even a decade that seemed as culturally homogenous as the 1950s can produce entirely opposing retrospective assessments. How much more diverse still are the reactions when we factor in developments over a number of decades, the varying impacts of class, gender, race, geographical location and age, as well as variations between individuals that cannot easily be accounted for by their social locations.

Many approaches to nuclear culture have restricted their range of reference, and where they have done so they have tended to home in on the early and high Cold War periods. This makes a lot of sense. The first decade and a half of the Cold War provide a fecund site for analysing atomic culture – it was the era in which nuclear issues were most obviously part of public discourse (although a similar claim might be made for the 1980s) – and, thus focused, such studies tend to be reasonably comprehensive in their analyses of the material they discuss. However, there is also a place for more wide-ranging, and necessarily more speculative, analyses.

The extended view is important because the building of the atomic bomb, and its emergence into a world that swiftly fractured along Cold War fault-lines, had long-term consequences. Although nuclear technology, both military and civilian, was less frequently a publicly discussed issue in the 1960s and 1970s, the cultural terms of reference established earlier in the Cold War continued to have an effect (indeed, it is for this reason that most of the preceding chapters include discussion of early as well as later Cold War texts: the latter emerged from the cultural matrix within which the former operated).

As the brief survey of developments since 1945 in the introduction will have made clear, cultural and psychological responses to nuclear anxiety were not static. Despite this, it is nevertheless worth asking what the various periods of the Cold War had in common. While nuclear weapons might or might not have been responsible for keeping the peace between NATO and Warsaw Pact forces for half a century, throughout the Cold War they defined the most terrible possible consequences of a projected war. Once the Soviet Union got the bomb, it was not long before any use of the weapon in conflict carried the possibility of escalating into all-out nuclear war. For all the changes in culture until 1989, for all the shifting contours of geopolitical alliances and rivalries, and for all the other more immediate struggles and experiences of people in this period, nuclear weapons induced a sense of stasis. They placed people's lives in a period of sustained suspension before a possible calamity. The Cold War period was many things at many times; it was always, to a greater or lesser degree, a state of suspense. A crucial factor in the production of this suspense and its cultural ramifications was one of the defining technologies of the period: nuclear weaponry (and, to a lesser extent, civilian nuclear energy technologies).

Choosing to focus on a much less tightly defined body of material is therefore a conscious attempt to broach this sense of Cold War nuclear anxiety as sustained and ongoing: nuclear weapons did not simply cease to have a psychological and cultural impact when they dropped down the public agenda after the Cuban crisis had safely passed. In spite of the difficulties thrown up by such a critical choice (the impossibility of being comprehensive; the necessity for a more speculative style of discussion; a focus on broad patterns of continuities between texts rather than an extended analysis of the specific cultural locations out of which each comes), it is therefore hoped that the choice to zoom out from detail shots of specific cultural moments, to a long shot of the Cold War period, has been productive, and might complement the excellent body of more specifically focused critical works.

In taking this long view, Bryson's comment that he did not feel scared, 'maybe because it [nuclear war] was too unthinkable', provides a clue to what at times during the Cold War was a seemingly muted cultural response. Nuclear war was unthinkable in at least three ways. Despite direct experience of atomic attack at Hiroshima and Nagasaki, it was only possible imperfectly to model the consequences of a broader nuclear conflict: the ecological, social and psychological fallout from multiple nuclear explosions defeated the imagination. It was also unthinkable because it was morally reprehensible: a willed human catastrophe on an unprecedented scale. Finally, and perhaps most significantly, it was unthinkable because very often it seemed so intangible: 'real' life, with its intellectual and emotional experiences, its hopes and frustrations, its joys and sufferings, was going on all the time, all around. It could be touched and felt and acted upon. The thought of its absolute negation, and the imposition of an entirely other reality, was frequently too uncomfortable to contemplate and always difficult to conceive.

Yet the unthinkable nature of post-holocaust reality did not mean that people were unaware of it, nor that they did not try to think it through with imaginative approximations of what it would involve. One way of thinking it through was to imagine it in terms of grand spectacles of horror, as in Jonathan Schell's attempt to forecast the impact of nuclear war in *The Fate of the Earth* (1982). Another was to focus on its impact on a family or a single community, as in Judith Merril's *Shadow on the Hearth* (1950), Philip Wylie's *Tomorrow!* (1954) or Pat Frank's *Alas, Babylon* (1959). Another was to turn it into a black comedy of the absurd, as in Kurt Vonnegut's *Cat's Cradle* (1963) or Stanley Kubrick's film, *Dr Strangelove* (1963). Yet another was to imagine it as part of a cycle of destruction and creation of civilisation as in Walter Miller's *A Canticle for Leibowitz* (1959) or Russell Hoban's *Riddley Walker* (1980). Yet another way was to try to create the sense of absence, of what would be gone, as in the empty city streets of Nevil Shute's *On the Beach* (1957).

Bryson himself clearly was aware of the bomb, and the chapter, 'Boom', of his memoir of childhood in the fifties, *The Life and Times of the Thunderbolt Kid* (2006), reveals a more complex response than his more blasé comment in the interview quoted above might suggest.[2] This is not to claim that he had a childhood blighted by fear of the bomb despite his assertions to the contrary, nor to deny that part of the complex cultural reaction to nuclear technology was that it was pretty 'neat'. Nuclear technology, for all the destruction it made possible, was also one of many seeming miracles of scientific and technological achievement. Nor was the destruction it could produce simply reviled: there was something alluring about absolute and sudden change to the world as the long tradition of 'last man' (men very often were their protagonists) texts, including Mary Shelley's *The Last Man* (1826) and M. P. Shiel's *The Purple Cloud* (1901), reveal.

It is because global nuclear war was both 'unthinkable' and, as a possible future for the world – the insecurity on which the world's security was based – a pressing issue, that I have taken nuclear anxiety as my subject in this book. I have not sought to claim, in line with the most extreme reading of Robert Lifton's 'psychic numbing' hypothesis discussed in chapter two, that everyone was psychologically damaged, whether they knew it or not, by the threat of world-ending war. However, Lifton's theory is useful in that it describes convincingly the sense in which it was generally easier not to think about nuclear war directly. Rather, nuclear realities were more frequently on the edges of consciousness, haunting contemporary reality. The shape of these realities was produced by the very specific strategic situation which moved fairly rapidly, even before it was named as such, toward Mutual Assured Destruction. In the United States, it was further inflected, at an early stage of its development (and thus with lasting significance) by extensive discourse about civil defence, by paranoia about communist influence within the country and by a culture that was centred on the domestic ideal and which generally embraced therapeutic, seemingly apolitical, adjustment rather than political action to tackle dissatisfaction (although by the 1960s the illusion of political consensus had begun to crumble).

By shifting the focus when we read conventional nuclear texts from the iconography of disaster, to their expression of an underlying state of suspense – the empty streets of *On the Beach*; the waiting within the home of *Shadow on the Hearth* – we can unearth a sense of lurking nuclear anxiety. This gives access to a more nebulous Cold War unease, rather than representing the period as one in which consciousness was dominated by sustained fear.

We can also find this focus by moving beyond texts like these. If there were nuclear dimensions to everyday reality after 1945, as there were, then their impact should be, and indeed is, felt in broader expressions of Cold War reality. It is in the asides about, the passing references to, and the indirect expressions of nuclear issues that nuclear anxiety's presence within the culture is most accurately charted. The more tangential representations of nuclear reality in postmodern texts like Thomas Pynchon's *Gravity's Rainbow* (1973), Leslie Marmon Silko's *Ceremony* (1977), Don DeLillo's *White Noise* (1984) and *End Zone* (1972), Robert Coover's *The Public Burning* (1976) and *The Origin of the Brunists* (1966), Jayne Anne Phillips' *Machine Dreams* (1984) and Paul Auster's *In the Country of Last Things* (1987), should therefore be considered equally valuable indicators of nuclear consciousness as those appearing in more directly nuclear texts.

Accurate understanding of culture in the second half of the twentieth century requires an appreciation of the subtle and wide-ranging impacts of nuclear technology and, while it is impossible to deal comprehensively with such a widespread nuclear culture, it is possible to make inroads by concentrating on the relevant motifs that link seemingly disparate texts. Nuclear weapons set the template for the confrontation between the United States and the Soviet Union, but they also established a context, as to a lesser extent did nuclear energy, for hopes, fears and debates that animated the Cold War period. Crucially, they established the possibility of the termination of culture and civilisation, and thus transformed conceptions of the future.

Yet, as well as these dramatic effects, they also had more subtle ones. Alan Nadel's and Elaine Tyler May's landmark analyses of 'containment culture' are important for the light they shed on the relations between foreign policy and domestic life. By showing discourses relating to self and home originating in Cold War contexts, they set up the possibility for an analysis of literary texts that understands their representations of domesticity to be linked to broad geopolitical circumstances. Although Nadel's and May's analyses focus on the early and high Cold War periods, subsequent cultures are largely the product of the 'fallout' from these earlier ones. As Nadel suggests, much of the energy of postmodernism comes from the instabilities inherent in the culture of the first decade and a half of the Cold War.

In providing the framework for foreign policy, and for competition between the superpowers, nuclear technology was a crucial component in the genesis and persistence of containment. One legacy of the first atomic age should, then, be a desire to make sense of the nuclear dimensions of Cold War culture. As chapter one suggested, although the largest output of criticism on this subject appeared from the mid-1980s to the mid-1990s, there is an important role for a contemporary nuclear criticism. It is vital to our appreciation of literature and culture from 1945 to 1989 that nuclear issues are not simply relegated to the margins and seen as inevitably less important than more frequently discussed topics. Indeed, they should not be seen as separate from them: 'containment' culture and its legacies suggest that we cannot simply bracket off nuclear consciousness from more palpably experienced principles of social organisation.

Another topic for a contemporary nuclear criticism is the persistence of a literary and cultural legacy from the first atomic age into the contemporary period, which might be considered to be a second atomic age. Central to such an understanding must be the realisation that we have an atomic consciousness. The perception of reality produced by our awareness of atomic science and technology cannot simply cease because the Cold War has passed. In particular, our relation to the world is fundamentally changed by our ability rapidly to destroy it even if, with the bipolar confrontation of the Cold War a thing of the past, such an outcome seems no longer to be imminent (although the continued newsworthiness of adjustments to the *Bulletin of Atomic Scientists*' 'Doomsday Clock' suggests the idea of nuclear holocaust has not become entirely unthinkable).[3] We might also usefully look for continuities between the deployment of terror in Cold War nuclear strategy, and the function of anxiety in the contemporary 'War on Terror'. The Cold War was intrinsically different, politically and culturally, but it was not entirely other to post-Cold War experience.

It is to some of these legacies and continuities that the remainder of this chapter turns, by way of providing an epilogue to the preceding discussion which has concentrated on the Cold War. As with earlier discussions, it seeks to be suggestive rather than comprehensive, proposing two avenues for exploring the continuing literary and cultural legacy of the first atomic age: the retrospective literary treatment of the Cold War, and the persistence in contemporary literature of nuclear motifs and concerns from earlier periods.

Literary reassessments of the Cold War: 'the bombs were not released'

Chapter two closed with a brief discussion of Douglas Coupland's short story, 'The Wrong Sun' (1994), arguing that it could usefully be read as a coda to the Cold War. As an overt expression of the state of suspense, of continually deferred expectation of nuclear attack, it retrospectively identified anxiety as a defining Cold War state of mind. Notwithstanding Tim O'Brien's *The Nuclear Age* (1985), it is perhaps in post-Cold War literature that the states of suspense of nuclear consciousness have been most directly explored.

During the Cold War, when nuclear issues were overtly broached, the tendency was to look forward to what might happen if open conflict between the United States and the Soviet Union broke out. This was the really pressing issue: if it had happened it would have been the defining, if terminal, feature of the struggle. Since the end of the Cold War, though, and looking back on it, nuclear conflict itself cannot be seen as definitive for it did not happen; it is, instead, expectation of that conflict which must now be seen as the defining experience of the period. When nuclear issues are now broached then (and there is a remarkable tendency to forget them, as if the anxieties of the past cannot match those of the present), the focus is more naturally on the experience of living with unfulfilled expectation of nuclear war; on, essentially, things not happening.

Don DeLillo's marvellous evocation of the second half of the twentieth century in *Underworld* (1997) is a case in point. Where it deals with nuclear issues, it is concerned more with nuclear anxiety than with nuclear explosion. Klara Sax's post-Cold War art project, 230 military airplanes arranged together in the desert, 'painted to remark the end of an age and the beginning of something so different only a vision such as this might suffice to augur it', are, she says, meaningful because 'we haven't actually fought a war this time. We have a number of postwar conditions without a war having been fought.' She comments in an interview on the planes: 'But the bombs were not released. You see. The missiles remained in the underwing carriages, unfired.'[4] The aircraft are emblematic of a war threatened but not delivered. They define the era precisely because they have not been used. Nick reiterates this point later in the book: 'But the bombs were not released. . . . The missiles remained in the rotary launchers. The men came back and the cities were not destroyed.'[5]

Retrospectively, the Cold War is defined by a sense of anticlimax: after all the build up there was no nuclear conflagration. When Nick eventually witnesses a nuclear explosion, it is in the former Soviet Union, and is an act not of war but of underground waste disposal. The sense of letdown is palpable: 'No ascending cloudmass, of course, or rolling waves of sound. Maybe some dust rises from the site and maybe it is only afternoon haze and several people point and comment briefly and there is a flatness in the group, an unspoken dejection, and after a while we go back inside.'[6] The rhythm of this sentence, produced by the repetition of the conjunction – 'and . . . and . . . and . . . and . . . and' – is indicative of a measure of time that does not move toward a conclusion. Unlike the expected doom of the Cold War period, this nuclear explosion exists merely as a bland continuation from the past into the future, moving toward neither telos nor climax.

If retrospectively the nuclear dimensions of the Cold War are defined in the book in terms of what did not happen, the episodes during the Cold War are represented in ways consistent with the motifs of nuclear anxiety I identified in chapter one. Rather than dominating life as an explicit fear, the nuclear context instead suffuses contemporary reality. It is part of everyday Cold War experience, breaking into conscious thought only sporadically. For instance, when news that the Russians have the bomb arrives, it briefly worries Cotter's mother before being pushed into the background by tangible physical sensations: 'I got worked up [about the news of the bomb] until I started up the stairs with those shopping bags. Thought I was going to pull my shoulder out of the socket.'[7] Although there are episodes directly concerned with the bomb (the Cuban crisis; Matty's work in weapons testing), it is more generally that the nuclear context is part of the 'underworld' of the novel, its traces more commonly apparent in the ephemera of the everyday. They are there, for instance, in the fluoroscopes used by shoe shops to picture children's feet, the safety of which Matty wonders about in retrospect; in a library in the Bronx named after Enrico Fermi; in a landfill site suspected to contain bomb waste; in an aircraft carrier that Nick sees sailing toward the Golden Gate bridge; in a street preacher talking of the coming apocalypse; and in the description of a moment as 'nuclear-packed with information'.[8] Nuclear reality, rather like the fallout shelter signs featuring in a Lenny Bruce skit ('Those yellow and black signs you've been seeing everywhere but never really noticed until six days ago'),[9] only registers in people's consciousness at the time of the Cuban crisis, and is described as generally so commonplace as to be unremarked upon. The nuclear reality for which these various incidents stand as signifiers only becomes apparent, only begins to be signified, when we seek their common root.

In chapter one I noted how in Thomas Pynchon's *Vineland* (1990) an alternative, secret United States was shown to be coded into the more readily acknowledged one, in the form of a hidden freeway designed as an evacuation route in anticipation of nuclear war. So, in *Underworld*'s depiction of the secret military installations in which Matty works, there is a United States concealed both by cartographic representations of the country, and in a surface architecture that is similarly blank, designed not to signify the reality underneath: 'white places on your map . . . the flats were map-white, on the page and in living fact, and a few low buildings . . . service[d] the underground operation in the Pocket, where weapons were conceived and designed'.[10] The 'white places' of both map and ground speak most profoundly through their apparent absence of signification; similarly, the novel shows Cold War consciousness of the nuclear threat, and of its attendant anxiety, to be repressed, surfacing in brief, cryptic traces and becoming meaningfully present only in the book's retrospective representation of the period.

The novel makes other familiar Cold War connections. I noted in chapter one that it invoked an agoraphobic sense of a threatening sky, and Matty's consequent preference for small, seemingly safe spaces. It also draws upon the idea of the family as offering psychological security in a dangerous, uncertain world. Janet, for instance, presents her desire to have children in precisely these terms: 'I want to have a child. . . . I want to be safe, Matthew.'[11] Yet the family is also shown to be permeable to threatening external environments, as in the densely suggestive portrayal of family life in the section, 'October 8, 1957', in which Erica Deming's unease in her suburban home is connected to various Cold War threats, most notably Sputnik, orbiting above, but also her son's emerging sexuality (as she does the dishes, he masturbates upstairs into a condom that reminds him of his 'favorite weapons system') and the more general permeability of her house and body to contaminants.[12]

Waste and contamination feature prominently, and are linked both to the radioactive fallout of nuclear explosions and concerns about nefarious communist influence. Sister Edgar, a 'cold war nun', is obsessive about cleanliness, putting on latex gloves that provide '[p]rotection against the spurt of blood or pus and the viral entities hidden within, submicroscopic parasites in their soviet socialist protein coats.'[13] In a Lenny Bruce routine, a woman listens to Kennedy talking on the television about 'swift and extraordinary buildup' and thinks it refers to grease in her oven rather than Soviet missiles in Cuba.[14] J. Edgar Hoover is portrayed as obsessed by cleanliness, getting a workspace built that is a 'white room manned by white-clad technicians, preferably white themselves, who would work in an environment completely free of contaminants, dust, bacteria and so on'.[15] Like William in *The Nuclear* Age, he dreams of being interred in a lead-lined coffin to protect him from 'worms, germs, moles, voles and vandals. . . . To keep him safe from nuclear war.'[16] In another echo of *The Nuclear Age*, where the home is described as an environment of 'Windex and wax', and of *The House in the Middle*, where cleaning the domestic environment is crucial, Nick finds, at a bomb test site in the former Soviet Union, American cleaning products on the shelves of houses built to test the effects of nuclear explosion: 'Old Dutch Cleanser and Rinso White, all those half-lost icons of the old life'.[17] Nick's nostalgic reaction can be read as a broader yearning, in the novel, for the lost world of the Cold War.

Underworld contains, then, a sequence of motifs relating to nuclear technology and anxiety that it inherits from Cold War culture. If anything, nuclear states of mind, the psychological and cultural articulation of nuclear realities, are more explicit in *Underworld* than they are in all but a few Cold War texts. The Cold War is defined as unfought (though not without casualties), a crucial distinction from earlier literature which could only define the Cold War as thus far unfought. Hence, it is not nuclear holocaust, but its possibility, that is definitive of the era.

Underworld is perhaps exceptional for the degree to which it makes nuclear issues a central subject in its representation of the United States in the second half of the twentieth century. However, it is by no means the only novel to perceive their importance. In Philip Roth's *American Pastoral* (1997), similarly applying itself to the grand project of making sense of United States culture during the Cold War, nuclear issues, though more muted, are present. When the narrator imagines giving a speech at a reunion of his classmates, he identifies the post-war mood as one of optimism related in part to the country's nuclear power: 'Let's remember the energy. Americans were governing not only themselves but some two hundred million people in Italy, Austria, Germany, and Japan. The war crimes trials were cleansing the earth of its devils once and for all. Atomic power was ours alone.'[18]

The novel's story, about the collapse of a seemingly perfect family, when Merry, the daughter of 'the Swede' and Dawn Levov, a high school sports champion and a former Miss New Jersey, '[b]rought the war home to Lyndon Johnson' by blowing up a rural post office,[19] is a complex interrogation of a long-standing United States theme: the corruption of the American dream – the replacement of the 'American pastoral' by the 'American berserk' ('the fury, the violence, and the desperation of the counterpastoral').[20] Although it is Vietnam that explodes most forcibly into the lives of the Levovs, the destructive forces of the American berserk are articulated, in part, through tropes that resonate with the nuclear culture discussed in previous chapters. The basement of the Levovs' house is described as being 'as technologically up-to-date as a nuclear submarine',[21] and it is powerful subterranean energies erupting within the family home that destroy the American pastoral of the novel's title.

In the midst of a family meal, the image of a 'monk going up in flames' intrudes from a half-watched news programme, and Merry is 'terrified for weeks afterward, crying about what had appeared on the television that night, talking about it, awakened from her sleep by dreaming about it'.[22] The explosive nuclear anxieties and energies in the home, familiar from Merril's *Shadow on the Hearth* and O'Brien's *The Nuclear Age*, are similarly present here.

While *American Pastoral* is not about a nuclear United States *per se*, it uses images identical with those of nuclear texts, particularly that of the destroyed home, to produce its central revelation: the discovery by the Swede's generation that everything by which they live is ephemeral; the confidence of a generation for whom atomic power was 'ours alone' is shown to be misplaced. Unsettled by the fragility of his family, like William in *The Nuclear Age* the Swede 'digs in', making love to his mistress 'like a person taking cover, digging in, a big male body hiding, a man disappearing'.[23]

Just as atomic technology functioned in part as a system of signification through which social stresses were articulated, so the truth Merry brings home to the Swede is in the end not about the Vietnam War itself. The 'war' is within the home, a disturbing domestic insecurity: 'He had thought most of it was order and only a little of it disorder. He'd had it backwards. . . . It was not the specific war that she'd had in mind, but it was a war, nonetheless, that she brought home to America – home into her very own house.'[24]

The Cold War continues, then, to be the subject of fiction and nuclear tropes persist, sometimes overtly, sometimes much less directly, in contemporary fiction. A new nuclear criticism need not, therefore, apply itself only to those texts published during the Cold War, but might usefully also consider the retrospective fictions through which it is reconstructed.

In addition to these overt attempts to make sense of Cold War culture, though, there are other, more subtle legacies of the first nuclear era. Paul Boyer suggests in relation to *Underworld* that, despite its interest in the cultural consequences of the Cold War, the novel implies that the impact of the East–West nuclear confrontation is 'now history . . . [that can] be grasped imaginatively and summed up novelistically'.[25] In other words, its retrospective perspective presents the Cold War era as closed. Perhaps this reading does not do justice to the ambiguity of DeLillo's text – it does, after all, depict the ongoing and developing post-Cold War lives of its protagonists – but the focus of the novel is certainly weighted toward the Cold War episodes, as it is in *American Pastoral*.

In the final section of this chapter, however, I turn to two novels where the emphasis has shifted to more recent events. Here the connection to earlier periods suggests ongoing cultural legacies of the first nuclear age of a different hue.

'Legacy waste' and 'Atomic World': cultures of anxiety since the Cold War

In Bobbie Ann Mason's novel, *An Atomic Romance* (2005), Reed Futrell, an engineer at a uranium-enrichment plant, reassures his daughter that rumours of contamination are nothing to worry about: 'They're talking about legacy waste, stuff from ages ago. They're cleaning it up. It's safe now.'[26] But the legacies of the Cold War are shown, by the novel, not to be safely dealt with, for the plant where Reed works, 'Atomic World' as he christens it,[27] is shown to be scandalously unsafe. Indeed, there is a continuity with the seemingly bygone era, which extends far beyond the physical contamination left over by the plant's Cold War work.

The novel shows the physical and cultural landscape of the United States to have been permanently changed by its Cold War nuclear past. As in *Underworld*, the contemporary United States is the product of economic, social and cultural nuclear energies. When Reed leaves town on his motorbike to go camping, at the beginning of the novel, he enters what appears to be a wilderness, although the simile used to describe cloud formations ('like fleecy foam insulation blown from a hose') gives a clue to a more industrial origin for this seemingly natural landscape. Sure enough, this is revealed to be an industrial environment – there are Quonset huts and electric towers from the uranium plant – transforming the natural world with which it coexists.[28]

The landscape only remains pure of this context in the careful framing of American experience as natural and authentic in popular cultural myths of the frontier West: 'When Hollywood filmed a frontier drama here, the source of the clouds remained just outside the frame of the Cinerama panoramas. A radiant green extended for miles, and the great mud and might of the river seemed unlimited. Even now . . . you might imagine an untouched old-growth forest.'[29] The industrial, atomic United States has to be edited out in order to maintain the founding national myth of the frontier.

Having drawn our attention to this atomic America, though, the novel does not pretend that we can simply mourn the passing of the frontier or the encroachment of an industrialised world into an imagined pristine landscape. The plant provides important jobs for the community, and *An Atomic Romance* convincingly portrays the mixed feelings of the workforce and their dependants about safety investigations that could destroy the local economy. Nor does the novel suggest that the difficulties at the plant are simply about 'legacy waste', the physical detritus of the Cold War.

Instead there are complex continuities with the past. While there is some consternation at the possibility that nuclear warheads passed through the plant during the Cold War, one of the hopes for the future is that the industry will be revitalised by new military investment, as an exchange between Reed and Jim, his superintendent, suggests:

'And if the D.O.E. comes in here wanting to start up a new phase of production, we can be ready.'

'You're talking nuke talk, Jim.'

Jim grinned. 'If it comes to that, they're going to need us, and toxic waste be damned.'[30]

Reed's complex and contradictory responses to revelations about the plant reproduce the anxieties of the Cold War period. He acknowledges there might be contamination but, at least at first, he convinces himself that it can be isolated: 'Of course the plant had hot spots, but he believed them to be contained.'[31] Yet, as during the Cold War, containment (whether literal containment of a physical threat, or psychological containment of disturbing social and cultural forces) is shown to be impossible. Reed imagines himself contaminated: 'He became conscious of the fillings in his teeth, imagining they were radioactive',[32] and as he works in the 'cascade' he imagines 'hot wind blowing through fissures in his moon suit'.[33]

Nuclear images, notably Cold War in origin, are used to render his current state of mind: a dream that haunts him lingers in his consciousness 'the way strontium-90 in global fallout settled in children's bones'.[34] Civilian and military contexts are conflated, as though neither peace nor war pertain: Reed's father, who once worked at the plant, and his co-workers are described as having 'sacrificed their personal safety for the safety of the country' by their involvement with nuclear energy.[35]

Reed's escape from these pressing worries is to imagine travelling through outer space – he collects images from the Hubble telescope on his computer – but such journeys, as with James Lovelock's response to images from space noted in chapter five, bring him back to a new consideration of the earth. This is partly because physics is a topic of conversation with Julia, a biologist working at the microscopic level, the relationship with whom is the 'atomic romance' of the title (although it can also refer to the United States' romance with atomic energy). Although Reed journeys outwards in his imagination, into space, Julia turns him back to the earth and the worlds within. Reed's imaginary journeys through space are also more directly reminiscent of Lovelock because, as with Lovelock, the perspective from space forces a reconceptualisation of the Earth: 'He tried to imagine what an astronaut would see, peering down on that patch of green earth with its gray scar, the earth still steaming from its wound.'[36]

Most interestingly, though, the novel suggests a continuation of the idea of suspense, associated with nuclear anxieties, beyond the end of the Cold War when we might more usually expect it to have been resolved. It is the uncertainty of nuclear doom – of, in Reed's case, whether he has been made sick by his work – that is the most debilitating aspect of his encounter with nuclear energy. Visiting his sick mother, a source of familial anxiety to place alongside that surrounding his job, he feels himself to be in suspense before an uncertain future: 'he had a broad view [from the hospital] of the plant, with the plumes rising out of the gray area. . . . He felt bolted in place, with his mother behind him. . . . Even though he apparently had been spared, for now, the impossible job of caring for his mother, he felt anxious, suspended.'[37] Although the feeling of being suspended is here produced specifically by uncertainty about his mother's future, it is significant that Reed experiences this suspension as he gazes at the plant where he works. It is his contact with nuclear energy that renders his life uncertain and suspended as much as it is his ailing mother.

An Atomic Romance is, then, an important text because it suggests the existence of a legacy waste that is about much more than poorly contained by-products of nuclear processing. There are ongoing psychological and cultural consequences to the United States' engagement with nuclear technology. It is still, in the twenty-first century, an atomic world.

Less overtly stated in the novel, but present nonetheless, are subtle hints that a contemporary defining context for the nuclear industry is the United States' involvement with the new world orders of the twenty-first century, particularly through the 'War on Terror'. For instance, in addition to the reference to a new phase in United States nuclear weapons programmes, in the conversation between Reed and Jim noted above, a co-worker cynically claims that if there really was a problem the plant would have been of interest to terrorist groups: 'If the stuff we've collected here is so powerful, why hasn't somebody been building dirty bombs with it?'[38]

This contemporary dimension of United States culture is dealt with much more directly in Jonathan Safran Foer's *Extremely Loud and Incredibly Close* (2005). Although the nuclear context is much less overt here – the novel is narrated predominantly by a nine-year-old boy, Oskar, who lost his father in an attack on the World Trade Center – this is also an 'atomic world', for nuclear tropes are used to make sense of contemporary anxieties.

The section titled 'Happiness, Happiness' begins, apropos seemingly of nothing, with the transcription of an interview with a Japanese woman, Tomoyasu, who tells the story of her struggle during the bombing of Hiroshima to find her daughter, who later dies in her arms.[39] Only when the interview stops do we realise that it is an audio recording used by Oskar for a school presentation. Sudden, unexpected atomic attack resonates with Oskar as he tries to process the dramatic transformation in the world brought about by the 9/11 assault.

Nuclear tropes appear elsewhere too. Oskar comments disapprovingly when he sees Oppenheimer, the architect of the Allied bomb, on a stamp commemorating 'Great American Inventors'.[40] Oskar also connects future terrorist threats and nuclear weaponry, through the familiar Western paranoia about weapons of mass destruction, fantasising a warning system for New York for 'when something *really* terrible happened – like a nuclear bomb, or at least a biological weapons attack'.[41]

Crucially, the experience of loss, the personal impact of contemporary anxieties, leaves Oskar stranded in his own state of suspense. Terrified that something like 9/11 will happen again, he often refuses to take public transport because it's 'an obvious target'.[42] He also keeps a scrapbook titled *Stuff That Happened to Me* in which he posts pictures of, for instance, a ferry accident and of children murdered and raped.[43] Significantly he makes sense of the world by placing himself in imaginary situations where the worst is coming to pass, just as Bertrand Russell and Jonathan Schell, as chapter three noted, described being haunted by visions of nuclear destruction. Oskar is placed in a state of suspense with its psychological and cultural roots in the Cold War.

Indeed, such connections are not only made in relation to Oskar. His grand-mother's realisation of what was happening at the World Trade Center on 11 September 2001 is rendered in a phrase, 'I was in the guest room when it hap-pened',[44] identical with that used to portray the moment of nuclear attack in Coupland's 'The Wrong Sun', discussed in chapter two ('I was by the fridge in the kitchen when it happened', 'I was having my hair done when it happened', and so forth).

The connection between Oskar and his dead father is articulated most directly through Oskar's memory of a story his father told about New York's Sixth Borough. The trope of suspense – of being poised before alternative futures – is crucial to this story. Although it is not directly identified as nuclear, it is linked in with contemporary anxieties about geopolitical cataclysm, the contemporary sub-stitute for Cold War concerns, through the novel's focus on the 9/11 attacks. In his father's story, the Sixth Borough is an island. Once a year, with much celebra-tion, the champion long jumper makes the leap to the Sixth Borough, and it is the moment when he is suspended between these two realities that is most inspiring:

> For those few moments that the jumper was in the air, every New Yorker felt capable of flight.
>
> Or maybe 'suspension' is a better word. Because what was so inspiring about the leap was not how the jumper got from one borough to the other, but how he stayed between them for so long.[45]

Yet suspension is not only a moment of possibility; it is also a moment of fear. In the story the Sixth Borough drifts away, reaching Antarctica where a different sort of suspense afflicts the frozen lives of the borough's residents: 'Middle-aged women are frozen in the middle of their lives. The gavels of judges are frozen between guilt and innocence. On the ground are the crystals of the frozen first breaths of babies, and those of the last gasps of the dying.'[46]

The story of the Sixth Borough is, among other things, a metaphor for Oskar's life, frozen in time by the death of his father. Its concern with boundaries, with the spaces across them, and with suspension of various kinds, is also about the transition between alternative realities: death and life; childhood and adulthood; fantasy and reality. More broadly it is about the geopolitical trauma of 9/11 and the consequences that flowed both from it and from the United States' reaction to it. Everyday reality is portrayed as fragile, liable to drift off like the Sixth Borough, and transitions between different realities can be sudden and disconcerting.

Such a concern with transitions, with disjuncture, similarly appears in the novel's depiction of Oskar's grandparents' experience of the bombing of Dresden. As with nuclear tropes during the Cold War, the emphasis is on the fragility of everyday reality, liable to be shattered by sudden change. There was no warning of the bombing: 'The night before I lost everything was like any other night.'[47] The moment of disaster is represented as the cusp beyond which nothing can be the same again ('[e]verything in the history of the world can be proven wrong in one moment'),[48] and once this is realised the world, just as when it was poised on the nuclear cusp, becomes catastrophically fragile, hovering perilously close to the point of radical disjuncture.

What *Extremely Loud and Incredibly Close* implies, like much of the discourse about the 'War on Terror' or about its origins and consequences, is that the cultural processing and representation of contemporary fears emerges from the legacy of the balance of terror through which the Cold War was held in stalemate. There is a tendency in contemporary discourses, nevertheless, to construct the past as somehow safer and more stable than the present, as if the anxieties occasioned by the Cold War nuclear threat were somehow less terrible than those of terrorism or the wars fought in the name of resisting terrorism. Indeed, the thriller writer, Robert Littell, has expressed the nostalgia that might arise from our cultural memories of the Cold War, and the contrasts we might draw with concerns about terrorism: 'Nostalgia comes not from the fact that it was safer – if anything it was more dangerous – but it was simpler in the sense that we knew who the enemy was, we knew where the enemy was and today we're sitting here in a much more complex situation where we're really not sure who the enemy is, we really have no idea where the enemy is, and we have not the vaguest idea what the enemy wants'.[49]

One of the roles a contemporary nuclear criticism might play is to remind us of the cultural history of anxiety out of which present articulations of geopolitical stresses emerge. Although this epilogue to *States of Suspense* can only gesture toward the ongoing role for nuclear criticism in understanding contemporary, as well as Cold War, culture, we should certainly be aware of continuities between the first and subsequent nuclear ages.

The nuclear past *is* qualitatively different to the nuclear present. In historian Michael Clarke's rather nice phrasing, '[w]e played the most dangerous game in history during the cold war but by very coherent means. Now we play far less dangerous games by frankly incoherent means.'[50] Nevertheless, the historical, cultural and psychological roots of the latter lie in the former.

It is discourse about terror, just as it was once discourse about Mutual Assured Destruction, rather than direct experience of these things, that most tangibly connects most of us to the perceived threats of the contemporary world. The legacy waste of the Cold War's psychologies and cultures shapes contemporary experience. Our world is still an atomic one.

Notes

1 Emma Brockes, 'Travels with a Superhero', *Guardian Weekend* (2 September 2006), p. 17. Brockes' ellipses. Gary Wilson, untitled letter, in 'Letters', *Guardian Weekend* (9 September 2006), p. 16.

2 Bill Bryson, *The Life and Times of the Thunderbolt Kid* (London: Doubleday, 2006), pp. 135–52. We should not, however, write off the excitement Bryson conveys at the idea of nuclear

energy, which is no less authentic a response than the fear others remember. Elsewhere, Bryson conveys the ambiguity of his response: 'Suddenly we were in a world where something horribly destructive could drop on us at any moment without any warning wherever we were. This was a startling and unsettling notion, and we responded to it in a quintessentially 1950s way. We got excited about it.' *Life and Times of the Thunderbolt Kid*, p. 220.

3 Since 1947, the clock, appearing on the cover of the *Bulletin of Atomic Scientists*, has signalled our closeness to a projected nuclear midnight. Since the moment of maximum 'safety' in 1991, just after the Cold War, when the clock stood at 17 minutes to midnight, the clock has, at the time of writing, crept forward four times: 1995 (14 mins), 1998 (9 mins), 2002 (7 mins) and 2007 (5 mins). The most recent of these made at least one front page in Britain. *Independent* (17 January 2007), p. 1.

4 Don DeLillo, *Underworld* (London: Picador, 1998), p. 126, pp. 69–70, p. 76. We should note, though, that one of the aircraft in Sax's exhibit, 'Long Tall Sally', is shown later in the novel being used during the Vietnam War (p. 607), demonstrating that, although nuclear conflict was avoided, the era was still defined by 'hot' wars of various kinds.

5 DeLillo, *Underworld*, p. 122.

6 DeLillo, *Underworld*, p. 799.

7 DeLillo, *Underworld*, p. 140.

8 DeLillo, *Underworld*, pp. 197–8, p. 232, p. 286, p. 305, pp. 352–4, p. 387.

9 DeLillo, *Underworld*, p. 593.

10 DeLillo, *Underworld*, p. 404.

11 DeLillo, *Underworld*, p. 455.

12 DeLillo, *Underworld*, pp. 513–21.

13 DeLillo, *Underworld*, p. 245, p. 241.

14 DeLillo, *Underworld*, p. 508.

15 DeLillo, *Underworld*, p. 560.

16 DeLillo, *Underworld*, pp. 577–8.

17 DeLillo, *Underworld*, p. 793.

18 Philip Roth, *American Pastoral* (New York: Vintage International, 1998), p. 40.

19 Roth, *American Pastoral*, p. 68.

20 Roth, *American Pastoral*, p. 86.

21 Roth, *American Pastoral*, p. 193.

22 Roth, *American Pastoral*, p. 152.

23 Roth, *American Pastoral*, p. 412.

24 Roth, *American Pastoral* p. 418.

25 Paul Boyer, *Fallout: A Historian Reflects on America's Half-Century Encounter with Nuclear Weapons* (Columbus: Ohio State University Press, 1998), p. 204.

26 Bobbie Ann Mason, *An Atomic Romance* (New York: Random House, 2005), p. 32.

27 Mason, *Atomic Romance*, p. 40.

28 Mason, *Atomic Romance*, pp. 4–5.

29 Mason, *Atomic Romance*, p. 4.

30 Mason, *Atomic Romance*, p. 145, p. 80.

31 Mason, *Atomic Romance*, p. 110.

32 Mason, *Atomic Romance*, p. 80.

33 Mason, *Atomic Romance*, p. 146.

34 Mason, *Atomic Romance*, p. 109.

35 Mason, *Atomic Romance*, p. 110.

36 Mason, *Atomic Romance*, p. 51.

37 Mason, *Atomic Romance*, pp. 84–5.

38 Mason, *Atomic Romance*, p. 110.

39 Jonathan Safran Foer, *Extremely Loud and Incredibly Close* (London: Penguin, 2006), pp. 187–9.

40 Foer, *Extremely Loud*, p. 105.
41 Foer, *Extremely Loud*, p. 38. Foer's emphasis.
42 Foer, *Extremely Loud*, p. 194.
43 Foer, *Extremely Loud*, p. 241, p. 243.
44 Foer, *Extremely Loud*, p. 224.
45 Foer, *Extremely Loud*, p. 218.
46 Foer, *Extremely Loud*, p. 223.
47 Foer, *Extremely Loud*, p. 313.
48 Foer, *Extremely Loud*, p. 232.
49 Robert Littell and Henry Porter interviewed by John Humphrys, *Today Programme* (BBC Radio 4, 2 July 2005).
50 Michael Clarke, 'Expert view: do not yearn for the return of the good old days', *Guardian* (9 January 2007), p. 9.

Appendix: bomb drills in New York 1951–61

Chapter three discusses a series of civil defence drills for atomic attack in New York City. The following is a comprehensive list of the dates on which these drills took place, with full references for the principal articles reporting each drill in the *New York Times*, and with brief notes where appropriate.

21 January 1951
Anon., 'Civil defense practice drills held here', *New York Times* (22 January 1951), p. 12.
Atomic context not specified; quite small scale.

14 November 1951
Thomas P. Ronan, 'City civil defense mobilized in drill for "atom bombing"', *New York Times* (15 November 1951), p. 1, p. 16.
Large scale but for civil defence personnel only.

28 November 1951
Thomas P. Ronan, 'Raid test silences city in 2 minutes', *New York Times* (29 November 1951), p. 1, p. 24.
First city-wide drill involving public.

3 April 1952
Anon., '2 "atomic bombs", one in harbor, keep 50,000 busy in raid drill', *New York Times* (4 April 1952), p. 1, p. 12.
Large scale but for civil defence personnel only.

30 September 1952
Alexander Feinberg, 'Civil defense tests disaster technique as city is "bombed"', *New York Times* (1 October 1952), p. 1, p. 18.
Large scale, but for civil defence personnel only.

13 December 1952

Kalman Seigel, 'Biggest raid test turns New York into a "ghost city"', *New York Times* (14 December 1952), p. 1, p. 72.

Public drill; all subsequent drills on this list involve public participation.

25 September 1953

Frederick Graham, 'Biggest defense test here called best', *New York Times* (26 September 1953), p. 1, p. 19.

14 June 1954

Milton Bracker, '54 cities "raided" in U. S. bomb drill', *New York Times* (15 June 1954), p. 1, p. 32.

First nationwide 'Operation Alert' test; also included some provinces of Canada.

15 June 1955

Peter Kihss, 'City raid alert termed a success', *New York Times* (16 June 1955), p. 1, p. 17.

First time drill assumes that the city is subject to a hydrogen bomb attack.

20 July 1956

Russell Porter, 'City at standstill in U.S.-wide atom raid test', *New York Times* (21 July 1956), p. 1, p. 6.

12 July 1957

Will Lissner, 'Streets cleared swiftly', *New York Times* (13 July 1957), p. 1, p. 3.

6 May 1958

Philip Benjamin, 'Millions here take cover in raid drill', *New York Times* (7 May 1958), p. 1, p. 30.

17 April 1959

Philip Benjamin, 'H-bomb test raid stills bustling city', *New York Times* (18 April 1959), p. 1, p. 3.

3 May 1960

Peter Kihss, 'Nation takes cover in air-raid alert', *New York Times* (4 May 1960), p. 1, p. 48.

28 May 1961

Foster Hailey, 'Streets cleared in defense drill', *New York Times* (29 April 1961), p. 1, p. 48.

Final large-scale drill for nuclear war in New York City.

Bibliography

Adam, Barbara, Ulrich Beck and Joost van Loon (eds), *The Risk Society and Beyond: Critical Issues for Social Theory* (London: Sage, 2000).

Altshuler, B. L. et al., *Andrei Sakharov: Facets of a Life* (Gif-sur-Yvette: Editions Frontières, 1991).

Amis, Martin, *Einstein's Monsters* (1987; London: Vintage, 2003).

Anisfield, Nancy (ed.), *The Nightmare Considered: Critical Essays on Nuclear War Literature* (Bowling Green: Bowling Green State University Popular Press, 1991).

Anon., '2 "atomic bombs", one in harbor, keep 50,000 busy in raid drill', *New York Times* (4 April 1952), p. 1, p. 12.

Anon., '2 get 30 days in alert', *New York Times* (16 July 1957), p. 20.

Anon., '9 pacifists seized in defying alert', *New York Times* (7 May 1958), p. 30.

Anon., '695,245 "victims" are counted among the city's school children as result of "raid"', *New York Times* (16 June 1955), p. 19.

Anon., '2,000,000 posters citing defense rules being distributed here to aid public drill', *New York Times* (10 November 1951), p. 5.

Anon., 'Air raid drill in capital', *New York Times* (8 December 1951), p. 3.

Anon., 'Air raid warnings set', *New York Times* (14 May 1951), p. 27.

Anon., 'Civil defense, called "useless", is eliminated by Portland, Ore.', *New York Times* (24 May 1963), p. 1, p. 8.

Anon., 'Civil defense practice drills held here', *New York Times* (22 January 1951), p. 12.

Anon., 'College suspends 53 drill critics', *New York Times* (15 May 1960), p. 69.

Anon., 'Exhibit will warn of atomic ruin', *New York Times* (19 January 1946), p. 1.

Anon., 'Family plan urged for civil defense', *New York Times* (30 August 1953), p. 36.

Anon., 'Five who defied air drill jailed', *New York Times* (25 April 1959), p. 3.

Anon., 'Gun thy neighbour?', *Time* (18 August 1961), pp. 104–5.

Anon., 'Liberty under law', *New York Times* (21 December 1962), p. 6.

Anon., 'L.I. girl suspended for refusal to join civil defense drill', *New York Times* (14 March 1964), p. 25.

Anon., 'New film to help in bomb training', *New York Times* (25 January 1952), p. 7.

Anon., *Nottingham After the Bomb* (Nottingham: Nottingham Medical Campaign Against Nuclear Weapons, 1983).

Anon., 'Pickets protest 26 drill arrests', *New York Times* (8 May 1960), p. 78.

Anon., *Protect and Survive* (1976; London: Government Bookshops, 1980).

Anon., 'Raid drill stirs parent protests', *New York Times* (6 November 1959), p. 31.

Anon., 'Raid shelters increase', *New York Times* (4 June 1952), p. 18.

Anon., 'The sound of sirens', *New York Times* (26 May 1951), p. 12.

Anon., *Survival Under Atomic Attack* (1950), at http://honors.umd.edu/HONR269J/archive/SurvivalBooklet.html (28 December 2006).

Anon., 'Teacher backed on shelter stand', *New York Times* (15 November 1962), p. 42.

Anon., *Whence the Threat to Peace* (2nd ed.; Moscow: Military Publishing House, 1982).

Atwood, Margaret, *The Handmaid's Tale* (1985; London: Vintage, 1996).

Aubrey, Crispin (ed.), *Nukespeak: The Media and the Bomb* (London: Comedia, 1982).

Auster, Paul, *In the Country of Last Things* (1987; London: Penguin, 1989).

Baldwin, Hanson W., 'Atom's Role in War', *New York Times* (23 October 1945), p. 6.

Ballard, J. G., *The Complete Short Stories* (2001; London: Flamingo, 2002).

Barclay, Dorothy, 'Film on atom war bad for children', *New York Times* (21 November 1952), p. 29.

Barclay, Dorothy, 'Group plans to study the effects of defense activities on children', *New York Times* (7 March 1952), p. 16.

Beckett, Samuel, *The Complete Dramatic Works* (1986; London: Faber, 1990).

Bell, Daniel, *Science, Technology and Culture* (Maidenhead: Open University Press, 2006).

Bellow, Saul, *Herzog* (1964; London: Penguin, 2000).

Bellow, Saul, *Mr Sammler's Planet* (1969; London: Weidenfeld and Nicolson, 1970).

Benjamin, Philip, 'H-bomb test raid stills bustling city', *New York Times* (18 April 1959), p. 1, p. 3.

Benjamin, Philip, 'Millions here take cover in raid drill', *New York Times* (7 May 1958), p. 1, p. 30.

Benton, Jill, 'Don DeLillo's *End Zone*: a postmodern satire', *Aethlon: The Journal of Sport Culture* 12:1 (1995), 7–18.

Black, Algernon D., 'Letters to the *Times* – "Civil defense drills"', *New York Times* (8 December 1962), p. 26.

Bodanis, David, $E = mc^2$: *A Biography of the World's Most Famous Equation* (2000; London: Pan, 2001).

Bourke, Joanna, *Fear: A Cultural History* (2005; London: Virago, 2006).

Boyer, Paul, *By the Bomb's Early Light: American Thought and Culture at the Dawn of the Atomic Age* (1985; new ed., Chapel Hill: University of North Carolina Press, 1994).

Boyer, Paul, *Fallout: A Historian Reflects on America's Half-Century Encounter with Nuclear Weapons* (Columbus: Ohio State University Press, 1998).

Bracker, Milton, '54 cities "raided" in U. S. bomb drill', *New York Times* (15 June 1954), p. 1, p. 32.

Bradbury, Ray, *The Martian Chronicles* (London: Flamingo, 1995). (Originally published as *The Silver Locusts*, 1951.)

Bradley, John (ed.), *Learning to Glow: A Nuclear Reader* (Arizona: University of Arizona Press, 2000).

Brewer, Ebenezer Cobham, ed. Betty Kirkpatrick, *Brewer's Concise Phrase and Fable* (London: Cassell, 2000).

Brians, Paul, *Nuclear Holocausts: Atomic War in Fiction, 1895–1984* (Kent: Kent State University Press, 1987).

Briggs, Raymond, *When the Wind Blows* (Middlesex: Penguin, 1982).

Brockes, Emma, 'Travels with a super hero', *Guardian Weekend* (2 September 2006), pp. 16–23.

Bryson, Bill, *The Life and Times of the Thunderbolt Kid* (London: Doubleday, 2006).

Buell, Frederick, *From Apocalypse to Way of Life: Environmental Crisis in the American Century* (New York: Routledge, 2004).

Canaday, John, *The Nuclear Muse: Literature, Physics and the First Atomic Bombs* (Madison: University of Wisconsin Press, 2000).

Carré, John Le, *The Spy Who Came in from the Cold* (1963; London: Sceptre, 1999).

Carson, Rachel, *Silent Spring* (1962; Middlesex: Penguin, 2000).

Chavkin, Allan (ed.), *Leslie Marmon Silko's* Ceremony: *A Casebook* (New York: Oxford University Press, 2002).

Clancy, Tom, *The Sum of All Fears* (1991; London: HarperCollins, 1993).

Clark, Clifford Edward, Jr., *The American Family Home 1800–1960* (Chapel Hill: University of North Carolina Press, 1986).

Clarke, Bob, *Four Minute Warning: Britain's Cold War* (Stroud: Tempus, 2005).

Clarke, I. F., *Voices Prophesying War: Future Wars 1763–3749* (2nd ed.; Oxford: Oxford University Press, 1992).

Clarke, Michael, 'Expert view: do not yearn for the return of the good old days', *Guardian* (9 January 2007), p. 9.

Coover, Robert, *The Origin of the Brunists* (New York: Grove, 1966).

Coover, Robert, *The Public Burning* (1976; New York: Grove, 1998).

Cordle, Daniel, 'Cultures of terror: nuclear criticism during and since the Cold War', *Literature Compass* 3 (2006), 1186–99. DOI: 10.1111/j.1741–4113. 2006.00378.x.

Coupland, Douglas, *Generation X* (1991; London: Abacus, 1996).

Coupland, Douglas, *Life After God* (1994; London: Scribner, 1999).

Coupland, Douglas, *Polaroids from the Dead* (1996; New York: ReganBooks, 1997).

Coupland, Douglas, *Shampoo Planet* (1992; London: Scribner, 1993).

Crockatt, Richard, *The Fifty Years War: The United States and the Soviet Union in World Politics, 1941–1991* (London: Routledge, 1995).

Crowther, Bosley, 'Screen: "On the Beach" ', *New York Times* (19 December 1959), p. 34.

Dear, Michael J., *The Postmodern Urban Condition* (Oxford: Blackwell, 2000).

Debord, Guy, *The Society of the Spectacle* (1967; rev. ed.; G B: Rebel Press, 1987).

DeLillo, Don, *End Zone* (1972; London: Penguin, 1986).

DeLillo, Don, *Underworld* (1997; London: Macmillan, 1998).

DeLillo, Don, *White Noise* (1984; London: Picador, 1986).

Denton, Jill, 'Don Delillo's *End Zone*: a postmodern satire', *Aethlon: The Journal of Sport Literature* 12:1 (1995), 7–18.

Detweiler, Robert, 'Carnival of shame: Doctorow and the Rosenbergs', *Religion and American Culture: A Journal of Interpretation* 6:1 (1996), 63–85.

Dewey, Joseph, *In a Dark Time: The Apocalyptic Temper in the American Novel of the Nuclear Age* (Indiana: Purdue University Press, 1990).

Doctorow, E. L., *The Book of Daniel* (1971; London: Picador, 1982).

Dowling, David, *Fictions of Nuclear Disaster* (London: Macmillan, 1987).

Dreishpoon, Douglas and Alan Trachtenburg, *The Tumultuous Fifties: A View from the* New York Times *Photo Archives* (New Haven: Yale University Press, 2001).

Drell, Sidney D., *Facing the Threat of Nuclear Weapons* (Seattle: University of Washington Press, 1983).

Edwards, Oliver, *The USA and the Cold War: 1945–63* (2nd ed.; London: Hodder and Stoughton, 2002).

Ehrlich, Paul R. et al., *The Nuclear Winter: The Cold and the Dark* (London: Sidgwick and Jackson, 1984).

Elder, J. H., 'A summary of research on reactions of children to nuclear war', *American Journal of Orthopsychiatry* 35:1 (1965), 120–3.

Ellin, Nan, *Postmodern Urbanism* (Oxford: Blackwell, 1996).

Escalona, Sibylle K., 'Growing up with the threat of nuclear war: some indirect effects on personality development', *American Journal of Orthopsychiatry* 52:4 (1982), 600–7.

Feinberg, Alexander, 'Civil defense tests disaster technique as city is "bombed" ', *New York Times* (1 October 1952), p. 1, p. 18.

Foer, Jonathan Safran, *Extremely Loud and Incredibly Close* (2005; London: Penguin, 2006).

Foertsch, Jacqueline, *Enemies Within: The Cold War and the AIDS Crisis in Literature, Film, and Culture* (Urbana: University of Illinois Press, 2001).

Foertsch, Jacqueline, 'Not bombshells but basketcases: gendered illness in nuclear texts', *Studies in the Novel* 31:4 (1999), 471–88.

Frank, Pat, *Alas, Babylon* (1959; New York: HarperPerennial, 1999).

Frayn, Michael, *Copenhagen* (London: Methuen, 1998).

Freedman, Lawrence (ed.), *Europe Transformed: Documents on the End of the Cold War* (London: Tri-Service Press, 1990).

Freedman, Lawrence, *The Evolution of Nuclear Strategy* (2nd ed.; London: Macmillan, 1981).

French, Perrin L. and Judith Van Hoorn, 'Half a nation saw nuclear war and nobody blinked?: *The Day After* in terms of a theoretical chain of causality', *International Journal of Mental Health* 15:1–3 (1986), 276–97.

Gaddis, John Lewes, *The Cold War* (London: Penguin, 2006).

Gaddis, John Lewes, *We Now Know: Rethinking Cold War History* (Oxford: Oxford University Press, 1997).

Gery, John, *Nuclear Annihilation and Contemporary American Poetry: Ways of Nothingness* (Gainesville: University of Florida Press, 1996).

Glad, Betty (ed.), *Psychological Dimensions of War* (London: Sage, 1990).

Goldman, Kevin L., 'Out of the past: fallout shelters', *New York Times* (21 November 1976), p. 268.

Graham, Frederick, 'Biggest defense test here called best', *New York Times* (26 September 1953), p. 1, p. 19.

Grossman, Andrew D., *Neither Dead nor Red: Civilian Defense and American Political Development During the Early Cold War* (New York: Routledge, 2001).

Hailey, Foster, 'Streets cleared in defense drill', *New York Times* (29 April 1961), p. 1, p. 48.

Hammond, Andrew (ed.), *Cold War Literature: Writing the Global Conflict, 1945–1989* (London: Routledge, 2006).

Heimann, Jim (ed.), *The Golden Age of Advertising: The 50s* (Köhn: Taschen, 2005).

Hennessy, Peter, *The Secret State: Whitehall and the Cold War* (2002; rev. ed.; London: Penguin, 2003).

Henriksen, Margot A., *Dr. Strangelove's America: Society and Culture in the Atomic Age* (Berkeley: University of California Press, 1997).

Herbele, Mark A., *A Trauma Artist: Tim O'Brien and the Fiction of Vietnam* (Iowa: University of Iowa Press, 2001).

Herman, Ellen, *The Romance of American Psychology: Political Culture in the Age of Experts* (Berkeley: University of California Press, 1995).

Herman, Robin, 'They turned old movies into a timely film about nuclear war', *New York Times* (16 May 1982), Section D, p. 21.

Hersey, John, *Hiroshima* (1946; 2nd ed.; London: Penguin, 1985).

Herzog, Tobey C., *Tim O'Brien* (New York: Twayne, 1997).

Hewlett, Richard G. and Francis Duncan, *Atomic Shield, 1947 / 1952*, A History of the United States Atomic Energy Commission II (University Park: Pennsylvania State University Press, 1969).

Hoban, Russell, *Riddley Walker* (1980; London: Bloomsbury, 2002).

Hoffman, Elizabeth Cobbs, *All You Need is Love: The Peace Corps and the Spirit of the 1960s* (Cambridge: Harvard University Press, 1998).

Hume, Kathryn, *American Dream, American Nightmare: Fiction Since 1960* (Urbana: University of Illinois Press, 2000).

Hutcheon, Linda, *The Politics of Postmodernism* (London: Routledge, 1989).

Huxley, Aldous, *Ape and Essence* (1949; London: Chatto and Windus, 1971).

Ibuse, Masuji, *Black Rain*, trans. John Bester (1965; Tokyo: Kodansha International, 1979).

Illson, Murray, 'Atomic neurosis feared for young', *New York Times* (5 September 1953), p. 12.

Isaacs, Jeremy and Taylor Downing, *Cold War* (London: Bantam, 1998).

Kahn, Herman, *On Thermonuclear War* (2nd ed.; Princeton: Princeton University Press, 1961).

Kanon, Joseph, *Los Alamos* (London: Little, Brown, 1997).

Kaufman, Michael T., 'War resisters enter 2d [sic] half century', *New York Times* (1 April 1973), p. 30.

Kennan, George F., *American Diplomacy 1900–1950* (New York: Mentor Books, 1951).

Kennan, George, 'The Long Telegram' at www.ntanet.net/KENNAN.html (25 January 2007).

Kermode, Frank, *The Sense of an Ending* (Oxford: Oxford University Press, 1966).

Kihss, Peter, 'City raid alert termed a success', *New York Times* (16 June 1955), p. 1, p. 17.

Kihss, Peter, 'Governor thanks workers in alert', *New York Times* (5 May 1960), p. 14.

Kihss, Peter, 'Nation takes cover in air-raid alert', *New York Times* (4 May 1960), p. 1, p. 48.

Knelman, F. H., *Reagan, God and the Bomb* (Toronto: McClelland and Stewart, 1985).

Kohn, Howard, *Who Killed Karen Silkwood?* (1981; London: New English Library, 1983).

Krock, Arthur, 'In the nation: the shelters are from harsh reality', *New York Times* (2 June 1962), p. 38.

LaFeber, Walter (ed.), *America in the Cold War: Twenty Years of Revolutions and Response, 1947–1967* (New York: Wiley & Sons, 1969).

Lauter, Paul et al., *The Heath Anthology of American Literature* (Boston: Houghton-Mifflin, 2002).

Lavery, David, *Late for the Sky: The Mentality of the Space Age* (Carbondale: Southern Illinois University Press, 1992).

Lenz, Gunter H., Hermut Keil and Sabine Bröck-Sallah, *Reconstructing American Literary and Historical Studies* (Frankfurt Am Main: Campus Verlag, 1990).

Lessing, Doris, *Memoirs of a Survivor* (1974; London: Picador, 1976).

Levine, George and David Leverenz (eds), *Mindful Pleasures: Essays on Thomas Pynchon* (Boston: Little, Brown, 1976).

Levine, Howard B., 'The psychology of the nuclear threat: a bibliography', *International Review of Psycholoanalysis* 14:1 (1987), 13–19.

Levine, Howard B., Daniel Jacobs and Lowell J. Rubin (eds), *Psychoanalysis and the Nuclear Threat: Clinical and Theoretical Studies* (Hillsdale: Analytic Press, 1988).

Lifton, Robert Jay, *Death in Life: Survivors of Hiroshima* (1968; new edn; Chapel Hill: University of North Carolina Press, 1991).

Lifton, Robert Jay and Richard Falk, *Indefensible Weapons: The Political and Psychological Case Against Nuclearism* (New York: Basic Books, 1982).

Light, Michael, *100 Suns 1945–1962* (London: Jonathan Cape, 2003).

Lissner, Will, 'Streets cleared swiftly', *New York Times* (13 July 1957), p. 1, p. 3.

Lovelock, J. E., *Gaia: A New Look at Life on Earth* (Oxford: Oxford University Press, 1979).

Lovelock, James, *The Revenge of Gaia: Why the Earth is Fighting Back – And How We Can Still Save Humanity* (2006; London: Penguin, 2007).

Luckhurst, Roger, 'Nuclear criticism: anachronism and anachorism', *Diacritics* 23:2 (1993), 88–97.

Lyotard, Jean-François, trans. Geoff Bennington and Brian Massumi, *The Postmodern Condition: A Report on Knowledge* (1979; Manchester: Manchester University Press, 1986).

Mandelbaum, Michael, *The Nuclear Question* (Cambridge: Cambridge University Press, 1979).

Mandelbaum, Michael, *The Nuclear Revolution: International Politics Before and After Hiroshima* (Cambridge: Cambridge University Press, 1981).

Mailer, Norman, *The Armies of the Night: History as a Novel; the Novel as History* (New York: Signet, 1968).

Mannix, Patrick, *The Rhetoric of Antinuclear Fiction: Persuasive Strategies in Novels and Films* (Lewisburg: Bucknell University Press, 1992).

Mason, Bobbie Ann, *An Atomic Romance* (New York: Random House, 2005).

May, Elaine Tyler, *Homeward Bound: American Families in the Cold War Era* (1988; 2nd ed.; New York: Basic Books, 1999).

May, Ernest R. and Philip D. Zelikow, *The Kennedy Tapes: Inside the Whitehouse During the Cuban Missile Crisis* (Cambridge: Belknap Press of Harvard University Press, 1997).

McCamley, N. J., *Cold War Secret Nuclear Bunkers* (Barnsley: Pen & Sword, 2002).

McCarthy, Cormac, *The Road* (London: Macmillan, 2006).

McHale, Brian, *Postmodernist Fiction* (New York: Methuen, 1987).

McMahon, Robert J., *The Cold War: A Very Short Introduction* (Oxford: Oxford University Press, 2003).

Merril, Judith, *The Best of Judith Merril* (New York: Warner, 1976).

Merril, Judith, *Shadow on the Hearth* (New York: Doubleday, 1950).

Merril, Judith and Emily Pohl Weary, *Better to Have Loved: The Life of Judith Merril* (Toronto: Between the Lines, 2002).

Millard, Kenneth, *Contemporary American Fiction: An Introduction to American Fiction Since 1970* (Oxford: Oxford University Press, 2000).

Miller, Walter M., Jr., *A Canticle for Leibowitz* (1959; London: Corgi, 1963).

Minca, Claudio (ed.), *Postmodern Geography: Theory and Praxis* (Oxford: Blackwell, 1996).

Mitter, Rana and Patrick Major, *Across the Blocs: Cold War Cultural and Social History* (London: Frank Cass, 2004).

Moore, Alan and Dave Gibbons, *Watchmen* (New York: DC Comics, 1987).

Morris, Christopher D., *Models of Misrepresentation: On the Fiction of E. L. Doctorow* (Jackson: University Press of Mississippi, 1991).

Nadel, Alan, *Containment Culture: American Narratives, Postmodernism, and the Atomic Age* (Durham: Duke University Press, 1995).

Nelson, Michael, *War of the Black Heavens: The Battles of Western Broadcasting in the Cold War* (London: Brassey's, 1997).

Newell, Diana, 'Home truths: women writing science in the nuclear dawn', *European Journal of American Culture* 22:3 (2003), 193–203.

Newkey-Burden, Chas, *Nuclear Paranoia* (Hertfordshire: Pocket Essentials, 2003).

Oakes, Guy, *The Imaginary War: Civil Defense and American Cold War Culture* (New York: Oxford University Press, 1994).

O'Brien, Tim, *Northern Lights* (1975; London: Flamingo, 1998).

O'Brien, Tim, *The Nuclear Age* (1985; London: Flamingo, 1987).

Phillips, Jayne Anne, *Machine Dreams* (1984; London: Faber, 1993).

Pinker, Steven, *How the Mind Works* (Uxbridge: Softback Preview, 1998).

Plath, Sylvia, *The Bell Jar* (1963; London: Faber, 1966).

Polyson, James, Jodi Hillmar and Douglas Kriek, 'Levels of public interest in nuclear war: 1945–1985', *Journal of Social Behaviour and Personality* 1:3 (1986), 397–401.

Poole, Robert and Steve Wright, *Target North-West: Civil Defence and Nuclear War in Region 10* (Lancaster: Richardson Institute for Peace and Conflict Research, 1982).

Poore, Charles, 'Books of the Times', *New York Times* (15 June 1950), p. 29.

Popper, Karl, *Unended Quest: An Intellectual Autobiography* (Illinois: Flamingo, 1986).

Porter, Russell, 'City at standstill in U.S.-wide atom raid test', *New York Times* (21 July 1956), p. 1, p. 6.

Pynchon, Thomas, *Gravity's Rainbow* (1973; London: Picador, 1975).

Pynchon, Thomas, *Vineland* (1990; London: Minerva, 1991).

Rayner, E. G., *The Cold War* (London: Hodder and Stoughton, 1992).

Rhodes, Richard, *The Making of the Atomic Bomb* (1986; London: Penguin, 1988).

Ronan, Thomas P., 'City civil defense mobilized in drill for "atom bombing"', *New York Times* (15 November 1951), p. 1, p. 16.

Ronan, Thomas P., 'Raid test silences city in 2 minutes', *New York Times* (29 November 1951), p. 1, p. 24.

Roth, Philip, *American Pastoral* (1997; New York: Vintage, 1998).

Roy, Arundhati, *The Cost of Living: 'The greater common good' and 'The end of imagination'* (London: Flamingo, 1999).

Tetlock, Philip E. et al. (eds), *Behavior, Society, and Nuclear War* (New York: Oxford University Press, 1989).

Ruthven, Ken, *Nuclear Criticism* (Melbourne: Melbourne University Press, 1993).

Rutter, Richard, 'Industry plans ways to survive nuclear strike', *New York Times* (1 October 1961), Section F, p. 1.

Sakharov, Andrei, trans. Richard Lourie, *Memoirs* (London: Hutchinson, 1990).

Sakharov, Andrei D., ed. Harrison E. Salisbury, *Sakharov Speaks* (London: Collins & Harvill, 1974).

Schell, Jonathan, *The Fate of the Earth* and *The Abolition* (Stanford: Stanford University Press, 2000).

Schumach, Murray, '"On the Beach" includes Moscow in 18-city premiere on Dec. 17', *New York Times* (30 November 1959), p. 27.

Schwartz, Richard A., *Cold War Culture: Media and the Arts, 1945–1990* (New York: Facts on File, 1998).

Schwenger, Peter, *Letter Bomb: Nuclear Holocaust and the Exploding Word* (Baltimore: Johns Hopkins University Press, 1992).

Seed, David, *American Science Fiction and the Cold War: Literature and Film* (Edinburgh: Edinburgh University Press, 1999).

Seed, David (ed.), *Imagining Apocalypse: Studies in Cultural Crisis* (London: Macmillan, 2000).

Seigel, Kalman, 'Biggest raid test turns New York into a "ghost city"', *New York Times* (14 December 1952), p. 1, p. 72.

Shabad, Theodore, 'Soviet twits U.S. on civil defense', *New York Times* (26 August 1961), p. 3.

Shalett, Sidney, 'New age ushered', *New York Times* (7 August 1945), pp. 1–2.

Shute, Nevil, *On the Beach* (1957; North Yorkshire: House of Stratus, 2000).

Silko, Leslie Marmon, *Ceremony* (1977; New York: Penguin, 1986).

Simak, Clifford, *City* (1952; London: Weidenfeld and Nicolson, 1961).

Simpson, Christopher, *Science of Coercion: Communication Research and Psychological Warfare 1945–1960* (New York: Oxford University Press, 1994).

Smith, Julian, *Nevil Shute* (Boston: Twayne, 1976).

Smith, Martin Cruz, *Stallion Gate* (1986; London: Macmillan, 1996).

Snow, C. P., *The New Men* (1954; London: Penguin, 1959).

Spencer, Steven M., 'Fallout: the silent killer', *Saturday Evening Post* (29 August 1959), at www.itseemslikeyesterday.com/Atomic/article_asp (25 January 2007).

Stearns, Laurie, 'Growing up in the bomb's shadow', *New York Times* (2 May 1982), Section WC, p. 24.

Steinbeck, John, *Travels with Charley in Search of America* (1962; London: Penguin, 1997).

Stengren, Bernard, 'Major cities lag in planning defense against bomb attack', *New York Times* (12 June 1955), pp. 76–7.

Stewart, George R., *Earth Abides* (1949; London: Millennium, 1999).

Tallack, Douglas, *Twentieth-Century America: The Intellectual and Cultural Context* (Harlow: Longman, 1991).

Taylor, Jessica, 'Let's build a bomb', *Guardian* (5 July 2006), Section G2, pp. 14–17.

Tetlock, Phillip E. et al. (eds), *Behavior, Society, and Nuclear War* (New York: Oxford University Press, 1989).

Turco, R. P. et al., 'Nuclear winter: global consequences of multiple nuclear explosions', *Science* 222 (23 December 1983), pp. 1283–92.

Vanderbilt, Tom, *Survival City: Adventures Among the Ruins of Atomic America* (New York: Princeton Architectural Press, 2002).

Veldman, Meredith, *Fantasy, the Bomb, and the Greening of Britain: Romantic Protest, 1945–1980* (Cambridge: Cambridge University Press, 1994).

Vonnegut, Kurt, *Cat's Cradle* (1963; London: Penguin, 1965).

Waggoner, Walter H., '"Direct action" drive in New York is led by young mother', *New York Times* (22 November 1961), p. 4.

Walz, Jay, 'Atom bombs made in 3 hidden cities', *New York Times* (7 August 1945), p. 1, p. 3.

Waugh, Patricia (ed.), *Postmodernism: A Reader* (London: Edward Arnold, 1992).

Weart, Spencer R., *Nuclear Fear: A History of Images* (Cambridge: Harvard University Press, 1988).

Wells, H. G., *The World Set Free* (1914; US: Quiet Vision, 2000).

Whitfield, Stephen J., *The Culture of the Cold War* (Baltimore: Johns Hopkins University Press, 1991).

Williams, Terry Tempest (ed.), *Atomic Ghost: Poets Respond to the Nuclear Age* (Minneapolis: Coffee House Press, 1995).

Wilson, Gary, 'Letters', *Guardian Weekend* (9 September 2006), p. 16.

Winkler, Allan M., *Life Under a Cloud: American Anxiety About the Bomb* (New York: Oxford University Press, 1993).

Witte, John (ed.), *Warnings: An Anthology on the Nuclear Peril* (1984; Eugene: University of Oregon Press, 2001).

Wittgenstein, Ludwig, trans. G. E. M. Anscombe, *Philosophical Investigations* (Oxford: Blackwell, 1974).

Wolfson, Richard, *Nuclear Choices: A Citizen's Guide to Nuclear Technology* (Cambridge: MIT Press, 1991).

Woods, Tim, *Beginning Postmodernism* (Manchester: Manchester University Press, 1999).

Wylie, Philip, *Tomorrow!* (1954; New York: Popular Library, 1963).

Wyndham, John, *The Chrysalids* (1955; London: Penguin, 1958).

Wyndham, John, *The Midwich Cuckoos* (1957; London: Penguin, 1960).

Young, John W., *The Longman Companion to Cold War and Détente 1941–91* (London: Longman, 1993).

Zur, Ofer, 'On nuclear attitudes and psychic numbing: overview and critique', *Contemporary Social Psychology* 14:2 (June 1990), 96–118.

Special editions of academic journals, runs of journals and complete editions of magazines

Diacritics (Summer 1984).

International Journal of Mental Health 15:1–3 (1986).

Journal of Adolescence 12:1 (Mar 1989).

Journal of Social Issues 39:1 (1983).

Life (15 September 1961).

Nuclear Texts & Contexts 1–8 (1989–92).

Papers on Language and Literature: A Journal for Scholars and Critics of Language and Literature 26:1 (1990).

Films

Atomic Café, The (US, Kevin Rafferty, Jayne Loader and Pierce Rafferty, 1982).

China Syndrome, The (US, James Bridges, 1979).

Dr. Strangelove, or: How I Learned to Stop Worrying and Love the Bomb (UK, Stanley Kubrick, 1963).
Fog of War, The (US, Errol Morris, 2003).
Hiroshima, Mon Amour (France / Japan, Alain Resnais, 1959).
On the Beach (US, Stanley Kramer, 1959).
Silkwood (US, Mike Nichols, 1983).
Thirteen Days (US, Kevin Costner, 2000).
War Game, The (UK, Peter Watkins, 1965).

Television series and plays, and films receiving their first showing on television

Atomic Attack (US, ABC, 1954).
Day After, The (US, ABC, 1983).
Edge of Darkness (UK, BBC, 1985).
Fail Safe (US, CBS, 2000).
Threads (UK, BBC, 1984).

Miscellaneous public information and news films and ephemera

A Day Called X (US, 1955).
A is for Atom (US, 1953).
Atomic Alert (Elementary Version) (US, 1951).
Duck and Cover (US, 1951).
House in the Middle, The (US, 1954).
News Magazine of the Screen: Atomic Energy (compilation of 1950s newsreels hosted at the Prelinger Archive: http://www.archive.org/details/NewsMaga1950_2, 27 January 2007).
Our Cities Must Fight (US, 1951).
Protect and Survive (UK, 1976).
Red Nightmare (US, 1962).
Shelter on a Quiet Street (US, 1962).
Sound an Alarm (UK, 1971).
Survival Under Atomic Attack (US, 1951).
Waking Point, The (UK, 1951).

Index

Note: literary works can be found under authors' names; film and television programmes are listed by title; 'n.' after a page reference indicates the number of a note on that page.